YURI & THE PIG

C W Lovatt

A Wild Wolf Publication

Published by Wild Wolf Publishing in 2023
Copyright © 2023 C W Lovatt

All rights reserved. No part of this book may be reproduced, stored in a retrieval system or transmitted in any form or by any means without the prior written permission of the publishers, except by a reviewer who may quote brief passages in a review to be printed by a newspaper, magazine or journal.

First print

All Characters appearing in this work are fictitious. Any resemblance to real persons, living or dead, is purely coincidental.

ISBN: 978-1-907954-85-6
Also available in E-Book edition

www.wildwolfpublishing.com

For the oppressed.
Never lose hope.

Acknowledgements

Many thanks are due to my friend, Olga Rudnitsky, for her suggestions pertaining to language and culture.

Thanks to my brilliant sister-in-law, Linda Lovatt RN (Diploma) BScN, CACE, ICP (retired), for her expert advice on any medical topics I encountered.

Thanks also go out to my friends, Pat Graham, Terry Wilkinson, Teresa Geering, and of course, Karen Sanchez for reading the manuscript in its rough form and for their invaluable comments on how to make it better.

As always, thanks to Wild Wolf Publishing for helping me bring another one across the finish line.

Preface

The idea for this novel came to me when I was halfway through the project I was working on at the time. As is my custom, I opened a file and made some notes before returning to my work in progress. Usually, this consists of a few paragraphs, but by the time I was ready to start, I had accumulated several pages, but it didn't end there.

Almost any writer will tell you of those nights when they're dead tired and about to drift off to sleep only to be visited by an idea that simply won't leave them alone. In order not to forget about it by the next morning, it's necessary to rise from our nice, warm bed, usually at the most ungodly of hours, and either scribble something down on a pad, or simply enter it into the computer straight away. As a general rule, this might happen half a dozen times per book. With this book, however, the story just wouldn't leave me alone. I was constantly up making notes, often three or four times every evening, for virtually the entirety of the first draft.

When the muse is speaking so forcefully, the writer is well-advised to listen.

Table of Contents

Overview………………...8

PART ONE
Chapter One……………..10
Chapter Two……………..20
Chapter Three……………29
Chapter Four…………….35
Chapter Five…………….44
Chapter Six……………...53
Chapter Seven……………63
Chapter Eight……………72
Chapter Nine……………81
Chapter Ten……………..89
Chapter Eleven…………94
Chapter Twelve………...103
Chapter Thirteen……….111
Chapter Fourteen……….121
Chapter Fifteen………...131

PART TWO
Chapter Sixteen………..141
Chapter Seventeen……..150
Chapter Eighteen……….160
Chapter Nineteen………169
Chapter Twenty………..182
Chapter Twenty-one…….191
Chapter Twenty-two……200
Chapter Twenty-three…..208
Chapter Twenty-four……217
Chapter Twenty-five……226
Chapter Twenty-six……..235
Chapter Twenty-seven….243
Chapter Twenty-eight…..252

Chapter Twenty-nine…………..259

Epilogue………………………..270

Afterward………………...……276

Overview

This tale concerns two countries in Eastern Europe. One, Zlaimperia, is very large. The other country, Xoraina, is much smaller and is situated on Zlaimperia's southern border. In times past, Zlaimperia was the core of a fearsome empire which, among many other countries, included Xoraina.

Now, also in times past – within the span of a lifetime ago – the Zlaimperian Empire was much weakened because of its struggle with the United States of America and her allies. Although still considered to be an empire by some, many of the vassal states, resentful of their Zlaimperian overlord, chose to go their own way, Xoraina being among them.

In the ensuing years, the divide between these two countries grew ever wider. Grasped in the iron fist of a dictator, Zlaimperia returned to its authoritarian roots. This dictator was known for his ruthless determination to cling to power, as well as his corruption. Xoraina, on the other hand, turned away from its past with Zlaimperia. Instead, they turned toward the western form of government that gave power to the people. In due course it began to prosper.

Now, the all-powerful Zlaimperian dictator lamented the lessening of what his country had once been and swore to regain those glories of the past. He also noticed that Xoraina had repudiated that past and embraced their old enemies in the West. Duly enraged by it, but he was also alarmed to have yet another democratic country on his border, especially a prosperous one, and *this* one most of all. To some degree, many in Zlaimperia and Xoraina shared a similar language and culture. Also, many people in Xoraina had friends and family in Zlaimperia, and vice versa. How long would it be, he wondered, before his own people, relating to life across the border, saw the benefits of democracy and wanted it for themselves? If such an unspeakable thing should occur, not only would it would be the end of all his dreams of returning Zlaimperia to its former glory, it would be the end of the dictator himself. Clearly, the status quo could not be tolerated. Therefore, girding the country in a blanket of lies, of how the erstwhile vassal state had now fallen victim to deplorable Nazis, he ordered his formidable military to invade Xoraina with two objectives in mind: to eradicate Xorainian democracy, and to absorb the country within a new Zlaimperian Empire.

However, having once tasted freedom, Xorainians were reluctant to surrender to the will of their old master.

Instead, they chose to resist.

PART ONE
Chapter One

On the western edge of Xoraina lies a remote valley bordering the Carpathian Mountains to the west and hemmed in by an immense forest to the east. Access to the rest of the country is gained via a single road cut through the forest. It had once been a fine road with a newly paved surface, but the years had taken their toll, until the pavement was potholed and riddled with cracks from neglect. However, not many people noticed or complained, because this was a region where few people came, and even fewer people left.

In this sliver of land lies the remote village of Homstood. Life is simple there, much slower than the hectic pace of the larger cities. In fact, it hasn't changed much since time out of mind.

As in many other rural communities, people went to church on the Sabbath. Largely, their prayers were dominated by pleas for good weather for their crops; for as anyone who has ever made a living from the land will tell you, the weather and the farmer have ever had an uneasy alliance. Afterward, they would often meet at the market square, to socialize and share the latest news, or gossip, as the case may be. The rest of the week was either spent tending their farms or working at stalls in the market to sell the produce thereof.

Year after year, this was their life with very little deviation. The rains usually arrived when moisture was needed, and the sun usually shone when it wasn't. Still, 'usually' should not be mistaken for 'always.' Growing crops was by no means a certainty. That was why whenever two or more of the villagers met at the square the conversation inevitably turned to the weather. Oftentimes they hearkened back to yesteryear with hyperbolic tales of the summer-of-the-knee-high-grasshoppers, or the winter-of-the-blue-snow. Sage heads would wag at the mention that Hans Gromp had cut his hay too early, or that

Vasily Pomkin had left his pumpkin harvest too late. To be sure, they would talk of other subjects, too, like rust in the wheat, or blight in the potatoes, or if the rains would fill out the heads of the barley, or if the plants were already too mature. The gist of it all, of course, was that the very real problems they faced were centred around husbandry of land that their fathers and forefathers had tilled before them, and their sons looked to inherit when they themselves were gone. If any mention was ever made of the world outside their valley, it was to do with the market price of their produce set in the far distant Capital, and to gleefully damn the politicians there, regardless of the party involved.

Now, just outside of this remote village was a farm at the foot of the mountain the village was named for, consisting of a few acres of rocky soil. It's current owner, Yuri Zavlov, was typical of that area, although even more typical than most. To Yuri, it was the farm that mattered, everything else was superfluous. One of the results of that philosophy was that he had never travelled more than a few kilometres from the village in his entire life. Certainly, he had never set foot on the dilapidated road that led through the forest.

A craggy faced man of perhaps fifty years of age, Yuri seemed to be a timeless figure carved from the land itself. Evidence of a lifetime spent tilling the soil was ingrained under his nails, and in the crevices around his eyes, so much so that it was difficult to tell where his features ended, and his homespun peasant garb began. If any of his fellow villagers was asked to describe him, they would universally mention his singularity of purpose. Whenever something – an issue, a problem, or what have you – became lodged in his mind, they declared that a crowbar couldn't pry it out until it had been resolved. They also declared that it was both his greatest and weakest personality trait, which was true, as we shall see.

A widower for some thirty years, Yuri lived with his mother-in-law, Oksana, two dogs, Pyotr and Borys, and Svetlana, the cat, all under the roof of the cottage his great grandsire had built many years before. As a household, they got along well. From sunup to sundown, Yuri and the dogs would be out working the fields, while Oksana busied herself about the house. At the supper table they would discuss the day's events in their quiet way, often damning the government out of habit, dating back to the days when Xoraina belonged to the Zlaimperian Empire. Of an evening they would sit by the fire, Yuri engrossed in a copy of the Farmers' Almanac, while Oksana, in her old rocking chair, peered short-sightedly at her knitting. Meanwhile, Pyotr and Borys would lie at one or the other's feet, while Svetlana daintily assumed the most privileged place of all on the hearth, closest to the glowing coals.

As for their outlook on life, both Oksana and Yuri viewed virtually everything through the lens of what was, or wasn't, good for the farm. If it was good for the farm, then it was good, if it wasn't, then it was bad, or at best, unimportant. Given the arduous nature of their existence, everything they owned had a purpose – even the dogs and Svetlana had to earn their keep – while luxuries were virtually unheard of. This included any of those modern electronic devices that were such the rage these days, or even a television. They did, however, own a radio that Yuri had been meaning to take to the repair shop for the last decade but constantly forgot.

Homstood was not a terribly prosperous community, and Yuri's farm exemplified that fact, which is to say that it was not prosperous at all. The reasons vary, depending upon whom you ask. Some say it was appallingly bad luck, which, given the nature of farming, is easy to believe. Others say that Yuri's obstinate streak was his own undoing, which is also easy to believe, as it could not be denied that there was a certain stubbornness to his nature. However, all agreed that the rocky land and thin topsoil might also be the culprits. The long and the short of it was that, while the land produced enough for them to subsist on, it did not allow the household to prosper. So it was that, one rainy evening in February, instead of sitting by the fire, we find Yuri at the kitchen table with a dog-eared sheet of paper in front of him while, with furrowed brow, he laboriously entered figures in a column with the broken end of a pencil. It was a chore he performed at this time every year and was of the gravest importance. He was planning for the coming growing season by deciding which crops should be sown, and where. Upon such momentous decisions the dubious fortune of Casa Zavlov would be made or lost.

"Well now, let's see," he murmured to himself. "I planted sunflowers in the north field last year, so I should plant wheat there this year, and there is still enough excess left in the granary to use for seed. I can do the same with the south field where I grew wheat the year before, using excess barley for seed. The west field has had crops grown on it for the last three years, so I'll leave it fallow this season to recuperate." At this point he paused, the pencil end poised over a square on the paper marked The East Field. Still murmuring, he said, "I would very much like to grow sunflowers here. The last time Mother Oksana went to the village, the farmers in the square told her that the price was through the roof – almost fifty lakons per demlo! The east field has the richest soil with the fewest rocks. If God is good, and the harvest is rich, I should be able to sell it for a fortune. If that were to be the case, then it would be possible to make repairs to the barn." Belatedly noticing the steady 'pat, pat, pat' of water dripping from the ceiling into the pot at his elbow, he added, "And, who knows, there might even be enough left over to re-thatch the roof of the cottage." Caught up in the thought, to Yuri, the future began to look bright ... until a shadow cast a pall over his dream. The problem was that the granary where he had kept his sunflowers had been swept clean months ago to pay for repairs to his truck, and he hadn't any left to replace them.

Frowning, he opened his booklet from the National Bank to check his balance and noted the hundred and sixty-five lakons penned neatly at the bottom. Then, laboriously calculating, he reckoned that he would need five demlos of sunflowers for seed, which, at eight hundred and thirty lakons per demlo, would cost two hundred and fifty lakons, leaving him eighty-five lakons short. Yuri sighed, and sat back in his chair, watching his fledgling dreams of riches dissipate into thin air ... but wait!

"My friend, Vasily Pomkin, has some leftover sunflowers. Perhaps he will be able to spare some for me at a reduced price. I will go to see him tomorrow with my proposition. The worst he can do is say no."

True to his word, Yuri caught up with Vasily the next day. He was forking manure onto a sledge but, of course, like any good Homstooder, ceased his exertions out of courtesy. After they exchanged the usual pleasantries, coupled with gloomy predictions about the weather, Vasily leaned on his fork, and said, "I know you are a busy man, my friend, as busy as I am myself. If you were to tell me the purpose of your visit, then we can both get back to our chores."

So, Yuri related his thoughts about planting sunflowers in his east field, and his lack of seeds. He went on further to recall that Vasily himself had mentioned that he had an excess of sunflower seeds, and would he be willing to part with five demlos of them, at fair market value, of course?

Yuri had mentioned fair market value only as a matter of pride and etiquette. It was no less than what was expected, just as he knew he could expect Vasily's counteroffer to be *less* than fair market value. The two men had been friends for many years and had often helped one another when times were hard, which they very often were. He saw no reason why that should not continue. As it turned out, he was partially right, but also partially wrong.

"Well now," said Vasily, his chin resting on the butt end of his fork, "it is true that I have an excess of sunflower seeds, and I will happily part with five demlos, and at a discounted price at that." Calculating quickly, he said, "What do you say to forty-five lakons per demlo?"

Yuri was careful to keep his features impassive – to show otherwise would not have been polite – but inside, his hopes for a field of sunflowers plummeted a second time. According to Vasily's offer, five demlos of seed would cost two hundred and twenty-five lakons. It would be a discounted price as his friend had promised, but it was still sixty lakons more than he could afford.

Forcing a smile, he said, "That is very generous of you, my friend."

However, Vasily was no fool. He could see through Yuri's polite smile and guessed that his offer was less than what he had hoped for, so he decided to explain.

"Look you, neighbour," he said, "I would happily sell it for even less, for I want the best for you and yours. But, you see, my oldest son will be leaving for university in the autumn and will need money for such things as clothes and tuition and books and such. So, I am afraid that I cannot go any lower than forty-five lakons per demlo." Somewhat defensively, he added, "Even then I would be taking a loss, for I could get fifty lakons at the market."

Yuri hastened to reassure his friend that his offer was more than generous, and that he would go home and ponder over it before deciding. "After all," he said, "two hundred and twenty-five lakons is a great deal of money."

Vasily readily agreed. It wasn't the custom of such folk to make precipitate decisions concerning the world of finance, so Yuri's vacillating came as no surprise. Therefore, after verifying that Yuri would not stay to share a glass of nalivka, Vasily wished his friend a good day before carrying on with his work.

That evening at the dinner table, Yuri idly swirled his spoon through his borscht, obviously deep in thought. At both knees, Pyotr and Borys stared with all the diligence of dogs willing table scraps to fall to the floor. Over by the old woodstove, Svetlana lapped contentedly at her saucer of milk.

Observing her son-in-law, Oksana, said, "What ails you, my boy? You have scarcely touched your food."

Roused from his thoughts, Yuri had no wish to cause Oksana to worry. So, stressing how insignificant it was, he confessed his seemingly forlorn hopes for the east field, and ended by saying, "It is nothing, really, Mother. I will plant the east field with potatoes, instead, and any dreams of wealth will have to wait for a better year."

Few words were spoken for the rest of the meal, aside from Oksana insisting that his borscht not go to waste, but she never stopped thinking about the problem until they were settled by the fire – her with her knitting, and Yuri with his ever-present almanac.

"Did you know," she began, "that I went into the village today?"

"Hmmm, yes?" said Yuri, without looking up from his book.

"Yes," she affirmed, "and guess who I ran into at the market?"

Still not looking up, Yuri said, "I have no idea, Mother Oksana." Then, dutifully, he added, "Who did you run into at the market today?"

"Hans Gromp," was her pert reply. "And guess what he told me."

Closing his book at last, Yuri looked at his mother-in-law, and smiled. "What is this, Mother? Are we playing A Hundred Questions? I have no idea what Hans Gromp told you. Perhaps you could enlighten me?"

Not wishing to string out the suspense any further, she said, "He told me that pigs are selling for two lakons per kilo."

Yuri regarded his mother-in-law with sudden interest, while a flurry of calculations progressed inside his head.

If Mother Oksana said that she had received the information from Hans Gromp, then he was inclined to believe it; for Hans Gromp was known as a virtuous man. Now, given that the old price was one lakon per kilo, a pig ripe for market of, say, fifty kilos for easy figuring, the profit would be fifty lakons. Obviously, this would still not be enough to purchase the sunflower seeds from Vasily Pomkin. However, with this new price of two lakons per kilo (a price never before heard of), his profit would be more than enough to purchase the seed, and still have some money left over.

It was a very attractive notion, for Yuri possessed two pigs, a young sow and a boar. It had been his intention to make his fortune raising pork, but the sow had been the runt of the litter and was still a shade under the ideal weight. Clearly, he could not send her to market. The boar on the other hand …

"There was something else," Mother Oksana ventured, not wishing to dash her son-in-law's hopes, but she knew it was best to put everything on the table from the start.

Recognising her tone, Yuri looked at his mother-in-law through guarded eyes.

"Yes?"

"Hans Gromp told me that the price of two lakons per kilo can only be paid by the Central Market in Lofstov. Which means, of course, that the pig would have to be shipped there on the train, and the National Railroad charges a shipping fee."

Yuri did his best not to heave a sigh of relief, for that would not have been becoming. He had shipped livestock in the past and knew that the travel fee was reasonable – possibly only ten centiems (one tenth of a lakon) per animal to reach the Central Market in Lofstov, which was easily affordable.

Of greater concern was that, having deprived himself of his boar, his pig-raising scheme would have to be put temporarily on hold. However, at fifty lakons per demlo, with the money he received for a sunflower crop, he would be able to purchase any boar he chose, possibly even one with papers. He smiled at the mere thought. If he had a boar with papers, the offspring would be worth double, or even ten times more than the market price. Not only that, he would also be able to charge stud fees from other farmers who wished to have their own sows serviced. With that in mind, selling his current, unregistered boar now, in order to realise sizeable profits in the future, appeared to be the obvious choice.

"That is very interesting news, Mother Oksana," he said, and the old woman flushed with pleasure at his praise. "Tomorrow I will go to the market myself and seek out Hans Gromp, to see if there is anything more he can tell me."

*

Early the next morning, Yuri found Hans Gromp at his market stall selling turnips. The conversation they had was short and confirmed what Oksana had said the night before. However,

Hans Gromp didn't seem to be terribly engrossed in the subject but was otherwise so preoccupied with something that he completely failed to mention the weather at all.

"Yes, that's right," he confirmed, "two lakons per kilo, payable at the Central Market in Lofstov." Then, revealing why he was otherwise preoccupied, he said, "But, that is a risky proposition now that the country is at war."

However, having had the good news confirmed, Yuri, with his singularity of purpose, was unwilling to pay much heed to Hans Gromp's warning. Too many things had fallen into place to make this anything other than a rare opportunity that mustn't be missed. Instead, he made an offhand remark, thanked Hans Gromp for his help, and returned to his farm, determined to get his pig to the station bright and early the next morning.

With his dreams finally within his grasp, Yuri slept more soundly, and peacefully, than he could ever remember, so soundly, in fact, that he never heard the distant rumble that might have been thunder but, tragically, wasn't.

*

As the pig snoozed contentedly in the ooze of the sty, he reckoned that he was the happiest pig in the world. The mud on the farm was of the highest quality, especially after it rained, making it just right for a good wallow. The swill was exceptional, too, for the squire never threw out any leftovers from his own table but saved the scraps for himself and the sow the next morning. The sow, who was the kindest, most beautiful sow in all the world, was equally contented, and had mentioned as much to him only a minute ago. She said that she was especially contented whenever he was near.

He wallowed deeper into the slime, relishing the memory. Then, as the grey light of dawn began to creep above the horizon, he thought that yes, it was a good life here on the farm, and he could see no reason why it shouldn't continue so for the rest of his days.

Just then, the door to the cottage swung open and the squire emerged carrying a fresh pail of swill. The pig grunted with pleasure and dove into the treasure as soon as it was poured into his trough. He was so engrossed that he never even noticed when the simple collar made of twine was slipped over his head.

Chapter Two

Yuri stood at the shipping agent's kiosk. In his pocket jingled the few coins needed to ship his pig to the Central Market in Lofstov. The pig in question stood obediently at his heel, snuffling contentedly through the grass.

Curiously, the shipping agent seemed as preoccupied as Hans Gromp had been the day before. However, just like his customers, he was first and foremost a Homstooder, which meant that several years spent at his occupation had ingrained a certain civility to avoid being rude.

"That is a fine hog," he said, although he was glancing nervously at the sky rather than at Yuri's pig. "Perhaps you could take him to the scale for me, please."

Obediently, Yuri took the pig to the scale beside the kiosk, and the pig, just as obediently, stood on it to be weighed.

"Fifty point four three kilos," the shipping agent nodded approvingly. Then, checking a table on a chart, he said, "That will be twenty-three centiems for shipping." As Yuri dug around in his pocket for the correct change, his hand froze when the shipping agent added, "And fifteen lakons for insurance."

Aghast, Yuri asked, "What did you say?" hoping against hope that he hadn't heard correctly.

More preoccupied than ever now, the shipping agent had paused with his head atilt, as if listening for something, but Yuri's response dragged his attention back to his duty, albeit only partially.

"What? Oh yes, that was just introduced. A new tax, they said, to cover the insurance of your cargo in transit." In a weak effort to ameliorate the shock, he added, "But you can continue to ship livestock on the same policy for one year before you are required to renew it."

"What other livestock?" an aggrieved Yuri asked. "I only want to ship one pig!"

"I am sorry, Yuri Yurivich," the shipping agent replied with a dramatic shrug, "but my hands are tied. It is the law."

"So, a new law, eh?" Yuri asked, expecting the shipping agent to share a knowing look with him, one that those of the village reserved exclusively for conversations concerning the government and taxes. However, the shipping agent had slipped away once more, staring at nothing in particular that Yuri could see, with his head tilted to one side as it had before. In the distance, the faraway drone of a jet engine drew rapidly nearer.

Diving beneath the kiosk, the shipping agent cried, "GET DOWN!"

The drone of the jet engine grew steadily into a roar until it filled Yuri's senses, while all around the rail station suddenly burst into chaos. People were running hither and thither, with women screaming, children crying, and men bellowing for no apparent reason. One man ran past him, his eyes wild with terror, while a woman huddled against the station wall, clutching a child to her breast. As he slowly turned, everywhere he looked the crowded station was surging with panic.

"How curious," he thought.

Then, with the roar of the jet engine drowning out a multitude of screaming voices, a few hundred metres down the railroad tracks, he saw fountains of earth suddenly burst from the ground, intermingled with twisted rails hurtling through the air. Even as he was struggling to come to terms with that, the deafening explosion caused him to stagger and clamp his hands over his ears. At his feet, the pig uttered a surprised grunt, and tried to run away, but was held firm by the leash in Yuri's hand.

After a long pause, when all the dust had settled, slowly, ever so cautiously, the shipping agent re-emerged from beneath the kiosk.

"I never had to pay a tax for insurance before," Yuri observed ruefully. "The government always covered the expense."

"What?" the shipping agent asked, in a distracted sort of way.

"The insurance," Yuri reiterated, "I have never had to pay for that before."

Still distracted, the shipping agent repeated, "What?"

After Yuri had morosely voiced his opinion of the new tax a third time, the shipping agent stared at him as if he had just grown horns.

"Well," he finally managed, "you have to pay it, it's the law. Now," he said, "I don't know about you, but I'm getting out of here before they return!" So saying, he began to close the kiosk.

Still ruminating about the new tax, Yuri absently asked, "Before who returns?"

On the verge of pulling down the shutters, the shipping agent cried, "The Zlaimperians, you fool!" Pointing a trembling finger to where the railroad tracks had so violently disappeared, he said, "The bastards who are responsible for that!" Staring as one might at an imbecile, he added, "My God, man, haven't you heard there's a war on?"

"Hmm," Yuri replied, in a disinterested sort of way. Then he said, "Well, it's not getting my pig any closer to market, now is it?" However, his words reached no one's ears but his own, for the shutter had already closed with a crash.

After glaring spitefully at where the shipping agent had been only a moment before, Yuri decided that there was nothing further to be done; so he left, with the pig trotting nervously at his heels.

He was still deep in thought twenty minutes later when the sound of a second jet engine roared into a crescendo, and having received a direct hit, the railway station erupted into a mountain of dust and debris behind him. Engrossed as he was in his single-minded way, he remained unaware of any of it.

Yuri's outlook on life was divided into two categories: things that could be explained, and things that just were. That sort of acceptance had served him well in the past, like, for instance, the time when he'd been about to harvest the wheat from his north field, and a sudden hailstorm had sprung from nowhere, flattening it to the ground. He hadn't cried out at his cruel fate, but had accepted that the hailstorm had happened, and doggedly set about preparing for the next growing season, instead. There was no use in complaining. After all, if anyone was responsible, it was God Almighty, and who was Yuri to question His motives? But this time was different.

Along with his philosophy of acceptance, perhaps incongruently, Yuri also possessed a finely tuned notion of justice; and the more he thought about it, the more he felt that this new tax was not just. Of the Zlaimperians and the war the shipping agent had spoken of, he thought nothing at all. What mattered was that his plan to sow the east field to sunflowers would never see fruition unless he was first able to purchase the seeds from Vasily Pomkin, and for *that* to happen, he had to get his pig to the Central Market in Lofstov, which wouldn't be possible because of the new insurance tax he couldn't afford to pay. To Yuri's mind, the tax wasn't '*the way things were*,' but neither could it be explained. Conveniently, he ignored the fact that the track had just been obliterated by the bombing at any rate. Until it was repaired, no one was shipping anything to the Central Market in Lofstov or anywhere else.

As Yuri puzzled over his dilemma, he and the pig approached the village market square. His awareness of any activity around him was so vague as to be virtually non-existent. However, in actual fact, the chaos in the village mirrored that which had been in the now equally non-existent rail station. People were running about in terror. Mothers scooped up their children, whisking them inside their homes, while the traffic in the streets – usually a trickle at this time of day – had suddenly grown to overflowing, with no resemblance to the sleepy crawl it had been in the past. The people inside their vehicles were as panicked as those running in the streets, with no thought to obeying the traffic signs whatsoever. Under such conditions, it was inevitable that a collision should occur at an intersection right in front of Yuri, when a car heading north ran into a truck (loaded with a household's worth of furniture, a crate of chickens, and a goat) heading west.

The sound of the collision directly in front of him penetrated Yuri's thoughts long enough to cause him to look up. A cacophony of aggrieved motorists, and equally aggrieved chickens, mingled with the panicked cries of everyone else. The goat, Yuri vaguely noted, appeared to accept the situation with stoic resignation. Stepping carefully, he (Yuri, not the goat) manoeuvred around the site of the crash and would have been on his way, but then he noticed that the driver in the vehicle behind the damaged truck was none other than the village administrator.

Without hesitation, he walked purposefully to the administrator's car, and ignoring the traumatised chicken on the bonnet, tapped on the driver's side window. Caught in the stalled traffic, unable to move in any direction, the administrator had little choice but to roll down the window.

Staring at Yuri in much the same manner as the shipping agent had, the administrator asked, "Yes, what is it?"

Peering inside the car, Yuri noted that the administrator's entire family was inside, all staring at him with varying shades of incredulity. Like any true Homstooder, he respectfully tugged the peak of his cap to them before returning his attention to the administrator.

"I want to speak to you about the new shipping tax for livestock," he said.

Glassy-eyed, the administrator asked, "What?"

"I think it's unjust," Yuri informed him, with a good deal of confidence.

From the back seat of the car, the administrator's daughter asked, "What does he want, Daddy?"

From the seat next to his, the administrator's agitated wife leaned over and touched his forearm to gain his attention. "Come, Yevgeny, we must flee to the countryside! Think of our children!"

Exasperated, the administrator indicated all the traffic filling the streets, which had now ground to a complete stop due to the collision. "How shall I accomplish that, my dear? We are hemmed in by that bastard truck in front of us and the bastard traffic backed up behind. We are unable to budge an inch!"

After advising him, in a dangerous tone, to be more careful with his language around their children, his wife shrilled,

"You are the village administrator! Have a party clear that truck off the road at once!"

Emitting a long-suffering sigh, the administrator reluctantly agreed. He got out of the car and walked toward the stalled truck in the intersection.

Trotting at his heels, with the pig in tow, Yuri reminded him, "About the shipping tax, sir …"

Preoccupied, the administrator turned at the sound of his voice, grasping him by the arm.

"Good, come with me." Then turning elsewhere, he said to some other men passing by, "You, you and you, help me get this thrice damned truck off the street."

"But sir, the shipping tax …"

Irritably, the administrator snapped, "Not now!" and led his party to the truck.

Coming around to the driver's side, they found an old grey beard and his wife lamenting the loss of their chickens.

Pulling his hair, the old fellow cried, "What shall become of us without my truck and my chickens?"

Still perturbed, the administrator snapped, "Never mind that, can you get this old heap moving?"

The old man's wife cried, "But our chickens, Your Honour, they won the blue ribbon at the Homstood County Fair last year, and I …"

Past all patience, the administrator cried, "I don't care if they won the Miss Universe Competition, can you get your truck off the street?"

Shocked by his callousness, the old man said, "There's no need to shout, Your Honour, and I'll thank you not to take that tone with my wife. After all," he huffed, "they aren't your chickens, are they?"

"But sir, about that shipping tax …"

Ignoring Yuri completely, the administrator grated to the old man. "Just try it, damn you!"

The old man did as he was ordered, albeit with some truculence. The engine turned over but refused to fire. At which point, everyone the administrator brought along to help chimed in with an opinion.

"It's flooded," said one.

"Take it out of gear," another directed.

"Put it in gear," said a third.

"The battery must be disconnected," said a fourth, obviously forgetting that the engine had turned over.

"Let's have a look under the bonnet," suggested yet another, which was deemed by all to be a reasonable course of action.

The men traipsed around to the front of the vehicle, where one of them managed to raise the bonnet. They gathered around, staring at the oil-caked mysteries within, each one unwilling to admit to the others that they knew nothing whatsoever about internal combustion engines.

Finally, one of them said, "It's no use, we'll have to push it off the road." It was then that Yuri elbowed his way to the fore.

Looking inside, he noticed that the engine was probably older than he was himself, and that a wire hung loose from the distributor. Pulling his Swiss Army knife from his pocket, he chose the pliers feature and soon had the wire tightened back onto its post.

Calling from under the bonnet, he cried, "Try it now!"

There was no response.

Looking up, Yuri, along with the rest of the men, peered through the windshield into the cab.

It was empty.

Frantically looking around, one of them finally pointed, and cried, "There they are!"

Following the direction indicated, Yuri saw the old grey beard with a chicken under his arm while he gave chase to another, with his wife following helpfully with the cage.

Taking hold of the man who had called out, he indicated the cab of the truck, and said, "Get in and give it a try."

The man blinked at the simplicity of the solution. Then nodding, he climbed behind the wheel and turned the key. The engine fired immediately.

After the administrator directed the man to pull the truck over to the shoulder of the road, he walked back to his car with Yuri and his pig trailing after him; but before he could speak, the administrator turned to him, as if suddenly remembering his presence.

"Look, Yuri Yurivich," he said in a harassed sort of way, "I understand your feelings about the new shipping tax, but the law is the law. There's nothing I can do."

"But, sir," Yuri insisted, "it's a stupid law and ought to be repealed."

The administrator uttered a dry, mirthless laugh. "Well, there it is, you see? I'm sorry, but I can't help you. Now, if you don't mind …"

The administrator climbed in behind the wheel of his car. By now, the streets were filled with the sound of horns blowing and angry motorists demanding to know why the traffic wasn't moving. If the administrator had simply got in his car and driven away that would have been the end of a rather unremarkable story. Left with no other choice, Yuri and his pig would have returned to their home, and nothing further could have been said on the matter. But the administrator didn't simply drive away. Instead, he happened to glance up and caught Yuri still standing there, wearing the most morose expression he had ever seen … and, of course, the pig standing beside him, looking even more morose than Yuri.

Reaching a decision, the administrator sighed, much as he had done with his wife earlier, and rolled the window down again.

"See here, Yuri, if it means that much to you, you can petition to have the law repealed."

With hope resurging by leaps and bounds, Yuri eagerly asked, "Who do I petition?"

"Why, the president, of course."

Yuri stared at him. "Do you mean to say …?"

"Yes," the administrator confirmed. "The only place that can be done is at the Capital, five hundred kilometres away, so that is where you would have to travel." Then, gesturing into the distance at the current inferno that had been the train station, he said, "But I would advise against it. Good luck." So saying, he drove off before Yuri could reply.

Deep in thought, Yuri watched him go, while the traffic, no longer stagnant, passed by perilously close.

"The Capital, eh?" He murmured to himself. "Hmmm."

Then, absently, he tied the pig to a lamppost and went to help the old couple collect their chickens.

*

The pig had been troubled earlier because of the nasty noise he had heard at the station, and all the screaming people running about with no one looking as if they knew where they were going. He could tell that the squire had been troubled, too, although he had no idea why. However, his concern began to fade as they neared the sights and smells of the market. When the squire tethered him to that lamppost before running off to help those old grey hairs with their chickens, he wasn't troubled at all, for he had discovered that a table, once stacked high with vegetables, had been overturned in the general panic ... and all that toothsome bounty was easily within reach.

Chapter Three

The remainder of that day saw Yuri caught up in an increasing state of perplexion. To begin with, the village administrator's advice required some serious thought. Given his single-minded nature, and his finely tuned sense of justice, it should come as no surprise that he concentrated far more on going to the Capital to plead his case than the administrator's final admonition that he not attempt it. However, first things first, he must confirm that the Kamaz was still up to the task.

Many years ago, when Xoraina was still part of the Zlaimperian Empire, the east field had produced a bumper crop of wheat. At the same time, the market price had been high due to famine in far-off Africa. That was one of those rare instances when the Zavlov family had experienced a time of plenty; so much so that a new washing machine had been acquired for his mother, and Yuri's father had purchased the Kamaz fresh off the assembly line. Painted a brilliant fire engine red, it was one of Yuri's first memories as a child. At the time, he thought it was beautiful. I must remind you, however, that this was many years ago.

Over time, the Kamaz had delivered dependable service, even as the fire engine red gradually transformed into a burnt brick colour that, in turn, blended in with the ever-widening patches of rust on the fenders. However, over the last decade, its dependability had begun to wane, requiring constant attention, and untold hours of maintenance. As a result, Yuri wasn't all that surprised when, taking it for a trial run, a radiator hose gave out, and the truck expired in a cloud of steam before it ever got off his land.

Yuri took a moment to consider his options. True, he could go to the village to order a new hose from the Kamaz dealer, which he would certainly do, regardless; but now that the decision had been made to go to the Capital, he was unwilling to countenance the delay. Therefore, he decided to ask Hans

Gromp if he could borrow his truck, instead. Perhaps he would even ask Hans to accompany him. As he set out on foot to the Gromp farm, he reasoned that, when it came to pleading his case to the President, it had to be acknowledged that there was strength to be found in numbers. As he walked along, the more he thought about it, the more Yuri came to believe that it was a brilliant plan, and for all we know, it might have been, if it had ever come to fruition. Sadly, it never did, for when Yuri arrived at the Gromps' cottage, he discovered that no one was home, and the vacant space beside the barn told him that, wherever he had gone, Hans had taken his truck with him.

This was a mystery, all the more so as it wasn't a market day; but even though a mystery, it wasn't entirely unheard of for his friend to leave with a destination in mind other than the village. It was rare, certainly, but as I said, not entirely unheard of.

Yuri puzzled over the matter for a good minute before he shrugged, accepted that it was '*just the way things were*,' and thought to himself, '*Never mind, I will ask my good friend, Vasily Pomkin, if I can borrow* his *truck, instead.*'

Except that the Pomkin household wasn't home, either. As was the case in the Gromp farm, here too Vasily's truck was gone, and not even so much as a chicken could be seen pecking in the yard.

How very curious, indeed.

Once more Yuri allowed himself a brief moment to ponder this imponderable, before giving up and proceeding to Plan C ... or was it D ... or possibly a furtherance of Plan A? By now it was difficult to keep track. Regardless, he said, "It looks as though I must go into Homstood to order a new radiator hose, after all."

Having reached this decision, he set off for the village straight away ... only to find that there was no one at the dealership, either. In fact, there didn't seem to be anyone in the village, at all. There is a possibility that, had he not been such a single-minded fellow so absorbed with getting his pig to market, Yuri would have been able to piece together the logjam of traffic from the day before with the absence of people on the streets today. As it was, this was duly noted, also filed under '*just the way things were*,' the same as he had done regarding the absence of both his friends earlier. Now, finding himself out of options, he returned to his home, where he puzzled over what his next step should be.

Well, actually, that isn't *quite* true. Yuri already knew what his next step would be, even before he left the village.

That night over dinner, he informed Oksana of the new shipping tax, and his conversation with the village administrator regarding having it rescinded. Yuri then went on to tell her about the burst radiator hose in his truck, and how his subsequent search to find an alternate means of transportation had failed.

When he had finished, Oksana, who had listened with interest, said, "That is certainly curious, is it not?"

Yuri, whose mind had already slipped back into the apparent dilemma, said, "Hmm? What is curious, Mother?"

"That both Hans Gromp and Vasily Pomkin are gone, not to mention the rest of the village. I wonder where they went?"

Yuri, as you may have gathered by now, was not gifted with as curious a mind as his mother-in-law. So, instead of attempting to answer her question, he asked one of his own.

"Mother, how far is five hundred kilometres?"

Oksana paused to consider. It was a simple enough question, Heaven knows, and yet she discovered that, not having travelled any further from the village than Yuri had himself, she was unsure of the answer.

Still, endeavouring to be helpful, she replied, "I don't know, my boy, but I think it is very far." Then, intrigued by the question, as it was not a topic that her son-in-law had ever shown much interest in, half in jest, she asked, "Why? Are you planning to take a trip?"

Instead of the laughter she had expected, Oksana was surprised to be met with Yuri's very serious expression.

Puzzled, Oksana asked, "Where are you planning to go?"

"Why, to the Capital, of course."

"Still?"

"Yes, certainly, why shouldn't I?"

"But you don't have a vehicle. How do you plan to get there?"

"On my own two feet," was the sturdy reply.

"But the Capital is five hundred kilometres away, my boy!"

"Exactly," said Yuri. "That is why I was wondering if I would need you to pack me a lunch?"

Oksana gasped, and thought that Yuri's mind had become addled, until she noticed that he was smiling.

"Oh, you rascal!" She scolded, "You tricked me!" But then the smile faded, and Yuri was thoughtful again.

"Only about the lunch, Mother," he told her. "I still plan to make my way to the Capital, and if necessary, on my own two feet.

Oksana studied her son-in-law carefully.

"But won't it be dangerous? What about this invasion everyone is talking about?"

Yuri shrugged as his face assumed a mulish expression that she was all too familiar with.

"The war has nothing to do with me," he told her. "Governments fight and the people just want to live their lives." Suddenly, he threw his hands up in exasperation. "Oh, what nonsense it all is!" he cried. "In years gone by, during the time of the old empire, the Zlaimperians and Xorainians were brothers. Then we are told that we are free of them. Does my life change? No! The soil still needs to be tilled, the cows still need to be milked, and," pointedly, he added, "the pigs must still be sent to market. Now the Zlaimperians tell us that we will be part of a new empire. Do I care? Do the crops care? Do the pigs and cows care? Again, no!

"The Zavlov family has belonged to the land for a thousand years and will continue to remain so for a thousand more. What do we care about the high thoughts and ideals of the great and powerful? Zlaimperian? Xorainian? Those are just words. What do I care what they choose to call me? I know who I am – Yuri Zavlov, son of Yuri Zavlov, and this is my land! The soil will still need to be tilled, and the pigs must still go to market. That is what matters, Mother Oksana. That is *all* that matters!"

Yuri paused, realising that, in his passion, he had risen from the table, and his voice had increasingly grown louder until he was almost shouting at his mother-in-law. Shamed by it, his eyes fell away as he resumed his seat.

"The Zlaimperians and Xorainians once were brothers," he repeated sullenly. "Why would they wish to bring harm to us? Do not concern yourself, Mother, I will be allowed to go about my business in peace."

Mother Oksana regarded her son-in-law with wide-eyed astonishment. She had no idea that he harboured such strong feelings on the matter. She knew Yuri better than anyone, and nothing could have surprised her more. Composing herself, she began collecting dishes from the table and carrying them to the sink. Finally, she ventured, "Well, if you think so …"

"I do, Mother."

"Then when will you start out?"

"Tomorrow morning. So, I must ask you to take care of things around here while I'm gone. It won't be too arduous," he explained. "Just see that the cow is milked, and that the sow is fed."

"The sow?" Oksana's brow wrinkled. "What about the boar?"

"He will come with me," Yuri explained, as if he had not just said the most astonishing thing she had ever heard, and after an entire conversation filled with astonishing things at that.

"Wait. You will take the pig to the Capital?"

"Of course."

"But what on earth for?"

Yuri reasoned, "The way I see it, this is his dilemma as much as it is mine. Therefore, it is fitting that he should accompany me."

Standing at the kitchen sink, up to her elbows in suds, Oksana gave this some thought.

"In that case," she said, "I will fix you two lunches instead of one."

*

It had been a disturbing few days for the pig. Accompanying the squire to the village had been a treat ... until those frightful explosions happened, and all those over-excited people in their machines began shouting and honking their horns; that had been unnerving, too, for he could smell the fear emanating off them in waves. But how fortunate he had been when the squire had tethered him next to all those tasty vegetables. The resulting feast had eased his stress considerably. Now he was back in his sty again, luxuriating in the mud, while the most beautiful sow in all the world took her ease in the adjacent stall and smiled at him.

Once more the pig reflected that, on the whole, life was good on the squire's farm, and he was becoming increasingly more successful at putting the unpleasant parts of the past few days behind him. He didn't question why life was so good, it simply was. After all, what creature in their right mind would question something that was good? Just take pleasure in the bounty was his line. Such a gift was meant to be enjoyed, and the pig felt that it was no less than his duty to enjoy it to the fullest. To make matters even better, he was exceedingly good at doing that, too.

While he was reflecting, the squire appeared as he usually did at that time of day, with the pail of swill in hand. But what was in his other hand? Was it his collar again?

'Oh, good,' *the pig thought happily,* 'we are returning to the village. I wonder if there will be vegetables for me this time, as well?'

Chapter Four

Just after dawn the next morning Yuri and his four-legged companion set out on the road through the forest for the very first time in their lives. As usual, there was very little traffic. In fact, truth be told, there was no traffic at all. However, there were signs aplenty that many vehicles had passed through the forest just recently, and at high speed.

All along the road lay a plenitude of items, from personal to functional, and everything else in between. Suitcases were predominant, many burst open, intimately revealing the lives of their owners, from undergarments, to dresses, to nightgowns, both frilly and sheer (which made Yuri blush just to look at them) to sensible ones made of cotton. One suitcase revealed a three-piece suit, which Yuri guessed belonged to the village administrator, because no one else in Homstood ever wore a suit, much less owned one. He reasoned, correctly, that these items had come adrift because they had been carelessly (or hastily) strapped down and become dislodged when they hit one of the myriad of potholes on the road.

Here he saw a kitchen chair, over there was a mattress, old and stained, and once he even saw a piano lying disconsolately on its back with its legs splintered into matchwood. He frowned as he studied all these things, for this wasn't '*the way things were,*' but as he travelled along over the days and weeks that followed, it got to the point where he scarcely noticed them at all.

Had Yuri possessed a more susceptible mind, he might have found that single ribbon of broken asphalt through the forest daunting, or possibly even haunting. The tall conifers cast such deep shadow, swallowing the light from the sky, and all those souls scattered along the road, as well. A more susceptible mind might have heard murmuring among the trees, and shadows flitting behind every bole, constantly working on his mind until he fled in panic. Had that been the case, Yuri would not have been the first to be so stricken, for it was certainly not unheard of for someone from the village to wander into the forest never to be seen again. Yes, it would definitely have been a possibility had Yuri not possessed such a pragmatic mind. As it was, the purpose of his journey kept him so preoccupied that he was barely even aware of the forest let alone whispering ghosts and lurking shadows.

The pig, on the other hand, required the occasional tug on his leash, although Yuri scarcely noticed that, either.

They paused at noon where a brook gurgled through the trees. The water, having tumbled all the way from the mountains, was cool and sweet, just the thing for two parched throats. Yuri tethered the pig with enough line for him to forage, while he himself sat beneath a drowsily swaying birch to partake in a meal of cheese, a small loaf, and a few sips of wine from his flask.

Having counted his paces from the outset, he reckoned that they had come fifteen kilometres, and with luck, would have travelled fifteen more by the end of the day. His feet were sore, and his joints ached, but that was due to his not having exercised them to this extent before. In fact, he was now further away from his home than he had ever been in his entire life, and every kilometre would take him further away still. But more to the point, he reckoned that thirty kilometres a day was reasonable to expect. Warming to the task, he set about ciphering how many days it would take to cover the five hundred kilometres to the Capital and was astonished when he arrived at a hundred and seventy days ... but then realised that he forgot to move the decimal point, and arrived at a little over two weeks, instead.

"Two weeks," he murmured to himself, "that shouldn't be too difficult." Thus heartened, he retrieved the pig, and they resumed their journey.

They reached the far edge of the forest by mid-afternoon, where their road debouched onto a highway. Thus far, the forest had completely sheltered them from the outside world, allowing them to proceed on their journey in relative peace and tranquillity, with birdsong the only sounds other than their footsteps on the pavement. But as they neared the intersection with the highway, a low rumble gradually became louder until it grew into a steady roar, quite unlike anything a true Homstooder had ever heard before.

It was traffic, of course, virtually bumper to bumper for miles upon miles. Sometimes racing, sometimes at no more than a crawl, the one thing they all had in common was that everyone was streaming toward the west.

There was a road sign at the intersection with pointing arrows. Alongside the arrow pointing west, in large black letters was LOFSTOV 1500 KILOMETRES. Beside the arrow pointing east was THE CAPITAL 480 KILOMETRES. Mindful that he still had much ground to cover before the end of the day, Yuri turned into the oncoming traffic, following the arrow pointing east.

As they progressed, Yuri noted that the steady stream of vehicles reminded him of what he had witnessed earlier at the village square, but on a much grander scale. As it was then, so was it now, with cars and trucks loaded with every sort of possession you could imagine stretching back to where the road ran out of sight around a bend, and the faces of those crammed inside gaunt with worry.

Another similarity was to the road through the forest. Here, too, was every item conceivable littered along the edge. There were even a handful of the vehicles themselves, abandoned and forlorn, waiting with sad resignation to be reclaimed by the earth. One difference was that this was all on the opposite side of the road. On Yuri's side there was nothing except a border of virgin grass flanked by the forest.

As they travelled along, the traffic would often slow, but this time it slowed until it came to a complete stop.

Instantly, car horns began to blare, mingling with the angry voices of those inside the vehicles. Some even exited those vehicles to exchange insults with owners of other vehicles. In at least one incident, they came close to exchanging blows.

Yuri happened to be close by when he saw a lad in his mid-twenties, dressed in blue jeans and a worn t-shirt, exit an old cream-coloured Lada with balding tires and rust on its panels, to confront another lad exiting a shiny new Mercedes. This one was dressed in a suit that looked far more expensive than any that the village administrator ever wore.

"Look, brother," the former explained, "you can honk your horn all day, but it won't make the line move any faster."

"I'm not your brother," the second replied with a fair bit of acid. "And if you can't make that heap of shit move any faster, you should leave it by the side of the road!"

"Who are you to be calling my car a heap of shit?" demanded the former, his hands suddenly clenching into fists.

"Who are you to say that it isn't?" jeered the second, his hands also curling into fists. "But then, trash likens to trash, does it not?"

The former, with the lean and muscular body of a labourer, took a step closer. Taking note of this threatening gesture, the latter took out an expensive-looking notebook, and gold-plated pen.

"What are you doing?" demanded the former.

"Writing down your licence number," replied the latter, who didn't appear to be anywhere near as muscular. "If you take so much as a single swing at me, the police will be able to track you down and make the arrest. Oh," he said smugly, "didn't I tell you? My father is the most expensive lawyer in the Capital."

With one swipe of his hand, the former sent the notebook flying. "The devil take your father," he said. "But the devil take you most of all."

Reaching out, he grabbed the latter by the front of his shirt, and drew his fist back, but before the blow could fall, Yuri intervened.

Catching the former by the arm, he demanded, "What's going on? This is no way for two lads to behave. Your mothers would be ashamed of you."

Two faces swivelled toward him, and Yuri could clearly see the fear etched on both of them.

"Who are you to interfere, old man?" sneered the former. "Besides," gesturing at the latter, he added truculently, "he started it."

Yuri bristled. "Who are you calling old? I'm the guy who is going knock some sense into you if you don't stop acting like a child." Turning to the latter, who was already pale from having come so close to being assaulted, he added, "Both of you!" to make it clear that he wasn't choosing sides.

Taking note of Yuri's stocky build and powerful hands, the labourer hesitated. Sensing incorrectly that he had an ally, the lawyer's son grew bold again.

"You're not such a bully now, are you?" he jeered at the labourer, and quickly found himself the object of Yuri's baleful gaze.

"If you don't shut your mouth," Yuri growled, "I'll shut it for you."

With both young men chastened to silence, Yuri stepped back, and said, "I don't know what you're afraid of or why, but this isn't helping." To the lawyer's son, he indicated the labourer, and said, "He was going slow because the traffic was going slow. Surely you're aware of this, and don't try to tell me otherwise."

Any show of defiance that may have begun to show on the young man's expression quickly melted away under Yuri's cold stare.

Turning to the labourer now, Yuri said, "And you, don't be so quick to show your fists, especially against someone who is weaker."

For a moment, it looked as though the lawyer's son was about to object to being referred to as a weakling, but upon noticing that Yuri's expression hadn't softened, he decided to keep any such objections to himself.

"I'm sorry, Father," he said, using the Xorainian gesture of respect. Indicating the direction from which that long stream of vehicles had come, he continued. "It's just that it's so horrible back there. People are on edge, including myself." Reaching out, he offered the labourer his hand. "I apologise for my boorish behaviour," he said. "That was unforgiveable of me."

Accepting the hand, the labourer replied, "No, Brother, this was my fault entirely." Tilting his chin down the road, he said, "Just as you say, it's a horror story back there. Everyone is on a short fuse."

Satisfied, Yuri said, "Good, now I suggest both of you return to your vehicles and continue in peace. Fast or slow, the important thing is that you arrive at your destinations safely."

The two young men were proceeding to do as instructed when, after a moment's reflection, Yuri called, "Wait!" Gesturing to where they had just come from (which happened to be the way he was going), he asked, "You mentioned something about trouble down the road. What sort of trouble?"

The two lads looked at Yuri with astonishment, then at one another, before returning to Yuri. Finally, the one whose father was the most expensive lawyer in the Capital said, "Why, the war is happening. The Zlaimperians are bombing everywhere."

"They bombed my village only yesterday," said the labourer, his face twisting with emotion. "They killed my sister." Then, baring his teeth, he said, "I'm taking my mother to Lofstov where she will be safe, and then I will return to fight!"

The other lad offered his condolences before proceeding to say that he, too, planned to return once he had seen his aged grandfather safely out of the country. An animated conversation ensued which Yuri was no longer part of. Therefore, finding himself ignored, he decided to continue on his way.

Once more this war business had reared its ugly head. The fear he had seen in those two lads had been palpable. It was true, young people are impressionable creatures, and prone to being overly dramatic, but the same could not be said for everyone in that long train of vehicles. It also had to be noted that, in spite of their fear, both young men had vowed to return to take up the fight. The courage *that* would require was, quite simply, something that he had never considered before.

Staring down the road, he realised that something was out there, some dark force that had devastating power, enough to drive all those people away in terror. Girding himself, he thought, well, that was certainly too bad, but he was willing to wager that all those who were suffering had been in defiance of the Zlaimperians. So, to a certain measure, it might possibly be said that they had brought their misfortune on themselves. At any rate, he was willing to bet that none of them had been trying to get their pig to market. War or no war, people needed to eat. Surely even the Zlaimperians could understand that.

*

That night he made camp by the side of the road but was assaulted by two men and a woman. Bedraggled creatures, they had crept close and attempted to steal his food. They might have succeeded if the pig hadn't squealed a warning. Forced to defend himself, Yuri had left both men unconscious by the fire while the woman took flight, shouting shocking obscenities at him as she fled into the dark. All this happened within a few feet of that seemingly endless stream of vehicles, but it never occurred to him to call for help. That was a concept that was completely foreign to anyone from Homstood, where everyone looked after themselves. The next night he moved deeper into the forest before making camp, specifically to avoid such encounters. Yuri was afraid of no man, but there was no use in taking unnecessary risks, either.

Even so, he was just settling into his bedroll when a twig snapped outside of the periphery of the fire's glow. Instantly alert, he called out, "Who's there?" When there was no immediate answer, he called, "Don't make me come out to find you!"

A moment later, the image of a young woman ventured into view, arms crossed protectively across her breasts.

"I'm hungry," she said. "Please, Father, if you have anything you could share …"

Unhesitating, Yuri unclasped his knife and cut off a length of sausage for her, as well as a good-sized portion from his block of cheese. Offering these, he invited her to sit by the fire while he unstopped his wineskin.

She accepted his invitation to sit, choosing a spot across the fire from him. Her eyes were as furtive and haunted as those of the two young men had been. She was a bit gaunt, maybe, but he was sure that, in better times, she would have had no shortage of young gentleman callers arriving at her door. As it was, he looked away out of politeness when she ravenously tore into her food.

At first, conversation was limited as she seemed reluctant to speak. But gradually the words began to flow, for although she still appeared *reluctant* to speak, it occurred to Yuri that she was unable to stop. The story she had to tell was short but powerful.

"The Zlaimperians came to my village," she said in a voice was filled with tension. "They took away the old and the sick. We never saw them again. Just like we never saw our men again, either." Her voice threatened to break when she added, "We just heard the gunfire coming from the woods."

Uncomfortable, Yuri murmured his commiserations but was ignored. Again, the woman continued as if she had no other choice but to speak.

"All the women were kept behind," she said, shivering at the memory, "for the soldiers. Each one of us was raped several times before I finally managed to escape." Her eyes mesmerised by the fire, she explained, "I didn't have a plan. I just ran as far and fast as I could."

Again, Yuri murmured something vaguely supportive, and again was ignored.

In a dreadful voice, rich with horror, she said, "But no matter how far I ran, or how fast, I couldn't outrun the bastard growing in my belly!"

Feeling the skin shrink on his scalp, Yuri asked, "Are you sure?"

Still with her eyes on the flames, she replied, "I'm sure."

The silence stretched on, growing more and more uncomfortable, until finally Yuri offered her his blanket, and with a false calm, said, "Here, take this. I can tell you're overtired. Get some sleep, and I promise you the world will look better in the morning."

Although she accepted the blanket, the woman didn't reply. She just sat, staring into the fire as if hypnotised by the flames.

As for Yuri, it had been a long day, and he wanted to get an early start in the morning. Reckoning that he had helped the woman all he could, he wished her a good night, and rolling up in his ground sheet, was soon asleep.

He was awake at the crack of dawn, and the first thing he saw was the woman hanging from the limb of a tree, his blanket knotted securely around her neck.

*

The pig had been disappointed that they weren't going to the village, after all, even more so as he had promised the sow that he would return that evening. What would she make of his absence? Would she miss him as much as he missed her? It wasn't that he was complaining, exactly, for he adored the squire, and sensed that they were on a great adventure like no other in the annals of swine lore. It just would have been nice if he'd had some prior notice, was all.

Thus far, it hadn't been a very consequential adventure, though. Their journey through the forest had been interesting with all those boxes burst open alongside the road. He had caught all sorts of interesting smells emanating from them and would have given them a good rooting over if the squire had let him. The fear he had smelled on those two young men had unsettled him, though, and later, it had been fortunate for the squire that the pig had been able to squeal a warning against those bad people. The scent of fear had been strong on them, too.

There hadn't been any fear on the woman last night, though, the one the squire had fed and loaned his blanket to. Instead, it was scent that was much, much worse.

It had unsettled him so much that he had almost been relieved when he watched while she hung herself from the tree.

Chapter Five

Yuri buried her that morning, caught between the tragedy of it all, and (to be honest) annoyance over the delay. Try as he might, he could not convince himself that this was '*the way things were,*' nor could he explain the woman doing something so apparently nonsensical as to take her own life. Finally, patting down the earth, it occurred to him that she had never told him her name. Therefore, instead of going to all the trouble of making a marker with an inscription, he simply fastened together a crude cross out of two sticks and placed it at the head of the grave. Then, still of the mind that this was nothing more than an unexplainable tragedy, he untethered the pig and began the day's journey.

It appeared that sometime during the night, the endless traffic had, indeed, finally ended, for when he reached the road there was no sign of a vehicle of any kind. He set off, thankful for the peace and quiet, with the pig trotting amiably at his heels.

However, they hadn't gone very far before the silence was broken by that same 'crump' sound in the distance that he'd first heard at the train station that day back in Homstood. 'Crump,' 'crump,' 'crump' it went, again and again, interspersed with the staccato sound of what could only be gunfire. Taking a firm hold on the leash, Yuri guided the pig off the road into the forest where they proceeded with all due caution.

On and on it went for almost an hour, and just when Yuri thought that it must go on forever, the terrible sounds stopped … to be replaced by a steady 'whop-whop' that grew louder by the second.

Retaining his firm hold on the leash, Yuri ducked behind a tree just as the sound grew to a roar, and three helicopters bearing the Zlaimperian insignia thundered low overhead. The noise was so deafening that he felt it vibrating through the bole of the tree while its limbs swayed wildly in the downdraft. Yuri hid his face in his hands, unable to move, transfixed by the thunder of the rotors.

The pig squealed with alarm and Yuri felt as if his arm had been dislocated from its socket as the young boar tried to run away from the terrifying sound; but his grip on the leash remained firm. He felt the pig struggle even harder as his squeals rose to vie with the tremendous din overhead. Falling to his knees, he struggled to wrestle the pig to the ground, which was no simple feat. Wrestling a pig at any time was bound to be exhausting but wrestling a pig in the throes of panic took all the energy he possessed.

The Zlaimperian helicopters were directly overhead now, but he didn't dare move a muscle lest the pig started up again. The ugly looking machines seemed to hover for an eternity, causing Yuri to reflect sourly that not one of them could have the least notion of how much trouble they were causing. Then, just when he was about to offer them a choice word or two, and maybe even toss a rock their way, the deafening sound of the rotors began to recede. Risking a peek over his shoulder, he saw the helicopters just above the trees as they followed the road to the west. He waited until they were gone from sight before stepping back onto the pavement. At first the pig didn't want to move, but a sharp tug on the leash soon got him mobile again. Then, with a last look over his shoulder, he continued on. Even so, every now and then another sharp tug was required to bring the pig to heel.

A kilometre further on, around a bend in the road, Yuri stopped in his tracks when he saw the results of the helicopters' grisly work. As far as he could see, until they disappeared over a rise, lay a long line of vehicles, some no more than charred and twisted metal, others burning furiously in the mid-morning sun. Still others were riddled with bullet holes, blood and gore splattered across shattered windscreens, mercifully shielding what was left of the occupants from view.

Yuri stood transfixed while his mind struggled to accept what his eyes were telling him. Any further thoughts that the people had been the architects of their own misfortune vanished in an instant, for no one could possibly have deserved such an end. Then, hearing a groan emanate from somewhere in that grotesque display, he leapt into action, forcing the pig to break into a trot in order to keep up.

Bracing himself, he peered into the side window of the lead vehicle and saw a young family inside. The father's head was missing, the mother was twisted into an improbable heap, held up by her seatbelt, the blood still pooling on the floor from a dozen wounds. In the back seat were two little girls, shredded to the bone, one still holding her doll.

Aghast, Yuri reeled away from the appalling sight, the smell of blood strong in his nostrils, and he was retching, again and again, as the contents of his stomach spilled out onto the pavement.

The pig, also smelling the blood, grunted nervously but, mercifully, didn't try to pull away.

Suddenly feeling very tired, every fibre in Yuri's body wanted to turn from the frightful sight and get as far away as possible. 'This must be a dream,' he thought, 'a horrible nightmare. I will open my eyes, and this will all be gone.' But then he heard the groan again and knew he had only been wishful thinking.

Willing his legs into motion, he staggered to the second vehicle, a truck this time ... or the shell of one – the blackened remains of the driver resting against the steering wheel. The groan sounded again, and he was able to sprint past the unidentifiable mass that was the third vehicle before reaching the fourth.

Once more peering through the side window, he saw two women, one old with grey hair and the other still in her twenties. The older woman sat upright in her seat staring sightlessly, with a fist-sized hole in her chest where her heart would have been. In the driver's seat, the young woman slumped over the wheel. Yuri was about to move on when he heard the groan a fourth time. It came from her.

Opening the door, he knelt on the pavement, and eased her back into the seat. Her face was a mass of blood, but she was still breathing.

"Where are you hurt?" he asked. She had a scalp wound, which explained the gore covering her face, but although ugly, it didn't look terribly serious. Nonetheless, he took out his handkerchief and pressed it against the gash to staunch the bleeding.

The woman grimaced and tried to pull away.

"Momma?"

More intent on saving the girl, Yuri spoke without thinking.

"She's okay, Miss. But I need to know if you're hurt anywhere else."

She began to cry, silent sobs, with her tears mingling with the blood smeared across her face.

"I'm sorry, Momma! Tell Yashi I'm sorry!"

"It's all right," Yuri assured her, not knowing if it was or if it wasn't, while he examined her for more wounds. "Just try to relax, and I'll see about getting you some help." Yet, even as he spoke, he realised how difficult that might be, if not impossible.

"Yashi's gone off to fight. He wanted us to be safe and I told him not to worry. Oh Momma, I'm so sorry!"

For a moment she appeared to become lucid and opened her eyes. She noticed Yuri for the first time.

Still drowsy, she asked, "Who are you?"

"I am no one," Yuri replied ruefully, "just a farmer trying to get his pig to market."

She stared at him with a frightening intensity, unsure if she had heard him correctly.

"Just … trying … to get your … pig …?"

She closed her eyes again and smiled, even managing to laugh – silent judders of mirth – as if this was the most absurd thing she'd ever heard; but it only lasted a moment, just as Yuri felt the shrapnel under his handkerchief.

Sobbing once more, she said, "This will break Yashi's heart."

Gently, Yuri removed the handkerchief and saw it – the nub of a splinter embedded in her skull. He had no way of knowing how deep it went.

Forcing himself not to panic, he asked, "And who is this Yashi?"

"Boyfriend," she replied drowsily, as if suddenly very tired. "We were going to be married, but Yashi said that the wedding could wait. He said first we must defeat the enemy …"

Her words trailed off as if she had fallen asleep, but when Yuri checked her pulse, he discovered she was already dead.

He bowed his head and regained his feet, wiping his blood-stained hands on his trousers. He regarded his handkerchief, now coloured a deathly red, and gently laid it on her lap before turning away.

For a full kilometre he walked along the edge of the road, but never heard another human sound. Either everyone involved in the tragedy was dead or had escaped. He tried willing himself not to look into any more of the vehicles but wasn't as successful as he would have liked. Glimpses here and there revealed the face of war as he'd never imagined. By the time he arrived at the end of that long caravan of vehicles, he had reached the conclusion that there was no dignity in death, nor sanctity, either. He paused for a moment, thinking of all those bodies with no one to attend to them. He continued on, trying to reason that there was nothing he could do, but struggled with an angry voice inside his head that accused him of deserting them all the same.

The rest of that day passed in a stupor. He was aware of leaving the road at least twice to avoid being seen by more helicopters. Sleek murderous bastards they were, bedecked with rocket pods and missiles slung under their stubby wings, and the barrel of a heavy machine gun projecting from each ugly snout.

Traffic was sparse, but he thought he recalled later that someone had enquired if he was all right and driving on with a mystified expression when he replied that he was merely trying to get his pig to market.

He made camp early that evening. Just the thought of spending another minute on that road, constantly afraid of what he might find around the next bend, was more than he could bear. He led the pig a good distance into the forest, until he reckoned he would not be seen by any passing vehicles.

Tethering the pig as before, he set about building a fire, and soon had a merry blaze underway, but the gladness of the flames never reached his heart.

Rummaging around in his knapsack for something to eat, he soon gave up when he realised he hadn't any appetite. Instead, he sat by the fire, filled with questions, staring into the flames as if hoping to find answers there.

Suddenly, he stood up and went to where the pig was tethered. He found him snuffling through last year's carpet of leaves in a lacklustre sort of way, as if he, too, had lost his appetite. His tail, usually curled into a jaunty devil-may-care attitude, now hung straight and forlorn as if exhausted. Untethering the beast, Yuri led him back to the fire.

Every evening at this time was when he and Mother Oksana would sit at the kitchen table and talk about their day. He hadn't realised just how much he missed those times until right at that moment, when he needed answers to so many questions, but at the same time, there was a reluctance to put those questions into words lest, somehow, they become too real. Just like it had for that unfortunate girl from the night before.

Dropping any pretence of searching for food, the pig sat and stared at him, his snout raised interrogatively, and his ears cocked forward. As with all animals, a change in routine was usually anathema to their conservative nature, but the pig seemed to recognise the urgency of the occasion. Absently, Yuri wondered if he might have questions of his own.

"Why would that woman take her own life?" Yuri wondered aloud. "She was scarcely more than a child with everything to live for."

The pig grunted encouragingly as if he had been wondering the same thing.

"Certainly, I know that rape is a terrible thing," he continued, in the offhand way that those who can't possibly comprehend tend to do.

However, in spite of our suspicions to the contrary, Yuri wasn't a stupid man, nor was he incapable of empathy. It was simply a case of his reluctance to delve too deeply into the tragedy. There was a time when he might have acted differently, but that was long ago when he had been a different person and believed the world to be a wonderful place. His reluctance caused him to attempt to push the subject from his mind and angrily demand to know what it had to do with running a farm. But changing the subject was no longer possible.

"I remember the look in her eyes, and how she spoke," he said. "As if she was being plagued by memories she was reluctant to recall, but was unable to avoid. How terrible must that feel?"

Finding it impossible to avoid the issue himself, he recalled opening his eyes that morning and seeing her hanging from the tree, her face horribly bloated beyond all recognition. He understood that this was the incontrovertible answer to his question. The depth of her pain had gone far beyond anything he could imagine.

Giving voice to half the argument, his brow furrowed when he said, "But that was before I saw what those Zlaimperian helicopters had done to all those people. How callous they had been, as if they hadn't recognised that Xorainians and Zlaimperians were brothers."

Just as it had been the case with the young woman, that had been barbarism on a scale he could never have imagined.

"Once having witnessed such evil, I can no longer pretend that it never happened," he said, and the pig sadly grunted that he agreed. "How lacking in humanity must someone be to inflict such destruction on fellow human beings – to rape and murder without remorse?"

The pig continued to stare at Yuri but remained silent. For he found the answer to be equally elusive.

"To behave with such savagery, what hate must lie in the hearts of those Zlaimperians?" He looked at the pig and slowly shook his head. "I simply can't fathom the depth of it." He hunched his shoulders, the palms of his hands facing the star-studded sky. "And for what?" he asked. "What did any Xorainian do to warrant such hate? For it is simply incomprehensible that humans could commit such acts without a soul filled with evil."

The coals were burning low, and true to his nature, after struggling over the issues to the point of exhaustion, Yuri felt that he could sleep at last. Stretching extravagantly, he yawned before curling up in his bedroll.

"Get some sleep, pig," he advised. "We have an early start in the morning. After all, we must still solve the problem of how to get you to the market in Lofstov."

Within minutes Yuri himself was sound asleep.

*

It had been an upsetting day for the pig. Certainly, he hadn't liked those flying machines with their thunderous 'whop-whopping' overhead, and it had frightened him to see them in a place where nothing but birds had a right to be.

The smell of death had been everywhere, too, from the time he woke up until he lay down to sleep.

He'd been seeing the ghosts ever since leaving the village – sad, lost creatures, not knowing what they had become or why they were there. As a rule, ghosts didn't frighten him – he had seen them all his life and was quite used to them – but the spirit of the female human who had taken her own life had made him feel uneasy. It was her sadness most of all, so overwhelming it was. Emanating from her in waves, he'd felt it enter him, and the weight of it had been terrible to bear.

However, it was when they were walking past that long line of charred and mangled machines that was the worst of all. The ghosts had been everywhere, reaching out to the squire, touching him with phantom hands, and crying out in anguish.

Lost, frightened, and oh so very sad. Their voices had risen in a chorus, soaring high above the trees, speaking of being wronged – lamenting their loved ones and those left behind.

He'd been glad when the squire had allowed him close to the fire. He didn't care for the flames, because fire was something that did *frighten him; it was listening to the sound of the squire's voice that soothed him. Even though he couldn't understand his words, it was still a comfort just to know that the horror could be rationalised, even if on a level only the squire could comprehend.*

But he had smelled the sadness on the squire, too.

Chapter Six

It is said that sleep is the great healer, but there was very little healing around the campfire that night. Both pig and man slept only fitfully, their dreams consisting mostly of faces of the dead. Both awoke the next morning feeling more tired than ever, filled with a creeping sadness that would have devoured them had they remained idle. It was only when they were on the road again that they were finally able to chase the black dog away.

Mercifully, they didn't encounter any more bombed-out caravans that day, but they did come across more and more signs of violence over the days that followed. The carnage was everywhere, and every night Yuri sat at his campfire, numb with shock, and discussed what he had seen with the pig.

By mid-afternoon of the seventh day, the occasional bit of traffic that he encountered was coming and going in both directions, consisting more and more of military vehicles bearing the insignia of Xoraina.

There was every type of vehicle imaginable – great lumbering tanks to nimble little scout cars and everything else in between. Those heading east (the same direction as Yuri) were filled with men with grimly determined expressions. In stark contrast, many of those heading west bore signs of ill use, scarred by unseen battles, wearing tired expressions but just as determined as their counterparts in the other lane. Very few paid him any attention. Those who did regarded him only with idle curiosity. None stopped to question him about his pig, or why he was there. All seemed preoccupied with whatever awaited them at their ultimate destinations.

It was mid-afternoon before he finally saw a soldier standing at a crossroad. Drawing nearer, Yuri saw that there were four other soldiers guarding the crossroad with him, all in tactical gear and carrying lethal-looking rifles. Some looked grim as they went about their work in a no-nonsense sort of way, while the others only seemed bored. Parked at the side of the road, in the shade of a birch tree, was an armoured vehicle surmounted by a heavy machinegun, manned by a fifth soldier wearing the grimmest expression of all.

There was a truck filled with soldiers waiting to pass through the checkpoint in front of him. The guards demanded to see their papers but gave each only a perfunctory glance before waving them through. Another truck, stopped at the opposite side of the intersection, was given considerably more scrutiny before it was allowed to proceed to the west. Finally, it was Yuri's turn.

Years earlier, Yuri had thought to get a licence for the Kamaz, when he had briefly considered hauling a load of grain directly to Lofstov, in order to avoid paying the shipping fee to haul it by rail. Of course, that was before he understood how reasonable the shipping fee actually was, and when the Kamaz still had a fighting chance of making such a journey. Naturally, the licence was well out of date by now, but it was the only identification he possessed. Even the papers he had been given, when Xoraina had still been part of the Zlaimperian Empire, had been tossed into the fire years before that and, after all, he wasn't driving, was he?

The guard was wearing dark glasses, so it wasn't possible for Yuri to see his eyes, but his expression of disbelief was plain even so.

He accepted Yuri's driver's licence, and with just a touch of impatience, said, "Hello, Father. And what can I do for you today?"

Another truck pulled up behind Yuri, and the guard motioned for it to wait a moment. By the brusqueness of the gesture, it was evident that he expected the moment to be a brief one.

"I'm going to the Capital to see the President," he was informed.

Meanwhile the guard had been studying Yuri's driver's licence.

"Hold on," he frowned, "this licence is twenty years out of date!"

"Do you see me driving?" Yuri asked.

"Well, no, but …"

"It's the only identification that I have," Yuri explained. "Nonetheless, although a good deal younger, you can tell by the photograph that I am who I claim to be, which is a simple farmer from the village of Homstood, bordering the Carpathian Mountains."

The guard was not used to irregularities. Indeed, he had not been trained for them, and this was an irregularity with a vengeance. As far as his duty went, he would demand to see a soldier's papers and have him arrested if said papers weren't in order. There was no question that this old man's papers weren't in order, but he was also a civilian. Therefore, the guard, quite simply, wasn't sure how to proceed.

"What seems to be the problem here," another soldier, this one with a corporal's stripes on his sleeve, had ambled over.

The guard passed Yuri's driver's licence over to him while Yuri explained a second time that he was going to the Capital to see the President.

Studying the driver's licence, the corporal arched an eyebrow. Then, passing it back to Yuri, he said, "You've come a long way, Father."

"Yes, I have."

"On foot?"

"As you can see."

"And what is your purpose for wishing to see the President?"

"I want him to repeal the new shipping tax." Yuri replied, as if he considered it a foolish question.

Hearing this, the corporal's mouth worked up and down so much that he had to look away. Finally, he was able to gesture at the pig, and ask, "And what about this fellow? Why did you bring him along?"

"The shipping tax affects him as much as it does me." Yuri confided, "It's quite unfair, you know?"

The corporal glanced at Yuri, then at the guard. Finally, he looked out at the horizon over Yuri's shoulder.

"You do realise there's a war on, don't you?"

"So I've heard," Yuri replied, grimly adding, "and seen along the way."

The corporal, fully aware of the obscene carnage that lay further down the road, frowned and said, "Yes, well, I'm afraid I can't let you pass."

"Why not?" Yuri demanded.

"For one thing, this section of the road has been reserved for military use only. For another," the corporal pointed to the east, "the Zlaimperians are barely five miles away. In order to reach the Capital, you'd have to go through them first."

His single-mindedness made it difficult for Yuri to deal with two 'things' at once. Therefore, deciding that the first 'thing' was the one that most pertained to his problem, he asked, "Who reserved this road for the military? I'm a tax-paying citizen," he said (which was occasionally true), "and this strikes me as being almost as unfair as the shipping tax itself."

The corners of the corporal's mouth worked up and down again.

"You'll have to take that up with the President, too," he said.

"So, the government then?"

"In short, yes."

"God damn the government!" Yuri said, in the time-honoured fashion of the true Homstooder, which is to say with a fair bit of gusto, and being a true Homstooder, he expected the corporal to reply in kind. However, much to his surprise, that worthy's reaction was exactly the opposite.

"That is your government you are referring to, old man," he replied acidly. "And as a soldier I am an extension of that government. We are currently at war, do you understand? Your *government* is under attack, and every day I'm risking my life on your behalf."

Yuri, whose own ire had begun to rise, had been about to retort that he hadn't asked the corporal to risk his life for him or anyone else, and further, judging by what he'd seen along the road to this point he wasn't doing a very good job. But he retained just enough self-control to pause and decided to try a more circumspect approach, even though it wasn't in his nature to back down.

"I didn't come all this way to argue with you, corporal. We could discuss the matter all day, but the long and the short of it is I still have a pig to get to market."

Not in the least ameliorated, the corporal snapped, "Well, you're not going to proceed any further along this road, and that's that." Exasperated beyond measure, he cursed, and said, "My god, man, can't you see I'm doing this for your own good?"

In fact, Yuri couldn't see that at all. Very well, there was a war. So what? There wasn't anything he could do about that, was there? It was just *the way things were*. However, regardless of how much he might urge the corporal to see reason, he soon understood that he could expect no help from that quarter. Therefore, any further argument he made would be fruitless.

Feigning contrition, he slumped his shoulders in defeat, and said, "I apologise, corporal, you are right. I will take my pig and go home."

The corporal, not ordinarily given to ill temper, nonetheless refused to let his guard down.

"See that you do!"

Yuri turned away, the pig trotting obediently at his heels. A plan was forming in his (Yuri's, not the pig's) mind. Glancing at the sun, he guessed there were still a few hours to go before nightfall. Very well, that should give him enough time to iron out the details.

*

The clouds had moved in after the sun went down. Shortly after, it began to rain.

Yuri made his way through the forest like a phantom, flitting from tree to tree. The pig, sensing the need for caution, followed without making a sound.

It was clear to Yuri that the corporal had never been a farmer, otherwise he would have understood how important it was that he got his pig to market. Instead, he hadn't shown the least inclination to even care. In Yuri's mind, there were two types of people: those who were farmers, and those who weren't. Any true Homstooder knew that all members of the latter party must be viewed with mistrust and suspicion.

After having left the checkpoint, he had retreated, following the road around the nearest bend, before slipping away into the forest. He'd continued on for a kilometre, making sure that the sun was over his right shoulder. Finding a clearing, he made camp but didn't dare risk a fire. Satisfying his hunger with a cold meal, there was just enough time before the clouds closed in to find the North Star. Placing it over his left shoulder this time, he searched for a landmark. Finding none, he noticed the wind was at his back. Provided it didn't change direction, he should be able to find the crossing point without any trouble.

He started out shortly after it began to rain, indifferent to the soaking he received from above, or from walking through saturated ferns that rose past his waist. Yuri didn't mind the rain. In fact, he considered it an ally. Odds were that any sentry on duty on a night like this would be too preoccupied with his own discomfort to spot anyone coming from a direction other than the one where an enemy might be expected.

Hour after hour, bit by bit, tree by tree, Yuri and the pig flitted through the forest. Progress was painstakingly slow, but the night was long. There was plenty of time.

"Halt! Who goes there?"

The voice was tense and challenging. More to the point, it seemed to be coming from directly in front of him, a mere handful of metres away, but although Yuri's eyes had long since adjusted to the darkness, he couldn't see a living soul.

He froze, raising his hands over his head, while the pig uttered a low grunt of surprise. His eyesight being inferior to begin with, the rain had also diluted his sense of sound and smell, rendering him as blind as Yuri was himself.

"Identify yourself!"

Yuri opened his mouth, on the verge of giving the disembodied voice his name, when a twinkle of light appeared some distance to his front, immediately followed by several more and the thunderous volley of dozens of firearms discharging at once. To make things even more confusing, this was instantly answered by an equally thunderous discharge and brilliant muzzle flashes of firearms coming from a narrow trench, virtually at his feet.

The first thing Yuri realised was that the disembodied voice hadn't been addressing him at all, but rather the unseen enemy. As dozens of bullets began zipping past his ears, the second thing he realised was that he was in terrible danger. Therefore, deciding not to wait for an invitation, he dove into the trench, dragging the pig in with him.

The sound was deafening and became even greater when a heavy machinegun opened up further down the line, sending a hail of tracer rounds into the midst of the muzzle flashes of the enemy. High overhead, a star shell burst, instantly transforming the forest into a sea of light and the eerily twisting shadows of trees and furtive figures as it began its slow descent.

The firing continued as Yuri cowered at the bottom of the trench with his hands over his ears. He could clearly see the tense expression on the face of the soldier standing above him, and the repeated jerking of his shoulder as it absorbed the recoil of his rifle.

On and on the battle raged, star shell after star shell revealing an inferno that Yuri never thought to see this side of Hell. The intensity increased even further when mortar shells began to rain down. An explosion further along the line was followed by the screams and groans of the injured.

Yuri's soldier grunted and grimaced as a bullet tore into his arm. Sagging to his knees, he saw Yuri for the first time.

"Who the hell are you?" he asked through gritted teeth. "And what are you doing here?"

Yuri saw the blood seeping through the soldier's clenched fingers. Instead of answering, he asked, "How can I help?"

The soldier gestured with a nod of his head to where some satchels lay. One of them was emblazoned with a red cross. "Get me a dressing for starters," he gasped.

Yuri retrieved the first aid kit, noting absently that the other satchels contained clips of ammunition. Returning to the soldier, he tore open his sleeve, revealing the wound.

"Not too bad," he observed. "It looks like the bullet just grazed you."

"I don't know about that," the soldier replied. "It hurts like a bastard."

"We'll have you fixed up in no time," Yuri assured him, hoping that was true.

Rummaging through the satchel, he produced a bottle. Peering uncertainly at the label in the wavering light, he hesitated until the soldier said, "Yeah, that's the right stuff."

Nodding, Yuri unscrewed the cap, adding apologetically, "This might sting a little."

"It always does," the soldier replied ruefully, and winced when Yuri poured a liberal amount of the disinfectant over the wound. "Goddamnfuckingchrist!" the soldier swore.

"Sorry," Yuri replied.

Producing a field dressing from the satchel, Yuri tore open the protective paper wrapping and pressed it against the wound.

"Jesus Christ, is that a pig?" the soldier demanded.

"It is," Yuri affirmed.

"What the hell is *it* doing here?"

"Same thing as me," Yuri replied, busily wrapping a bandage around the soldier's arm. "We're on our way to the Capital."

"The Capital?" The soldier seemed to be having trouble understanding. "What the hell for?"

"To get the new shipping tax rescinded," Yuri replied, almost adding 'of course,' but contented himself by confiding, "It's quite unfair, you know?" Then, pinning the loose end of the bandage in place, he asked, "Is that too tight?"

"No," the soldier replied, "it's fine."

"Do you need morphine?"

The soldier gingerly flexed his arm, considered for a moment, and said, "No, I'm good."

"In that case, I think I'm done," Yuri replied, not quite believing that he'd just administered first aid in the middle of a battle.

"Will I be able to play the piano when this is healed?" the soldier asked.

"I doubt it," Yuri replied, recognising the old joke. "Not if you've never played one before."

"Huh," the soldier replied ruefully, "Looks like I need new material." Then, seizing his rifle again, he rose to his feet. "Cheers, mate," he said, "I hope you get that shipping tax thing sorted." Then, for some reason, he offered a brief nod to the pig before resuming firing into the inferno.

The firefight continued and was so intense that it wasn't long before calls went out up and down the line. "I'm out! I need ammo!"

Eyeing the satchels filled with clips, Yuri slung one over each shoulder.

"On its way!" he cried, before turning to the soldier who was still blazing away into the night. "Watch my pig for me, will you?"

"Roger that," the soldier replied without taking his eyes off the battlefield.

Up and down the line Yuri went, thrusting clips into the waiting hands of the soldiers. So intense was the fighting that not one of them turned to see who had delivered the precious ammunition.

Finally, it seemed to Yuri that the firing from the opposite side of the field was beginning to wane. Someone cried, "They're retreating, lads!" and the intensity of the firing from the trench redoubled.

Well, Yuri thought, that was a good night's work, but I've been fortunate to get this far. I'd best be on my way before someone else starts asking me even more foolish questions. He made his way back up the line to where his soldier was still firing with the pig's leash looped around his good arm. Retrieving it, Yuri said, "Thank you very much. I'll be on my way now."

Still without turning his attention from the battle, the soldier said, "Good luck," and Yuri hoisted the pig out of the trench with a mighty heave before following a short second later. Then, stumbling through the dark, he led the way back into the forest.

*

What, with one thing and another, the pig had formed a definite opinion of all the noise, flying machines, ghosts, and creeping through the forest in the dead of night. However, all was not doom and gloom. When the squire led him back to the clearing where they had first started out, he noticed that the rain had turned the ground into a sea of mud. A good wallow was just the thing for his over-stressed nerves, and he made the most of the opportunity, happily content while he listened to the squire tell him about his day.

Chapter Seven

Yuri's determination to cross the lines remained unflagging, but one thing was certain, it wasn't going to happen tonight.

"Rain or no rain," he told the pig, "after such an intense battle, this sector of the front is sure to be on high alert for some time to come."

Luxuriating in the mud, the pig regarded him through half-lidded eyes.

"So, what shall our next step be?" Yuri wondered aloud. "The way I see it, either we wait, or we try somewhere else further on."

He regarded the pig as if seeking an answer, but the pig merely regarded him in turn, volunteering nothing.

"Hmm," Yuri mused, "I see you're playing your cards close to your vest, pig. Some comrade you are."

The pig, too clever to be so easily drawn out, delivered a long, luxurious exhale before squelching deeper into the mud.

Arching an amused eyebrow, Yuri stretched out on his groundsheet, wondering if he dare risk a fire before reluctantly deciding against it. If the soldiers saw the flames, they might be inclined to shoot first and ask questions later. Besides, even though the rain had let up, there wasn't a dry stick of wood for miles. Resigned to an uncomfortable night, he spared a moment to envy the pig's affinity to mud.

"It's all right for some," he accused. "You haven't a worry in the world. As far as you're concerned, it makes no difference if you catch a bullet out here or have your throat cut at the market in Lofstov. It will all have the same ending. But I have a farm to run and sunflowers to grow. Then, pig, just wait and see; I will be able to mend the barn and buy a real boar, one with papers, whose offspring will be worth ten times anything your mongrel seed can produce. We'll see who gets the last laugh then, won't we?"

The pig grunted contentedly and exhaled, blowing bubbles in his current domain.

Ordinarily, his farm was where Yuri's mind tended to travel in times of stress. How intimately he knew every field, every rock and cranny, every rise and hollow of the undulating ground. He liked to feel the pride of ownership surge through his veins and know that no one else in the entire world was as familiar with his land as he was himself. No matter how meagre the circumstances, or how dire his bank account, the land always remained, and would continue to do so until the end of time.

However, these weren't ordinary times. '*The-way-things-were*' no longer allowed the luxury of such pleasant reflections. This war had nothing to do with him or his farm, therefore it was bad, but it still affected the farm indirectly. It was an obstacle on the road to the Capital where the president held office, and it was only the president who had the power to rescind the shipping tax. Be that as it may, obstacles weren't unduly upsetting – in one form or another Yuri had been dealing with them his entire life – and this obstacle was no different. All that was required was to give it sufficient thought, and in due course, the answer would reveal itself. The fact that the answer to this current obstacle remained elusive merely meant that it required further cogitation. This was indeed fortunate, for after all that he had witnessed this past week, culminating in tonight's firefight, the war played heavily on Yuri's mind whether he wished it to or not.

"I've never been in a battle before," he told the pig, who twitched his ears to acknowledge that he was listening. "It was frightening," Yuri said. "All those bullets, people getting shot, maybe some even killed. Yes, it was all very frightening. Didn't you think so, too?"

The pig's ears twitched, first one way and then the other, in a *comme ci comme ça* sort of way.

Yuri regarded the pig sardonically, sure that his leg was being pulled.

"Well, I was afraid and I'm not too proud to admit it. Not like some I could mention." He favoured the pig with a knowing squint before continuing. "But when that soldier was hurt, I didn't hesitate. Did you see? Something just came over me." Struggling for words, he said, "It was like it is on the farm, yes, quite similar to that. When confronted with a problem I attend to it, because if I don't no one else will. Yes, it was exactly the same as that. And don't you know? There was no time to be afraid."

Yuri sat back, caught up in the wonder of it all. The pig burbled some more bubbles through his snout.

"I wonder," he said, "if that means I'm brave?" Certain that the pig would agree, Yuri continued with a great deal of pride. "I must say that the camaraderie I felt with those men was quite uplifting, and knowing that when the time came, I measured up." But then, as soon as he gave voice to his feelings, an uncertain frown settled on his face. "People died," he said. "I'm sure of it." Remembering the explosion down the line, he grimaced as he recalled the screams of the injured. Had some of those lads died? Had others? What of the Zlaimperians? Almost certainly there had been casualties on both sides, and the knowledge humbled him. Whatever course of action he chose to take, he would no longer congratulate himself on his bravery. Compared to those boys, who risked everything, day after day, he was nothing.

"That's another thing," he said, thinking aloud, "the Zlaimperians are a fearsome enemy, are they not?"

The pig appeared to have no opinion on the matter, so Yuri expanded this thought without benefit of any other contribution, porcine or otherwise.

"They may not be as mighty as they were in times past," he mused, "back when they were the mightiest empire in the world. But Zlaimperia is still an empire and, reduced in strength though it may be, it is by no means a weakling state. Why, compared to Xoraina, it is a giant."

Once more Yuri recalled the battle, the fierce resistance against all those twinkling lights and fleeting shadows under the eerie glare of the star shells. After only the United States of America, it was said that those fleeting shadows still belonged to the mightiest army in the world. In a moment of clarity, using the same brutal honesty that he had practiced all his life, Yuri realised that Xoraina's position was hopeless.

"But those boys," he said, "those brave lads, they never thought for one second that their cause was hopeless, had they? Indeed not, they had stood up to the Zlaimperian horde and seen them off." Musing further, he said, "But for how long can that continue?"

And there, he thought, was the rub.

"Zlaimperia has far more tanks, more planes, more artillery, more soldiers, more everything than Xoraina, and more modern equipment, too. True, those brave unassuming lads had fought them to a standstill, but what about the next time, or the next, or the time after that? Fighting spirit is one thing, but clearly it's not enough. Surely, sooner or later, the Zlaimperians must prevail. It only stands to reason."

Luxuriating in his bed of mud, the pig regarded him solemnly, as if to ask, "*And how do you feel about that?*"

How, indeed?

"I have no argument with the Zlaimperians," Yuri reasoned. "Therefore, it should follow that they have no argument with me."

Again, the pig seemed to ask, "*How can you be so sure that it follows as you say? Your memory is short. Have you forgotten that charnel house on the road? Don't you remember saying that the Zlaimperians did not behave as brothers should? Why is that d'you suppose?*"

"I don't know," Yuri admitted. "In the past, we used to be brothers, as you said, pig, but how can a brother behave with such barbarism to his own brother?" Suddenly, he threw his hands up in exasperation, much as he had when discussing the war with Mother Oksana all those days ago. "Oh, the devil take it," he cried, "It's all so confusing!"

Angrily, he turned away from the pig, determined not to discuss the matter any further. It was fine for him, he thought, one way or another his fate was sealed. What difference did it make if a Zlaimperian or a Xorainian consumed his chops? Surely, as far as he was concerned, it was all one and the same.

"And Zlaimperian money is just as good as Xorainian," he muttered. "The market is still the market. The price is still the price. Lakons or Zlaimperian gold, it makes no difference. The sunflowers in the east field won't care which banner they grow under. And that's just as well, for it is all but a certainty that Xoraina must become part of Zlaimperia once again. We can only hope that they leave enough of us alive to make it worth their while."

"To which I will say again, is that how a brother should treat a brother?"

Yuri spun around, staring defiantly at the pig. But of course, it wasn't the pig who had spoken rather than his own subconscious.

"Very well then," he said irritably. "We are no longer brothers. Why? I don't know, but the 'why' of it no longer matters. One day the Zlaimperians will come with their tanks and their soldiers and their planes, and there will be no one left to oppose them. So what? The soil still needs to be tilled, and pigs must still be sent to market. That's all, and there's nothing anyone can do about it."

"But would you even if you could?"

The question, to be frank, startled Yuri. Where had it come from? From his subconscious, to be sure, but never in his wildest imagining had he suspected that it lurked in those dark corners of his mind. The cold implication caused him to scowl uncomfortably, but …

"Very well," he said, "the question has been posed. Therefore, it must be dealt with."

He recalled the two young men he had come across earlier in the week. They had come close to blows and almost certainly would have if he had not prevented them. Later, they had both voiced a desire to return to fight the Zlaimperian invasion once their current duties had been performed. Then, yet again, he recalled the battle just that evening, of the determined men in the trench and the brief camaraderie he had felt with them as he lent assistance. Impatiently, he made a warding off gesture with his hands, as if he was trying to erase both memories from his mind.

"Fools!" he said, yes, even himself. To be caught up in the moment was to turn a blind eye to the certainties that lay ahead. All that grim determination, all that bravado, all their heroic endeavours could only end in failure. Ultimately, Zlaimperia must prevail.

"Besides," he muttered, "all governments are despicable. They care nothing for the people – less than nothing for the poor farmer who only wants to send his pig to market. Why should I believe Xoraina's is any better than the government of Zlaimperia? While it's true that I don't completely understand the inner workings of either, I am sure that this is so. Just as an example, take the new shipping tax," he said, clinching the point, "that was a Xorainian government's decision, not Zlaimperian. So, why should I lift a finger to try to prevent the inevitable? Perhaps a Zlaimperian government will even rescind the shipping tax and save me a lot of trouble." In conclusion, he said irritably to his subconscious, "You wanted an answer? There it is. Now let me sleep."

But sleep wouldn't come for a long time after. The very admission of his uncertainty played with Yuri's mind. While it was impossible to ignore the cold hard facts of the matter, it did not escape his attention that such thoughts might be construed as treasonous by others, or even by himself and his own vague notions of what was right and what was wrong. Still, while Xorainians and Zlaimperians may no longer be brothers, and every day bore witness as to why it was impossible to harbour any love for them, two irrefutable facts remained – Zlaimperia would prevail, and it was vital that the pig be sent to the Central Market in Lofstov.

*

Yuri woke early the next morning, lack of sleep making him tired and out of sorts, or possibly his unsettled conscience was the cause. He thought that the argument of the night before had followed him into his dreams. He had a vague recollection of those moments when he had administered first-aid to the soldier, only in his dream he was unable to stop the blood from flowing. It continued to run from the soldier's arm to the floor of the trench until it rose to their ankles. He remembered tossing the old dressing aside and applying a new one, but still the blood wouldn't stop, no matter how much pressure he applied. All too soon this dressing became saturated, as well, and needed to be replaced, as the blood rose to their knees. Again and again, Yuri changed the dressing, but the blood continued to flow while the soldier leaned against the side of the trench, a cigarette loosely dangling from his lips, as he waited patiently for Yuri to save him. But now, the blood had risen waist high; thick and viscous, forcing their comrades to wade through it in slow motion while it covered them from head to toe. As hard as he tried to staunch the flow, not one of them showed their resentment, or accused him of failure, even as they were struck by Zlaimperian bullets and sank beneath the crimson sea. He had been startled awake when the level of the blood had reached his chin.

 He broke camp in a surly silence, forced himself to swallow a cold breakfast, paused to stare back the way he had come, reached a decision, and turned south, leading the pig deeper into the forest.

 The sun had fallen by the time he made a second attempt to cross to the Zlaimperian-controlled area several kilometres further on. However, this turned out to have an even higher concentration of soldiers than his first attempt, so he was forced to turn back, yet again. The next day he tried in a different area, and again the day after that even further on, but each time there were just too many soldiers to make a crossing possible.

 It wouldn't be fair to say that Yuri was disheartened – a true Homstooder didn't know the meaning of the word – but it *was* fair to say that he had become frustrated, even to the point where he thought he might have to consider trying a different approach. However, on the fifth night his luck finally changed.

 The sky was clear and a full moon at its zenith the night when he arrived on the outskirts of a village. With the pig in tow, he crept forward to where he judged the lines must be and found them almost immediately with depressing precision. The soldiers manning the trenches seemed as alert as everywhere else he had been.

Cursing silently, he whispered to himself, "Well that's that, then. Obviously, this plan isn't working. I'll have to come up with a new idea."

Then, just as he was about to turn back, he heard an explosion that must have been several miles down the line from the direction he'd just come, followed closely by another, and then another after that.

Clamping his hand over the pig's snout to keep him quiet, Yuri murmured, "The Zlaimperians must be attacking again. I'll see if I can get closer." Tethering the pig to the nearest tree, Yuri blackened his face with rich forest loam and inched forward on his belly. He had succeeded in travelling perhaps thirty metres when, to his amazement, he heard a voice crackle over a radio.

"*Alpha B, this is Alpha A, come in, over!*"

Yuri frowned, for the voice sounded tense and also very near, even though peering into the dark revealed no one in the vicinity. Almost immediately the call was answered.

"*Alpha A, this is Alpha B, reading you four by four, over.*"

Again, the voice came from directly beneath Yuri, and he soon deduced that he was lying on top of a covered dugout. The reply came through loud and clear.

"*Alpha B, this is Alpha A! We are currently under attack! I repeat, we are currently under attack! We've taken casualties from accurate artillery fire, and the enemy is advancing with heavy armour and a brigade-sized force of infantry! We need reinforcements NOW! Send us everything you've got! Over!*"

Without hesitation, Yuri heard, "Alpha A, this is Alpha B. Roger that. Help is on the way. This is Alpha B out."

Within seconds, a head appeared from the ground in a cleverly designed opening for the dugout. Fortunately, it was turned away from him. The man was talking on a handheld radio, summoning junior officers to prepare their men to move out. As he talked, he continued to ascend the steps from the dugout until he was standing in the open, mere inches from where Yuri lay.

After a last flurry of rapid-fire instructions, in very short order, troops began leaving the trenches, making their way to the rear where their transport awaited them. Scores of men, hundreds, possibly even thousands, ran past on the double, none of them noticing the misshapen form lying at their commander's feet. Finally, the flow of men dwindled to a trickle until it stopped altogether. Then and only then, did the commander take his leave, as well, still ignorant of Yuri's presence.

A minute passed, then two, before Yuri worked up the courage to creep forward to inspect the trench.

It was empty.

He waited five more minutes to make certain before regaining his feet. Then, retracing his steps to fetch the pig, he set off toward the Zlaimperian lines, never dreaming that achieving this leg of his goal would ever be so easy.

*

The pig was overjoyed to see the squire return. Ever since they'd been apart he hadn't any appetite to root through the undergrowth, which was saying a great deal.

He had smelled enough of death to do him a lifetime and being left alone like that soon had his nervous imagination wondering if the squire had abandoned him. But then he reasoned, 'No, not the squire. He would never desert me. The squire is my friend.' And, sure enough, the squire had appeared a minute later.

However, before he could utter a greeting, he saw the halo of danger hovering over the squire's head.

Chapter Eight

As it turned out, crossing the lines was even simpler than Yuri imagined. For apart from the numbers in the Xorainian trenches being left much reduced, it would appear that the Zlaimperian lines had also been denuded, presumably to aid in the attack further to the north.

Still, Yuri had to assume that there were enough soldiers left behind on both sides to necessitate proceeding with caution. Consequently, the sun was just beginning to rise by the time he could conclude with any certainty that they were through. Washing the loam from his face in a nearby stream, he took up the pig's leash and resumed his journey to the Capital. By mid-morning, it felt as though he and the pig had wandered into the depths of Hell, instead.

He saw the pall of smoke rising in the darkened sky from several kilometres away. It was still visible when he made camp that night, after having passed by column after column of burnt-out armoured vehicles – convoys of death, each one reminding him of the columns of civilian vehicles he'd seen similarly destroyed on the Xorainian side. The true Homstooder in him couldn't help thinking that the price of just one of those tanks would see his farm operating in the black for the rest of his natural life. Separate and apart from the loss of so many lives, the realization brought home to him just how monumentally wasteful this war actually was.

He reached the place from where the smoke was emanating by noon the next day. It was a village … or rather, it had been.

Street after street he walked, winding his way through rubble, from one end to the other. Only a handful of houses were still standing, the rest reduced to ashes and blackened piles of bricks. Once he saw a lone emaciated cur worrying something on the ground. It paused long enough to give Yuri a hard stare as he approached before slinking off. Drawing nearer, Yuri could smell the object of the dog's attention, and when he saw it, he immediately wished he hadn't.

An old woman, her hands tied behind her back, lay face down on the side of the street in a pool of congealed blood. The flesh of one calf was crudely torn from the leg, the canine teeth marks clearly visible.

It was obvious that the victim had been executed and left to rot, but why?

Wondering, Yuri murmured to the corpse, "What could you possibly have done, Grandmother, to make them behave so barbarically?" Then, giving into his revulsion, he recoiled from the sight, fervently hoping that he would not discover any others, but he did, a full score altogether – some with their hands tied behind their back like the old woman, but all had been shot in the back of the head, clearly executed.

Shocked, Yuri reeled away, determined to put as much distance as possible between himself and this accursed village before the sun went down. The pace he set was so fast that the pig was forced to break into a trot to keep up, while over and over again, Yuri murmured to himself, "This can't be *the way things are*, they just can't," in spite of the evidence he had seen with his very eyes.

Running blindly now, struck by the horror he'd left behind, he had no idea how long he'd been on the road, only that the sun was lowering toward the horizon when he came to the farmhouse.

Truth be told, he might not have noticed it at all if he hadn't heard the woman call out to him. The interruption was welcome, as it jarred Yuri from his thoughts.

"Hey stranger, where are you going with that pig?"

Turning, he saw her standing just outside the door of the cottage – a woman somewhere in her forties with a haggard look about her, dressed in wellington boots, men's trousers, and a heavy woollen jumper. Tendrils of greying curls poked out from the multi-coloured scarf covering her head.

Seeing the state Yuri was in, she stepped down from the stoop and approached him, clutching the sweater close around her neck. As she drew nearer, Yuri could see the haunted look in her eyes and silently shuddered. In their way, those eyes were almost as bad as the sights he'd left behind at the village. They had a story to tell, but he wasn't at all sure he wanted to hear it.

"Where are you going?" she repeated, studying him closely.

Numbly, Yuri heard himself reply. "To the Capital."

The lines on the woman's forehead grew deeper.

"The Capital? Oh, what nonsense that is!" Then, squinting suspiciously, she asked, "What is your business there?"

"I want the shipping tax rescinded," Yuri replied automatically.

"The shipping tax?" the woman parroted. Looking closer, she studied Yuri more intently, as if to reassure herself that he wasn't insane. Then, looking down, she motioned to the pig, and asked, "And what do we have here?"

Yuri heard himself reply, "It's a pig," without any discernible inflection or feeling.

"Yes, I can see that," she replied wryly. "What on earth is it doing here?"

"It's my pig," Yuri said, as if that answered her question.

"Yes, of course it's your pig, and a fine one, too, by the look of him, but ..." It seemed that she was about to enquire further, but something caused her to reconsider. Instead, she said, "I think you had better come inside." At which point, she turned and led the way back to her cottage. Yuri, still shocked by his experience at the village, followed obediently behind her.

Reaching the cottage, the woman held the door open for him, but Yuri had just enough wherewithal to hesitate.

"What about my pig?" he asked.

Forcing a smile, the woman regarded the animal, who was standing politely at Yuri's heel.

"You'd better bring him inside, too. If you leave him tethered out here, he's bound to be scooped up by the first Zlaimperian that happens by. Mercy, it's a wonder they haven't taken him already!"

Seeing the wisdom of her words, Yuri edged past her through the door. The pig, never having been inside a cottage before, hesitated at the threshold, sniffing the air suspiciously. Absently, Yuri gave a tug on the leash and the pig, trusting the squire, allowed himself to be coaxed inside.

The cottage was neat and freshly swept. A gas stove and an ancient refrigerator took pride of place in the kitchen, next to plain wooden cabinets and a table and two rickety-looking chairs. Through a passageway, Yuri could see a sitting room with a rug over the weathered planks of the floor. At the far end, an icon hung over the fireplace.

The woman produced an earthenware jar and two glasses from a cupboard. Motioning to one of the chairs, she invited him to be seated.

Hesitantly eyeing the chair, Yuri sat on the edge, ready to leap to safety if it decided to collapse.

Pouring the dark red liquid, the woman said, "It's nalivka, from my own private recipe." Holding out one of the glasses for him to take, she said, "Here, get this inside you, you'll soon feel right as rain."

Yuri accepted the glass gratefully. At that moment, the only thing that mattered was getting the brandy into his stomach. Pausing only briefly to hold up the glass to her in a toast, he said, "Long life to you," and downed its contents in a single swallow.

Yuri grimaced and grasped his throat as the fiery liquid coursed through his system. He was no stranger to nalivka – every farmer in Xoraina produced their own version of the spirit every year after harvest – but this woman's recipe was far more potent than most. The fire continued to build and build inside his body, and though he struggled to prevent it, he burst into a violent fit of coughing.

Primly sipping from her own glass, the woman nodded approvingly, and said, "There now, I'll wager you feel better already, don't you?"

Yuri was incapable of answering. In fact, simply breathing seemed to be a tall order. Whenever he tried to inhale, the potent fumes brought on another fit of coughing, until he felt himself getting quite red in the face. Far from feeling better, he now felt he was in some danger of choking to death. However, just when he was verging on panic, a sharp blow to his back seemed to set things in order again.

While Yuri gratefully gasped in great lungsful of air, the woman raised an eyebrow, and said, "My husband had the same reaction, but then *his* mother was from the city, and taught him city ways."

For a true Homstooder, reviling people from a city was the only subject that even came close to their real passion on matters outside their farms, which, of course, was damning the government on no uncertain terms. Therefore, the woman's acid comment about her mother-in-law was one he could warm to. In fact, the triumvirate of the nalivka in his veins, the slap on his back, and that comment miraculously made him feel close to his old self again in no time at all.

Stifling one final cough, he managed to whimper, "City people have no idea what real drinking is."

The woman regarded him for a long moment, her eyebrow still raised in wry judgement; but instead of pressing the point, she enquired, "If you don't mind my asking, where are you from, stranger?"

Gingerly massaging his throat, Yuri replied, "From Homstood, in the far western region, at the foothills of the Carpathian Mountains."

The woman nodded sombrely. "I can believe it. It is known that the people there are all *nevcheniy*."

Roughly translated, *nevcheniy* meant backwards and uneducated.

Taking her in, from her booted feet to the ruddy complexion of her face, Yuri was about to reply with an angry retort, but managed to stop himself just in time. After all, the woman had invited him into her home and treated him kindly. Under the circumstances, it would be unworthy of him to take exception to what was a commonly held opinion for people living on this side of the forest anyway. He held his peace, but he did raise an eyebrow of his own.

Watching his reaction with some amusement, the woman then asked, "And how on earth did you get here without being murdered by the Zlaimperian scum?"

So, Yuri related an abridged version of his tale, only briefly mentioning some of the horrors he had witnessed, for he had no wish to revisit any of them. He ended by relating how he'd crossed the battle lines just the day before. When he had finished, both the woman's eyebrows were raised.

Letting out a long, low whistle, she said, "You are very fortunate, my friend, and very foolish to have come all this way in the first place, which only proves that you are *nevcheniy*."

Somewhat defensively, Yuri replied, "Fortunate yes, but I fail to see how that makes me *nevcheniy*. To my mind, there is what is just and what is unjust. The shipping tax falls into the latter category. That is enough."

The woman studied him for a long time. More than once, it appeared as though she was about to reply, but couldn't find the words. Finally, dismissing the subject with an impatient gesture, she rose from the table and. taking a large pot from its hook on the wall, she proceeded to fill it with water from a handpump set in a corner of the room.

"My name is Hanna, by the way, Hanna Gorchenko."

"Yuri Zavlov," Yuri replied laconically.

Filling the pot, Hanna placed it on the floor in front of the pig who regarded it uncertainly before glancing up at Yuri. Yuri nodded encouragingly, and said, "It's okay," whereupon the pig thrust his snout into the pot and began to drink with greedy dedication.

"That was kind of you," Yuri said.

"Yes, well," Hanna said, brusquely waving off the compliment, "I thought he was thirsty. I'll wager he's hungry, too."

To which Yuri shrugged, and replied, "Of course, he's a pig."

Hanna studied the creature with some speculation, and for the second time, observed, "And a fine specimen he is, too."

She paused to consider, then said, "I have some turnips in the larder, and some beets, as well. Perhaps ..."

Yuri interrupted her.

"No, that would be taking food from your own table. But perhaps if you had some swill?"

Hanna shook her head. "I regret that I do not. The Zlaimperians took away my own pigs weeks ago. They stole everything – our cow, chickens, everything. And besides," she said with telling simplicity, "there is little enough left after a meal, even the rinds are consumed, along with the water the vegetables are boiled in."

For the first time Yuri noticed how gaunt Hanna's face was, and guessed that beneath her jumper, was even more evidence as to how closely she was flirting with starvation.

'*The Zlaimperians did this to her*,' he thought, once more confirming – if confirmation was, indeed, still necessary – that they were no longer their brothers. '*This is nothing more than cruelty for its own sake. Why do they hate us so?*'

Yuri picked up his knapsack, hefting it thoughtfully. His own provisions were getting very low. Indeed, he had planned to rummage through the village grocery when he passed through hoping to refill his supply, but the place had so unnerved him that he'd been reluctant to tarry. But to be honest, he hadn't been so much reluctant as frightened out of his wits. The bodies of the innocent lying abandoned in the streets, left to rot or be consumed by dogs; the total destruction of homes and way of life, all combined to form a conclusion that this was not an invasion of conquest but of annihilation – to wipe Xoraina completely off the map. The concept was so incredible that Yuri's mind rebelled against it.

'*No*,' he thought, '*I must be missing something. This is the 21st Century, no one commits such atrocities for no reason anymore.*' Taking another glance at Hanna's emaciated face, he thought, '*Still, whatever the reason, it's a heavy price to pay.*'

Continuing to heft his knapsack, he said, "I have some food – a heel of cheese, another of sausage, both made with my own two hands." He offered a faint smile, realising he had mimicked words Hanna had spoken regarding her nalivka.

Hanna stared at him, her haunted eyes making her scrutiny all but unbearable for Yuri. The mere mention of food had brought her to the edge of her seat.

"Yes?" she said eagerly.

Yuri looked away, clearing his throat uncomfortably.

"I thought we might combine them with whatever you have. Perhaps we could make something suitable to eat?"

"I could make soup," she replied, so quickly that Yuri suspected that she had been planning that very thing as soon as he had listed his few meagre provisions. Then Hanna did the strangest thing, she allowed her gaze to fall back on the pig. "Such a fine pig," she said yet again, with just a hint of wistful desperation, "No doubt he will produce the most savoury chops."

The room grew chill as Yuri shifted uncomfortably in his chair. Hanna's suggestion was plain, but he was finding it difficult to believe what his ears had just told him. It was true, he wanted to help her. She had been kind to him, so it was only natural that he wanted to repay her, but the pig …?

The sudden tension threatened to become unbearable when, suddenly, Hanna burst out laughing. It wasn't an unpleasant sound, although her eyes remained haunted.

"Oh!" she said, still giggling, "you should see your face!" Placing a careless hand on his knee, she confided, "Of course I was only joking."

Unmollified, Yuri continued to squirm uncomfortably in his chair. "The pig is destined for the market in Lofstov."

"Yes, of course."

"I need the money to purchase sunflower seed for the east field."

"I completely understand."

"If it wasn't for that damned shipping tax I wouldn't even be here."

"I said I understand!"

Hanna's sudden fury caused Yuri to freeze and the pig to grunt with surprise.

"I only meant ..."

Flustered with herself, Hanna gave his knee a second pat.

"Yes, of course, I understand," she said airily. Then, reaching down, she scratched the pig under his chin, and smiled. Mimicking the voice women use when addressing small children, she said, "Don't worry, Mr Oinkers, you're safe in this house."

As a general rule, the pig delighted in attention, but now he jerked away from Hanna's caress.

Acknowledging the rebuff, Hanna all but leapt to her feet, as if eager to change the subject.

"Let's see about making that soup!"

Producing the items from his knapsack, Yuri, grateful for the change of conversation, and equally eager to regain their easy rapport, apologetically added, "We might have had wine with our meal, but I finished the last of it only yesterday."

"Ah," Hanna replied brightly. Patting the earthenware jar beside her, she said, "I wouldn't worry about that, my *nevcheniy* friend. There's plenty more where this came from."

*

Every day caused the pig to grow more and more uneasy. The smell of death was even stronger in this new country, and the ghosts, oh my, the ghosts were everywhere, but especially in the ruins of the village where they had lingered too long for his liking. He had been grateful when they left, but he would rather the squire had chosen a different route out of town. But then, he couldn't have known that he had led them right past the mass grave on the outskirts.

Chapter Nine

The meal, while unconventional, was a success. The fact that they were both famished only served to heighten their appreciation.

Hanna had put a large kettle of water on the stove, cut up a turnip and some beets, added slivers of Yuri's sausage, along with a sprinkle of salt, and settled in to wait.

"I thought we could have the cheese afterward," she explained, pouring them each another glass of nalivka.

Yuri concurred. "That is an excellent idea."

Sitting back in his chair, now completely unafraid that it might collapse on him, Yuri, caught up in a feeling of well-being, felt the pleasant sensation of the liquor warming his insides. However, he reminded himself that he mustn't get too comfortable, for there were still chores to be done to pay for his keep.

While the water came to boil and simmered long enough to cook the vegetables, he went outside to cut some wood for the fire. Hours later, he returned inside with an armful of split logs, after having left a stack against the side of the cottage high enough to reach the eave. Soon he had a blaze burning merrily in the fireplace.

With the fire and the nalivka (this was now his third glass), and the aroma of the soup permeating the kitchen, he felt quite the domesticated man. Then, of course there was the company of this pleasant woman to make it all complete. What a strange thing to experience amidst a land so ruined.

Hanna must have felt something equal to the occasion. Between the fireplace and the stove, the cottage grew so warm that she had felt safe to divest herself of her jumper. Then, seized with an idea, she had disappeared into her bedroom at the back of the cottage, reappearing with a freshly powdered face and gloss on her lips, while wearing a dress with a string of pearls around her neck. One other thing: the haunted look in her eyes, if not altogether gone, had somehow become more diminished, causing her to look ten years younger.

"Of course, they aren't real," she said of the pearls, then, laughing shyly, she added, "It's just that it's been so long since I've had a man about the house, I wanted to dress for the occasion."

Now, halfway through his fourth glass of nalivka, Yuri regarded her with an appreciative eye.

As she busied herself about the kitchen, he decided that Hanna wasn't a bad looking woman. The jumper had done an effective job of hiding her bosom, but now, with all her feminine splendour on display, its fulsome roundness was clearly visible; and when she bent to retrieve a ladle from the cupboard, he became aware of a stirring in his nether region that he hadn't felt in many a year.

While their meal simmered over the fire they talked of peaceful things and did not speak of the war. Hanna served the soup when it was ready, and poured Yuri his fifth glass of nalivka before sitting down to her own meal. She'd placed a candle on the table earlier, citing the fact that there had not been any electricity for weeks. Whether that was true or not made little difference insofar as the atmosphere was concerned. Although the world outside had gone insane, inside the cottage it was as pleasant as anyone could hope for. If pressed, he would have said that it was all to do with that undefinable quality known as 'a woman's touch.'

The soup was piping hot, but he savoured every mouthful. His taste buds, having been lulled into boredom due to the plain fare that had sustained him over the past few weeks, had responded appreciatively as the savoury broth roiled in his mouth. Hanna rose in his esteem with every spoonful.

After his first taste, he barely restrained an ecstatic moan, and said, "This is delicious Hanna Vasilova. I must compliment you on your cooking."

Hanna feigned indifference but looked pleased, nonetheless.

"I'm glad that you like it, Yuri Yurivich," she said, and was there something about the way she spoke his name that made the evening even more intimate than it already was?

"Have you always been so gifted in the kitchen?"

"Oh no," she said with a self-deprecating laugh. "I was quite hopeless when I was younger. My husband had to put up with some lamentable efforts throughout the first years of our marriage."

Yuri's expression remained impassive, but for some unknown reason an anxious knot formed in his stomach.

"Where is your husband now?" he asked, blowing gently on his spoon.

A cloud seemed to form over Hanna at the question, poised to ruin the evening, although he could see her trying valiantly not to let it.

"He went off to fight," she said, setting her spoon aside.

Sensing the worst, Yuri paused with his own spoon poised between bowl and mouth. "Have you heard from him at all?"

She shook her head. "Not from him, but *of* him." Explaining, she said, "I was told that he was killed in the fighting around the Capital two weeks ago."

"I'm very sorry to hear that," Yuri said and was relieved that it felt sincere rather than a meaningless reflex.

He felt for the girl, how could he not? He had seen so much death already, each one a tragedy for those left behind to grieve. The Zlaimperians were responsible, of course. There would be a great need for forgiveness when they became Xoraina's new overlord, so much that he wondered if it was even possible.

Seemingly of its own volition, his hand crept across the table until it rested atop of Hanna's. It was a gesture of sympathy, completely innocent, or so he told himself. Still, it was gratifying when Hanna grasped his hand in return.

"Thank you," she whispered.

The moment began to drag, threatening to put a pall over the evening, but as much as he tried, Yuri couldn't think of a thing to say. Fortunately, it was Hanna who stepped up to save the day.

Picking up her spoon, she said, "I didn't want him to go, of course. It seemed such a futile gesture. I mean, the Zlaimperians were invading, and as much as we might wish otherwise, there was nothing we could do about it. Nothing. Xoraina would succumb as it had in the past."

Finding his own thoughts coincided with hers, Yuri stated more than asked, "But he didn't listen."

A shrug. "Of course not. Men seldom listen to women, even less so during times of war. The allure of fighting against insurmountable odds was just too great for him to resist. It was the noble thing to do, you see."

Yuri was surprised by her lack of bitterness and remarked upon it.

"That's just it," she replied, "I wasn't speaking facetiously, it *was* noble. Taking up arms against a tyrant is always the right thing to do, and although I begged him not to go, I was secretly proud that he did." Gesturing helplessly, she laughed, and said, "You must think that I've gone completely mad."

Naturally, Yuri assured her that it was the furthest thing from his mind, although, this time, he *was* speaking reflexively.

More seriously, she continued. "In truth, I'm not sure that I haven't. Grieving is a terrible thing. It stabs into your vitals, so deep that I marvelled that my body could contain it all, and the pain it inflicts is beyond measure. With all that running amok inside, it's difficult to believe that something hasn't been nudged off the rails, wouldn't you say?"

Again reflexively, Yuri wanted to agree with her, but couldn't bring himself to venture to that extreme.

She laughed a mirthless laugh. "Take tonight, for instance. He's only been dead for two weeks, and already I have another man at my table. It would be foolish not to acknowledge that the next obvious step was my bed." This time placing her hand on top of Yuri's, she said, "Come, Yuri Yurivich, would you not say that was madness?"

Yuri opened his mouth, but no words would come. He wanted to deny that she was mad, telling himself that it was for her own peace of mind; but a small whisper in his head asked if there might be a different reason, that by acknowledging her madness he would be placing her out of reach? In the grand scheme of things, it was such a small sacrifice and one that he should be happy to make. Certainly, respect for her dead husband demanded that of them both, yet he still hesitated, because he realised that he didn't want to make that sacrifice at all.

Instead, he said, "Who knows the ways of the mind? Each one of us is different. If you are mad, that is understandable. It is not for me to judge."

Caressing his hand, Hanna regarded him with gratitude.

"No, Yuri," she said, "it's not for you to judge. Only God, and God has deserted Xoraina, so I am free to do as I please." Then, in a sudden change of topic, she leaned down and scratched the pig under his chin again. Lulled by the pleasant warmth inside the cottage, this time the pig did not jerk his head away. "In the meantime, what about this fellow, he hasn't had a bite to eat all evening."

Surprised, Yuri regarded the pig, feeling a twinge of guilt for having forgotten about him.

"I know," Hanna brightened, "we can take him out to my garden where there are grubs and all sorts of toothsome things for him to eat. We can take the cheese and nalivka out with us so the time will pass pleasantly while we keep an eye on him. Again, she sighed, and said, "What a fine specimen he is."

To Yuri's befuddled mind, this seemed like an excellent idea, for the cottage had grown uncomfortably warm. Surely the fresh air would do him good.

Moments later, the pig was rooting happily away in Hanna's back garden, while the two humans sat on the step, sipping nalivka and sharing what was left of Yuri's cheese. For a while gaiety returned to the evening, even if Hanna's was somewhat forced; but it was Yuri who decided to return their conversation to more serious matters.

"I agree with what you said earlier, about the Zlaimperian invasion, and how there is nothing that can be done. They will reconquer Xoraina, that is a certainty, but do I care?" He regarded Hanna. "You and I, we both can remember when Xoraina was part of the old empire. Was life so bad then?"

"Yes."

Surprised by her answer, he asked, "How so? Do we not till the soil as we did before? Do we not take our produce to market, just as we did back then? How have things changed so much that your husband felt that Xoraina was worth dying for?"

Quietly, she replied, "I feel that way, too. I'm very proud of him."

Chastened, Yuri replied, "Yes, of course. It wasn't my intention to besmirch his memory," and he fervently hoped that was true. "What I mean to say is that, while I would rather this continued to be sovereign Xorainian territory, I fail to see a drastic change in our lives if it does not remain so.

Hanna regarded him and laughed, the closest to genuine laughter he had heard all evening.

"You Homstooders," she said wonderingly. "How to explain anything to a *nevcheniy*?" Linking her arm through his so that he didn't take offence, she pondered the question for a moment before she said, "Very well, I shall try.

"Do you recall the commissars from the old empire, those political officers who had so much power over us? They could send anyone to the gulag if they said anything that didn't align with the state philosophy."

"Yes, of course," Yuri replied, smiling. "Ours was old Niko, a harmless fellow who let us do and say as we liked, just as long as it didn't bring any unwanted attention from the secret police. Given that he was the conduit to their ear, there was very little chance of that."

"You were fortunate," she replied. "Ours was not so affable. He was an uneducated man drunk with power and sent many to the gulag for the least infraction, my own father among them."

Yuri shifted uncomfortably, but before he could reply, she continued.

"And where are the commissars now? Where are the secret police? They are gone because the people said that we do not want them. With the coming of democracy, we have a voice, Yuri. Do you understand? A *voice*. We no longer serve the government, the government serves us, instead. We are free to do as we like and say what we please. Now we have the law to protect us, not subjugate us. Do you understand?"

"That is not entirely true," Yuri replied. "We can*not* do as we like. We must obey the laws, just as we did before, and for that the police are no longer so secret, but openly subjugate us to their will."

"Oh?" she asked. "And how do you know this, Yuri Yurivich? Have you ever been in trouble with the police?"

"Not in so many words," Yuri replied evasively. "There are only two policemen in Homstood, and both of them are drunks."

Amused, Hanna said, "How fortunate for you."

"They were unemployable," Yuri admitted, "so the village administrator decided to deputize them, in order to keep them out of jail."

Hanna laughed outright, a sound unadulterated by restraint.

"And in the meantime, the criminals run free like foxes in the chickencoop!"

"No," Yuri replied seriously. "Criminals are rare in Homstood. It's just that the government sends us money to pay for a police force." Regarding her soberly, he said, "We had to spend it somewhere."

Yuri warmed to the sound of Hanna's laughter even though he didn't fully understand it. Whatever the reason, it turned the evening onto a more pleasant path.

Rising to her feet, she held out her hand for him to take.

"I think Mr Oinkers has had enough for one night, don't you?" Then, in a tone heavy with meaning, she added, "It's time for bed."

Mystified but content, Yuri readily agreed.

*

The pig liked the nice lady, insofar as it went. She had given him water and scratched under his chin, which, although initially hesitant, he had come to enjoy.

Still, he was uneasy. There had been something about her, something he couldn't quite understand but instinctively knew to distrust. He rolled over on his side on the bed of old blankets she had made for him. Without a doubt she had been kind, and he tried not to feel ungrateful, but he couldn't put that veiled hardness in her eyes from his mind.

Unfortunately, that was something the squire couldn't see.

Chapter Ten

Yuri was naked when he awoke in Hanna's bed. He was also alone with the trace of a hangover and an urgent need of the outhouse in the back garden. Looking from the room's single window, he could see the grey light of the pre-dawn stealthily creeping over the horizon. Still groggy, he massaged his aching skull while calling out to Hanna but received no reply.

Muttering under his breath, he flung the duvet aside and stumbled out of bed. During the act of fumbling one leg into his trousers, he happened to look out the window a second time, and with the different angle, saw Hanna in the back garden with the pig. One hand held him firmly by his leash, in the other was a knife with a long, wicked-looking blade. In a trice, he was out the door, still struggling to pull his trousers past his knees.

"Stop!" he cried. "Hanna, what are you doing?"

Hanna froze with her back to him, but she didn't release the pig or the blade.

"He's such a fine pig," she said, the wistful inflection having returned.

Yuri stumbled a step closer, managing to pull the waist of his trousers over his hips.

"Give me the knife."

"No!"

The ferocity of her reply made him pause.

"Hanna, what's going on?"

"Isn't it obvious?" she asked. "I have so little. You have a pig. We could share him."

Standing there, without shirt or shoes, Yuri began to shiver in the early morning chill.

"The pig is mine," he said, meaning to sound forceful, but he was shivering so violently that it came out more as a whimper.

"You owe me a debt," she said, not backing down.

"A debt? What sort of debt?" Yuri took another step closer.

"A debt of hospitality," she said. "I invited you into my home and fed you."

"And I'm grateful," he said. "But are you forgetting that I chopped the wood and contributed to the meal?"

"I let you take me!"

Yuri froze, dumbstruck both by her vehemence and to what she was insinuating.

At last, trusting himself to speak, he said, "So, was that all that was – just an elaborate hoax to put me in your debt?" The scorn in his voice was intended to sting and it did.

Hanna's shoulders abruptly sagged, and the hand holding the knife fell to her side. For the first time she turned to him, and Yuri saw that the haunted look had returned with a vengeance.

Bursting into tears, she said, "No, it wasn't that!"

"Then what?"

Yuri took another step closer and, reaching out, eased the knife from her hand.

Hanna looked at him through a blur of tears. Yuri fought off an impulse to fold her into his arms. She had fooled him once. There would not be a second time.

"I've been so lonely," she said miserably. "So lost."

Coldly, Yuri replied, "Designing woman, it's only been two weeks since your husband's death."

Lashing out, she said, "You didn't protest so much last night!" before relapsing into tears.

Yuri stood, shivering, with the knife in his hand, not knowing which way to turn. It was true, he hadn't protested. Even if her intention had been to seduce him, he had gone willingly to her bed. Still, he wasn't about to surrender the point.

He said, "I didn't take you. What happened last night was something we shared."

Warily, he waited for another retort, but instead, Hanna acknowledged meekly, "You were very gentle."

Gesturing helplessly, he repeated, "Then why?"

Instead of answering, for the first time Hanna took note of Yuri's insufficient state of dress, and said, "Come inside. You can warm yourself by the fire while I explain." So saying, she walked past him with the pig in tow. Left with no alternative, Yuri followed.

Minutes later, flames were dancing in the fireplace and Yuri, wrapped in a blanket with a mug of tea, huddled as close to it as he dared. Hanna sat on a threadbare sofa, looking down at her hands folded neatly on her lap.

"It's true," she began, "when I first saw your pig, I wanted it for myself. So, I invited you into my home with designs of somehow enticing it away from you." Her shoulders gave a slight shrug as she endeavoured to explain. "It's been difficult ever since the Zlaimperians came and took everything from me, even ..." she gestured weakly toward the bedroom.

In spite of his determination not to be fooled again, Yuri asked, "They raped you?"

"Several times," she acknowledged, her apparent lack of emotion causing Yuri to shiver even more than he already was. "And they weren't nearly as gentle as you. I wanted to die, of course, but this was before the news came about my husband, so I made myself live for him." Bereft of hope, she slowly wagged her head, back and forth, "But it has been unbearable ever since."

Awkwardly, Yuri began, "But that still doesn't explain why ..." Giving up, he contented himself by merely gesturing toward the bedroom.

"Don't you see?" she asked through her tears. "You came along and, although you couldn't give me hope, I *could* pretend." Hurrying to explain, she said, "I could pretend that my husband wasn't dead. I could pretend that he had come home to me. If you only knew how hard it has been, you would know what a gift that was. Last night was so wonderful by its mere simplicity – the warmth, the food, the laughter and ... the other thing." Raising her head, she looked almost defiant. "I gave you my body because that's what all men want, and because it was what I wanted, too, to be possessed ... by him, one last time. So, I pretended!"

At another time, with another woman, Yuri might have felt insulted, to be so used. But seeing Hanna sitting there, so lost in her grief, it simply wasn't in him to feel angry. Still, it was an awkward situation, and he didn't know how to respond, so he was almost relieved to discover that Hanna had more to say.

"But then the morning came, and the spell had been broken," she said. "I could no longer pretend. The reality of my life closed in on me again, and once more, I became who I was – a pathetic wretch with designs to steal your pig." She looked at Yuri and laughed, but it was an ugly sound, like a crone cackling over a boiling cauldron. "If it had taken you one minute longer it would have been too late. I would have slaughtered your fine pig and, who knows? If you had still been asleep, perhaps I would have slaughtered you, as well. After all," she said with a hideous wink, "dead men tell no tales. With this wicked war raging all around there are already so many dead. What difference would it make if there was one more?"

The chill that passed through Yuri had nothing to do with the cold. It was the sort of chill that fire couldn't touch; only putting distance between himself and this unfortunate woman could release him from its icy grasp. However, it was true what she claimed: there was still a debt to be paid.

Rising to his feet, he took the mug (now empty of tea) and the knife in his hand. Running his thumb along the edge of the blade, he decided that it would do.

"I can't let you have my pig," he told her. "But I can let you gain some sustenance from him. He is, as you say, a fine animal, and I can spare you that much."

With that said, he straddled the pig, holding him immobile, and quick as lightning, nicked a vein in his neck with the knife. Then, holding the cup beneath the wound he collected the flow of blood. The procedure was performed so quickly, and the knife was so sharp, that the pig never moved, or otherwise made any complaint, whatsoever. When the mug was full, he handed it to her while busying himself binding the wound with his handkerchief.

While he was tying the knot, he said, "You can put that in with the rest of last night's soup, or …"

Looking up, he saw her already lowering the cup from her lips, her tongue licking the red stains clean from around her mouth.

Yuri stared but said nothing, nor did she volunteer to say anything more. Thinking it best to take his leave, he collected his belongings with indecent haste and was chivvying the pig out the door, giving the forlorn figure – still standing where he left her – the most hurried of nods as he took his leave.

*

The pig hadn't cared for the look in the strange woman's eyes when she had approached him with that evil-looking knife and had been relieved when the squire had come to take him away. He had seen how she regarded the blade, as if it was a means to an end, and he had also seen the aura of death already forming over her head.

Chapter Eleven

The road wound through the rolling hills of the countryside. The stubble from last year's crops lined either side for kilometres all around, looking so barren that it was difficult to believe that those same crops had once been green and alive. In the distance, the darkening of the horizon promised more forest in the days ahead.

Also on the horizon, even more distant than the forest, other plumes of smoke roiled into the sky, with low thunder-like grumblings constantly rolling across the plain, marking a point of conflict and his ultimate destination, the Capital.

Yuri saw neither the stubble nor the forest, nor even heard the distant rumbles. All he saw of the road was the ground in front of his boots. He was too lost in thought to pay any heed, which was a dangerous situation to be in when travelling through the heart of occupied territory.

As he walked along, convoys of Zlaimperian soldiers passed him by, heading in one direction or the other. Great armoured vehicles and artillery of every description, along with endless streams of trucks carrying men and supplies. The odd soldier would look and idly wonder about the simple peasant and his pig, but most were too caught up in their own thoughts to pay him any heed. As for Yuri, he never noticed them at all. The destruction of the village and the trauma of his encounter with Hanna Gorchenko had greatly unsettled him.

He was thinking of the woman and the tragedy of her life. He told himself that he had done all he could for her, but that didn't lighten the weight he felt pressing down on him now.

"Maybe I should have shared the pig with her," he mused aloud. "He is, after all, a fine pig and is bound to produce the most delicious chops, just as she said. And there really is nothing like a full belly to make a person see the sunnier side of things."

However, even as he spoke the words, he knew that, if given another chance, he would not have acted any differently.

"Perhaps if her intentions had been honest, I might have reconsidered," he conceded grudgingly. "However, her intentions *hadn't* been honest. She had planned to cheat me, possibly even murder me in my sleep – she had admitted as much herself – therefore she had placed herself outside the bounds of humanity." Belligerently, he mumbled, "The pig is mine, after all. I haven't come all this way to save the world, but merely to protest an unfair tax, nothing more. As a true Homstooder, I feel the injustice of this war, but that is beyond my ability to change. I just want to be able to send my pig to market at a price that I can afford."

At this point, Yuri had not travelled so far that, if he had bothered to look back, he would have seen the flames beginning to flare through the windows of Hanna's cottage and the smoke rising from the thatch of the roof. He had no way of knowing that all hope had deserted her before he had even walked out the door, and that her last act just prior to slashing her wrists (with the very same knife she had intended to use on the pig) had been to set fire to her home.

So, in his ignorance, he continued along, voicing his arguments over an issue that was already beyond his ability to resolve. Thus it was that he was also unaware of the single tank that rumbled by him and came to a stop on the side of the road.

The Zlaimperian lieutenant, dirty and bedraggled, with a bandage wound around his head, had noticed the Xorainian peasant with the pig. His tour at the front had been bloody beyond anything he'd ever experienced before, with many of his comrades dying in the flaming cauldrons of their own vehicles. Those bastard Xorainians were fighting back harder than anyone had predicted, and he was looking for some hapless victim on which to vent his pent-up fury. The first that Yuri noticed him was when he called out in Zlaimperian.

"Stop, Grandfather, I wish to speak with you."

Yuri looked up and saw the lieutenant sitting atop the tank's turret and knew by his haggard appearance that he hadn't stopped for idle conversation. From his cockpit in the front, the driver's head appeared through the hatch. If anything, he seemed even less inclined to observe the social niceties than his commander.

Yuri stopped as ordered, and the lieutenant climbed down from the tank, followed by the driver and the gunner. The faces of all three, smeared with oil and spent powder, bore identical scowls.

Yes?" Yuri asked, for he spoke Zlaimperian, as most Xorainians did to some degree. "What do you want with me?"

"Never mind that," the lieutenant brusquely replied. "What business do you have on this road?" As he came nearer, he drew his pistol causing Yuri to gape with surprise … and then transform into anger.

"This is a Xorainian road," he said in defiance, "and I am a Xorainian citizen. By what right do you question my business in my own country?"

The lieutenant walked up to Yuri and placed the muzzle of his pistol against Yuri's forehead.

"This gives me the right," he snarled. "Xorainian scum!"

However, Yuri, ever a true Homstooder, didn't cow so easily.

"And why do you insult me?" Yuri demanded. "There was a time when Xorainians and Zlaimperians were brothers."

"I'm not your fucking brother," the lieutenant sneered, and was joined by the angry murmurs of his crewmen standing close behind him. The lieutenant gestured at Yuri for their benefit, and said, "What say you, lads? Let's have this damned Nazi's shirt off!"

The two crewmen stepped forward, and first divesting Yuri of his coat, tore his shirt from his body.

Protesting, Yuri cried, "That was my finest shirt! By what right …?"

But the Zlaimperians ignored him. Instead, they were closely examining Yuri's torso, front and back.

"Nothing," said the driver.

"Doesn't mean anything," said the other crewman. "He could still be a fucking Nazi."

"A what?" Caught up in one indignation after another, Yuri was finding it difficult to comprehend their behaviour.

"Don't pretend you don't know what we're talking about," hissed the lieutenant. Then, to his men, he said, "Let's have his trousers off, too. Maybe they're on his legs."

The two crewmen advanced on Yuri a second time, and in a trice his trousers were tugged down around his ankles.

Virtually naked now, Yuri shivered in the cold, caught between indignation and outrage.

"What's the meaning of this?" he cried but was again ignored as the Zlaimperians examined him from head to toe.

Finally, "Still nothing," the driver said.

And again, the other crewman opined, "Still doesn't mean anything."

Acidly, Yuri interjected, "Perhaps if you told me what you're looking for I could help."

"Your tattoos," the driver accused, "what did you do with them, you Nazi bastard?"

Genuinely confused, Yuri replied, "Tattoos? What tattoos?"

"Don't play the innocent with us," the gunner growled. "Better come clean or it'll be the worst for you."

"But I don't know what you're – oof!" was as far as Yuri got before the driver's fist drove into his stomach, toppling him to his knees.

"Fucking Nazi," he said.

Meanwhile, having been deprived of any obvious clues, the Zlaimperian lieutenant tried another tack.

"Check his pockets," he told his two cohorts. "He's sure to have a camera hidden away somewhere." When this produced no results, the lieutenant said, "Check his pack, then. I'll eat my shirt if this bugger isn't a Nazi spy."

Still holding his stomach, Yuri managed to wheeze, "Just who are you calling a Nazi?"

Pugnaciously, the lieutenant replied, "I'm calling you a Nazi, Grandfather. Got it?"

Struggling to his feet, Yuri glowered at the lieutenant. "And just who the hell are you calling 'grandfather'?"

Yuri wasn't known as a particularly tall man back in Homstood, but he topped the lieutenant by a good six inches. Even the driver and gunner looked small by comparison.

Pretending not to be intimidated, the lieutenant took a casual step back, suddenly not so sure if Yuri was as fragile as he'd first assumed. If he hadn't been so preoccupied with tattoos, he would have noticed that there were still muscles rippling across that broad chest.

Gesturing with his pistol, he said, "All right, you can get dressed now." Then, to the two crewmen who were busily rummaging through the contents of Yuri's knapsack, he snapped, "Anything?"

"Nothing, Lieutenant." The driver sounded disappointed. "Not even a cell phone."

The gunner swore. "He's got it hid somewhere."

"Maybe a cavity search will reveal the truth," the driver opined, but after a minute had passed, amidst much hemming and hawing, it soon became apparent that no one was inclined to pursue that hypothesis any further.

However, the mere threat of being subjected to a cavity search caused a return of Yuri's defiance. Once again decently clothed, he ignored the contents of his knapsack scattered all around as his hands clenched into fists.

"Maybe he's not a Nazi after all," the lieutenant suggested.

"It's possible," the gunner agreed.

"I mean, they can't *all* be Nazis, can they?" the driver asked.

"I've never met a Nazi," Yuri grated, before adding meaningfully, "Although my grandfather killed his share of them back in the Great Patriotic War. Also, I've never had a tattoo in my life."

Annoyed with the lack of progress they were making, the lieutenant snapped, "Yes, we can see that."

"It's not a total waste of our time, though," said the gunner seizing hold of the pig's leash. "We've got this fine pi …" and the next thing he knew, he was sprawled across the road minus a tooth.

"The pig is mine," Yuri warned, his fists still clenched.

Sensing the situation slipping away from him, the lieutenant further added to the debacle by hesitating. It must be said that, in ordinary life, he was a decent man, with a wife and child back in Zlaimperia. It was the war that was to blame, that and seeing so many of his comrades die so horribly. Layer by layer, it had peeled away at his humanity until his only thought was to kill. Kill for vengeance, for a higher ideal, or just for the pure bloody-mindedness of it, it made little difference. Part of him wanted blood and that's all there was to it. Except, of course, it wasn't.

Neither was the lieutenant a coward, nor was he terribly brave, but it wasn't purely intimidation of Yuri's muscular build and obvious anger that caused him to hesitate. It was their mistreatment of a helpless and obviously innocent man that caused the return of at least one layer to his humanity in the form of shame.

Having hesitated, he knew that the time for him to pull the trigger had come and gone, and the longer the moment stretched out the more he knew that he no longer wished to kill.

"Let the old man keep the pig," he said, ignoring the reproachful look from the driver. "We're not thieves, after all."

The driver was not so sure about that, but he had the good sense to keep any objections he may have felt on the matter to himself.

"And who are you calling old?" Yuri challenged, his fists still clenched.

Laughing nervously, the lieutenant said, "I meant no disrespect, Grand – that is to say 'Father.'" Motioning for the driver to return Yuri's possessions to his knapsack, he said, "We were looking for Nazis, that's all."

"Well," Yuri said, still glowering, "I'm not a Nazi, and I'll repeat that I've never known any."

"But how can that be?" the driver asked. "Xoraina is full of Nazis."

"Who told you that?" Yuri demanded. "It's a lie."

"The Leader told us," said the driver, sharing an uneasy glance with the lieutenant.

"Then he lied to you," said Yuri. "Surely you're not so gullible that you would believe such a thing?"

"Of course not," said the driver.

"The very idea!" the lieutenant snorted, and once again shared an uneasy glance with the driver.

Belatedly, it dawned on Yuri to ask, "Wait a minute, is that why you invaded Xoraina in the first place?"

"Don't be ridiculous," scoffed the driver.

"Yes," the lieutenant admitted. Then, musing, he added, "As much as we love our Xorainian brothers, we hate Nazis more."

"And so you should," Yuri replied with some vehemence of his own. "But there are no Nazis here." Then, summing up his feelings on the matter, he said, "Go home."

"If only it was that simple, Father," the lieutenant said wistfully.

"I don't know why we're here in the first place," said the driver. "We were told that we were to take part in manoeuvres and the next thing we know we're in Xoraina."

"You were supposed to welcome us," the lieutenant accused.

Yuri shrugged. "I would have had no thoughts on the matter," he said. "Zlaimperians have always been welcome in Xoraina, but not with guns. Not with tanks, and bombs, and planes. Not if you come to slaughter our people and take our land."

"All in the name of rescuing you from oppression," the lieutenant murmured thoughtfully under his breath.

"Let me speak plainly," Yuri said. "If this war continues, Zlaimperia must prevail. You are big and we are small, so it's only natural. Now, I have no use for Nazis, and I don't especially care for any government, yours or ours. They only interfere with an honest man's labour. But, Lieutenant, the only one oppressing me is you."

Feeling foolish, the lieutenant felt the gun in his hand begin to waver. Then, having reached a decision, he returned it to its holster. Gesturing at the gunner, who was just now beginning to regain consciousness, he said to the driver, "Come on, help me get him back in the tank."

Stooping low, they managed to get the unfortunate man to his feet, and with one of his arms slung around each of their necks, they returned to their vehicle. Unceremoniously dumping the gunner through the driver's hatch, the lieutenant turned to Yuri, and asked, "Where have you come from, Father?"

"From the village of Homstood," Yuri replied, just now unclenching his fists. "At the foot of the Carpathian Mountains, on the far side of the forest."

The lieutenant ruminated for a moment. "You have come very far," he said wonderingly, "even farther than myself, and with a pig, at that? What is your purpose for making such a dangerous journey?"

"I'm on my way to the Capital," Yuri replied, feeling a sense of déjà vu. "I'm going to ask the President to repeal the new shipping tax. It's quite unjust, you know."

Both the lieutenant and the driver stared at Yuri as if he had just arrived from another planet, then the lieutenant began to laugh, so hard that the driver had to take hold of his shoulders to prevent him from falling over.

Finally, he managed to say, "I advise you to stay off this road, Father. Regretfully, not all of my countrymen can be counted on to see the humour. With that in mind, it may not go so well for you if you are stopped a second time." Pointing due north, to where the columns of smoke rose in the sky, he said, "Yonder lies fifty kilometres of Zlaimperian controlled ground. After that, you'll have to find some way to cross the lines again, and that may turn out to be a very tall order. Tread carefully, Father, and good luck."

Then, climbing back inside their vehicle, the driver started the engine, conjuring a cloud of diesel fumes. He gave Yuri a final wave before putting the transmission into gear causing the behemoth to lurch forward down the road.

As for Yuri, his mind brought back to the present by the potentially dangerous encounter, returned the wave, counted his lucky stars, and continued in the opposite direction.

*

The pig hadn't cared for the strange men in their giant rumbling machine and had been prepared to bite an ankle or two if the squire decided to fight. That the strange men had gone away was as much a mystery as it was a relief. Now they were free to resume their Great Adventure, but all the same, he was happy when the squire led him off the road at the end of the day.

Chapter Twelve

They came upon another village later that afternoon. Unlike the one from the day before, there didn't appear to be any signs at all that the war had reached this far, regardless of the fact that it was situated in the middle of Zlaimperian-controlled territory. With the buildings intact, the streets were teeming with pedestrians going about their daily business. In fact, the only signs of a Zlaimperian presence was the flag flying over the town hall and the armed sentries at its entrance.

Stopping outside a grocery shop, Yuri tethered the pig to a lamp post prior to entering. After his stay with the unfortunate Hanna Gorchenko, his provisions had run out altogether, and he was relieved to find the shop open with shelves well-stocked with goods.

The portly woman behind the counter regarded him with suspicion the moment he walked through the door. Yuri had anticipated as much; strangers entering Homstood were often regarded the same way until the family had settled in the area for at least two generations. Realising the best course of action to ameliorate the situation, he intended to engage her in friendly conversation straight away. However, it was the woman who spoke first.

Looking past him with a perplexed frown, she demanded, "Is that a pig?"

Turning to look through the plate glass window, Yuri saw his pig tethered to the lamp post exactly where he had left him. He seemed to be taking an equal interest in the passers-by as they were taking in him. At one point, he even suffered a little girl to scratch him behind his ears, just prior to her mother yanking her fastidiously away.

Bemused, he turned back to the woman. "Why, yes, it is," he said. "A real fine one, isn't he?"

Unmollified, the woman demanded, "Do you have a permit for him?"

Surprised by the question, Yuri replied, "He's my pig, if that's what you mean. I bought him for a single lakon from my friend, Vasily Pomkin, when he was just a piglet." Infused with the pride of ownership, he spared another, more appreciative glance at his property, and added, "He should fetch a good price when I get him to market, don't you think?"

The woman didn't even so much as shrug.

"A permit is required to take pets outside their homes."

"Oh, he's not a pet," Yuri assured her. "On my farm everyone must earn their keep, even my two dogs, Boris and Pyotr, and my cat, Svetlana. That fellow," he said, indicating the pig, "will earn his keep just as soon as I can get him to the market in Lofstov."

The woman scowled. "You're a long way from Lofstov."

"Yes, I know," Yuri replied absently. "First I must go to the Capital and have the new shipping tax rescinded."

The reason why Yuri spoke so absently was the same reason he failed to see the woman roll her eyes at his reply. After all that he'd endured thus far on his journey, simply mentioning the names of his old friends and companions caused Yuri to be struck with a sudden pang of homesickness, and he wondered how things were back on the farm. No doubt, after a hard day of mousing, Svetlana would be busily grooming herself in the kitchen window, while the dogs, having terrorized the rat population, would be sitting in earnest obedience, hoping to be tossed a morsel, while Mother Oksana busied herself about the kitchen making them all some supper. The warm domestic image came upon him so suddenly, and so unexpectedly, that he had to speak very carefully lest he betray his emotions.

Not privileged with the same vision, however, the woman shook her head, causing several of her chins to wobble disconcertingly. "Doesn't matter. If it's on a leash you need a permit."

Having recovered – for, although powerful, the image had only been a fleeting one – Yuri leaned over the counter in a confidential sort of way, careful to keep his feelings well hidden.

Dipping her a clandestine sort of wink, he said, "I won't be in your beautiful village long enough to purchase such a permit. So, perhaps you could let it go just this one time, eh? Otherwise," he said, capping off his gambit, "I'll be forced to take my leave from your charming shop and spend my money elsewhere."

It worked, of course. Even though the woman made a great show of indecision and went on at some length about the village being overrun by pets, Yuri knew she would eventually see reason. Forced to choose between greed and her love of making life more difficult for others, there really was only one choice.

Still, running a sceptical eye over his unkempt form – for living weeks on the road hadn't been conducive to Yuri's appearance – he could tell that she didn't entertain any high hopes of his contributing to her wealth in any meaningful way. Hoping to nip that scepticism in the bud, he produced the money that Mother Oksana had slipped inside his pack when he wasn't looking. The note that had been pinned to it explained that it was for just such an eventuality.

The woman's close-set eyes lit upon the bills, as she licked the slabs of liver that passed for her lips.

"I think I could be persuaded," she allowed, in a marginally more congenial tone. "How can I help you?"

Minutes later, Yuri was filling his knapsack, item by item, as the woman entered the price into the till. In the process, he thought to strike up a conversation to satisfy his curiosity.

Briefly recounting his experience of the other day, he mentioned the previous village he had come across that had been completely destroyed. "And yet here all appears to be unharmed."

The woman never looked up from her work. "That was a Xorainian village," she said.

Yuri frowned. "Isn't *this* a Xorainian village, too?"

"Not anymore," was the pert reply. "We have sworn allegiance to Zlaimperia." Pause. "Most of us anyway." Another pause. "Well, the mayor did," she said, adding, "and a few others."

By the way she spoke, Yuri could tell that the woman was one of those few.

Perhaps realising how unconvincing she sounded, the woman offered, "Regardless of how many, those who count chose to join Zlaimperia." Then, dismissively, she said, "The others will simply follow along."

"I'm sure you're right," Yuri replied politely; but at the same time, he thought that, while this woman obviously considered *herself* to be one of the few, Yuri felt that she would just as easily have placed *him* with 'the others.'

However, whether it was his intention or not, Yuri had finally found the one subject this corpulent woman could warm to.

"I mean, it's all one to them, isn't it? Whether we're Zlaimperian or Xorainian, democratic or authoritarian, why should they care? All governments are the same."

"Yes," Yuri replied, "that is my own sentiment, exactly."

However, he didn't say it with as much conviction as he might have a minute earlier. This woman seemed to hold the same views as he did, but he didn't feel the affinity towards her he thought he should have. He was reasonably sure that it wasn't because of her prodigious girth. No, it was because she was so unlikeable, and being unlikeable, it caused the first, tiny shift in the foundation of his belief. Meanwhile, the woman continued.

"Xoraina is a small country no one really cares about, but Zlaimperia is an empire that must be regarded with respect."

Yuri might not have been the wisest of men, but he didn't have to be to understand that when the woman spoke of respect, she meant fear. Still, it was best to keep in her good graces, as he might have to stop by here again on his way back to Homstood.

Forming the statement into a question, he asked, "I'm sure your mayor is happy with the arrangement?"

Instead of answering, Yuri was surprised when the woman became evasive, choosing her words carefully.

"The mayor is no longer with us," she said haltingly. "He had ... an accident ... in his automobile."

"Oh dear," Yuri replied, "what a shame."

"Yes," the woman agreed. "He lived in a fine house on the hill just outside of town and was coming in for a meeting at the town hall. His brakes failed, causing his car to go off the road. Of course, there are gossips who claim that someone cut the lines, but that's a ridiculous notion."

She offered Yuri a look, challenging him to say otherwise, but he merely shrugged, and politely repeated, "I'm sure you're right." Then, in an effort to move away from the subject, he said, "At least a Zlaimperian government would never have imposed a shipping tax for the railroad."

"Eh? What's that?" she asked before considering. "A shipping tax?" She shrugged indifferently. "Perhaps, perhaps not. What's important is getting the pigs to market. Isn't that right?"

"Yes, of course," Yuri replied, unconvincingly. Then, venturing, he said, "But just suppose the farmer can't afford to pay the shipping tax. What then?"

Still dismissive, she said, "Then he will soon go out of business, won't he? What does an empire care for a farmer or two? Besides," she said, "the future is in larger farms that can be run more efficiently."

Looking around, Yuri wondered if the same might apply to little shops, as well, but thought it best to hold his peace. Instead, troubled by the conversation, he absently bid the woman a good day before taking his leave.

He had entertained thoughts of finding lodging in the village for a night, but there was something about the place that made him feel uneasy. Perhaps he was being unjust and was looking at it through the filter of the storekeeper's narrative; but whatever the reason, he soon felt better when he'd collected his pig and left the village behind.

They made decent progress for the rest of that day, even considering that they no longer used the road. Once or twice, they were forced to lie low when a Zlaimperian convoy passed by, but they were a good ten kilometres further along when he decided to make camp for the night.

He chose a hollow nestled in a stand of birch on the premise that his fire wouldn't be visible from the ground. Between the storekeeper and his earlier encounter with the Zlaimperian soldiers, he was even more uneasy now than ever and thought it wise to avoid meeting strangers from that point on.

Once his fire was burning well, Yuri checked the wound he'd inflicted on the pig's neck that morning and applied a salve. After all, it was only good husbandry to look after one's animals, wasn't it? Yes, of course it was, and taking pains to be gentle was just a sound and sensible extension of that truism. At least that was what he told himself when they settled in after a hearty meal.

Addressing the pig, as had become his habit, Yuri said, "It would be accurate to say that I am troubled by my experiences since setting out on our journey. Much of what I've witnessed has challenged my beliefs and much has outright destroyed them. One that is glaringly obvious is that the Zlaimperians and the Xorainians can no longer be considered brothers. As much as we all might wish it were otherwise, those days are irrevocably gone.

"While I am under no illusions that Xoraina must eventually succumb, after all the barbarity I have witnessed, I have become equally sceptical that any Zlaimperian victory will erase the animosity that has grown between our two nations.

"There is something else worth mentioning, pig: out of all my compatriots, from the two lads who had come close to blows with one another in the convoy to Lofstov, to the solders fighting in the trench that night, there has been a universal sadness, and the burden of a crippling pain that had been unimaginable to bear just a few weeks earlier. However, in the face of all that, they had not succumbed to the inevitable but, instead, had chosen to meet it with a defiance I have to admire, regardless that it will only prolong their suffering. Even Hanna Gorchenko, to whom I fear no good end will come, even if – Heaven forbid – it results in her death, she will have chosen defiance over submission." Speculating further on the unfortunate woman, he explained to the pig, "I was helpless to save her, you know. The cup of your blood that I gave her was only a token, woefully insufficient to match her suffering."

Sitting opposite to him, across from the fire, the pig uttered a sad grunt that could easily be mistaken for commiseration.

"Then, just look at those Zlaimperian soldiers we ran into," Yuri invited. "What a sad lot they were, convinced that there were Nazis behind every tree. *Nazis*, if you please! Who would tell them such a thing, I wonder? How could they be so misled? While it is true that we in Homstood may not be the best informed on such issues, and while it is also true that *some* Nazis may exist among us, I would wager the farm – yes, even the east field – that there are no more Nazis in Xoraina than there are in any other country in the world. So, while I may not be aware of the specifics, I am quite comfortable stating that their accusations are ridiculous.

"Then, take that nasty woman in the shop this afternoon. While we are in agreement that the Zlaimperians must prevail, I find her relishing that thought as repugnant. It seems obvious that there are others who would refute her claim, as well. For instance, I would wager the new boar I will purchase with the proceeds from my sunflowers that the mayor's brakes didn't simply fail but were sabotaged, just as the rumours claimed. There now, pig, what do you think of that?"

The pig stretched out on the ground, resting his head on his forelegs with a long, relaxed sigh, stating unequivocally that he didn't think much of anything that didn't involve a good feed of swill or the undeniable luxuries of mud.

Not realising that he did so, Yuri managed the ghost of a smile at the pig's disinterest. Then, stifling a yawn, he said, "With regard to the two villages, while it must be admitted that the one which had stood in defiance had paid a terrible price and the other had been spared, I do question that woman's assertion that the opinions of 'those who count' carry more weight than 'the others.' Obviously, the mayor's opinion no longer carries any weight at all, for while his home had been spared, he too had paid a heavy price, his life, in fact." Staring into the flames, he said, "*'The way things are'* has gone insane, pig. This war has driven the entire world mad." Recalling the reasons Hanna Gorchenko gave for her husband going off to war, he mused, "I am told that we now live in a democracy. What do I care? I have never paid much attention to government, outside of how it affects my farm, or voted in an election, either. Governments are all the same. What do I care what silvery-tongued vagabond occupies the Presidential Mansion? One is as bad as the other."

Then, having reasoned himself to exhaustion, he curled up in his bedroll to sleep … but could not elude the uncomfortable notion that he had failed to reach a conclusion.

*

The pig hadn't minded the stares of the people as he had waited patiently outside the shop, and he had certainly appreciated the attention of the little girl when she had scratched behind his ears. All the same, he had sensed something about those villagers that made him feel uncomfortable. It was as though they were walking about in a dream from which they were unwilling to waken; but although it had been carefully masked, the pig knew that it wasn't a good dream at all. Frankly, he had been relieved when the squire had returned to lead him away.

Chapter Thirteen

By noon, after several Zlaimperian military convoys had forced them to stay ever further from the highway, they reached a heavily guarded crossroad. Through his binoculars, Yuri could easily see a sign there, with an arrow indicating that the Capital lay twenty kilometres to the north. Underneath a crudely spelt 'GO FUCK YOURSELF' freshly painted on the signboard, he could just make out 'ZLAIMPERIAN BORDER 150 km' next to an arrow pointing east.

"We're getting very close to our destination," he murmured to himself, but hadn't required the road sign to tell him that. All morning the sounds of war had been drawing closer the further they proceeded, so much so that the not-too-distant rumble of artillery had grown until it had become very nearly continuous.

Seeing that there was no point in attempting to travel further east, Yuri had backtracked to a heavily wooded area and crossed the road at a sprint when the traffic had thinned sufficiently for him to do so without being noticed. Then, with the leash fastened to his belt, he continued to the north with the pig trotting apprehensively at his side.

Sensing the pig's unease, Yuri said, "I don't blame you, that artillery is getting closer than ever before. It's making me nervous, too." Then, through a break in the trees, Yuri saw the ever-present columns of smoke marking the battle raging around the Capital, rising so high that it was necessary for him to crane his neck to see the top. Was it his imagination or had those columns multiplied several times over since he had last checked; or was it because they were closer now that the signs of war were much more visible?

"I could speculate all day and still be none the wiser," Yuri muttered to himself. "Nor will it bring me any closer to my goal." With a gentle tug on the leash, he said, "Come along, pig," but he was beginning to feel a sense of dread that they were heading into trouble.

Progress was much slower now as, time after time, they were forced to circle around a Zlaimperian position that he could just make out through the trees. More than once he was forced to retrace his steps when he found one avenue after another blocked by soldiers bearing the red, white, and blue shoulder patches of what Yuri had come to regard as the enemy.

The day stretched on with very little progress. Even when he thought one line had been successfully crossed, it was only to be confronted by another, each one successively filled with more Zlaimperian soldiers than the last.

Throughout this time the din of artillery continued, although by now Yuri had become so acquainted with the sound that he could tell that most of it was from Zlaimperian batteries sending outgoing rounds to Xorainian positions around the Capital, with comparatively few incoming rounds in return. Even so, more than once he'd had to dive for cover when a shell landed close by, and in one particular occasion, the subsequent explosion was followed by curses and cries of pain from a grove as it apparently found its mark.

As they pressed deeper through the increasing bedlam, dodging Zlaimperian patrols in one instance, and increasing rounds of Xorainian artillery in another, Yuri was gradually forced to accept the fact that it was futile to attempt to go any further.

Reaching a decision, he told the pig, "We'll find a spot to lay low for a while and try our luck after dark."

If the pig didn't necessarily seem in agreement, he appeared even less so when faced with the *status quo*. In spite of that, however, he didn't feel inclined to argue when, after some length of time had passed, Yuri succeeded in finding a hollow much the same as the one where they had made camp the night before.

"This will have to do," he told the pig anxiously, remarkably for the first time wondering what he'd got the both of them into. "At least we should be safe from anything but a direct hit, and if we cover ourselves with some of these boughs torn loose by the barrage, we will be safe from the prying eyes of a Zlaimperian patrol, as well."

So saying, Yuri gathered a considerable number of branches, and shortening the leash, forced the pig to lie down. Then, lying down beside him, he covered them both with the boughs until they were invisible from anything but the most intensive scrutiny.

Meanwhile, the artillery duel continued.

Tucked beneath their veil of branches, Yuri and the pig lay face to face. As the steady 'crump' of artillery continued, Yuri could see the whites of the pig's eyes and feel the tension in his body, coiled like a spring, threatening to give into his fear at any moment. Reaching out, he placed a hand on the animal's chest and felt his heart racing fifteen to the dozen. Curiously, his touch seemed to, if not calm, at least ease the pig's tension ever so little, and he offered Yuri a small grateful grunt in return.

Yuri couldn't blame the beast for feeling frightened. Truth be told, he was pretty frightened himself, and once again wondered belatedly at his foolishness that had gotten them into this fix in the first place. Lying there beside the trembling animal, the façade of the past weeks fell away as though he had woken from a dream.

All his life, he'd been cursed with a single-minded stubbornness and lying there, with artillery shells exploding all around, he was struck with a moment of clarity. He had to admit that while that stubbornness had gained him a certain reputation among the villagers of Homstood, it had seldom done him any favours, least of all now. When he thought of all the warnings he'd ignored, beginning with his friend, Hans Gromp, then the shipping agent at the rail station, the village administrator, Mother Oksana, and the Xorainian soldier at the checkpoint, he felt a stab of shame. All had tried to warn him of the danger, but he had been too single-minded to listen. From the beginning, the war had seemed a mere inconvenience, one that could be overcome through sheer determination and that single-mindedness he was so famous for. Never had he suspected the wanton brutality that he would be facing, of the destroyed convoys and villages, both filled with the charred remains of people whose only crime was to have been born a Xorainian citizen. Somehow his mind had been able to absorb those horrors and eventually accept that this was just *'the way things were.'* Even so, little by little, bit by bit, it had begun to erode his convictions but, sadly, not enough to turn him from this folly until he was well and truly in the thick of it. Well, there was no going back now. To retreat posed as much danger as there was pressing forward. That is, he reminded himself, if they survived long enough to do either.

As the crash of exploding rounds drew ever nearer, the pig began to wriggle frantically in an attempt to escape and it was only with the greatest difficulty that Yuri was able to restrain him. Cursing, he muttered to himself, "Poor fellow, he's terrified and who can blame him? But even worse, he senses my own fear and is panicked by it. I must find a way to calm him and quickly, for if he escapes, this will all have been for nothing."

Hesitantly, as this was a first time for him, he began to stroke the pig's flank, the same as he would have Borys or Pyotr back home. At the same time, he began to croon such things that he thought might reassure the beast. "There, there," he said, "it will be all right, you'll see," at the same time praying that this was the truth.

However, the pig wasn't reassured. Instead, a second effort had to be made to restrain him when a shell landed closer than any of the others. It exploded with a loud BOOM, shaking the very ground where they lay, dislodging branches from the overhanging trees that came tumbling down all around them.

Strangely enough, it was his fear that saved the day. Never before had Yuri been faced with the prospect of his own death, not even when Jasmine, his cow, had been startled by a rat and kicked out blindly, breaking two of Yuri's ribs. True, the pain had been excruciating but he had never even considered that he might die. He had simply sent Pyotr to fetch Mother Oksana and that had been the end of it. This was different.

Here there was no Pyotr and no one to send to for help even if there was. There was just this hollow – that had seemed safe enough only moments earlier, but now appeared to be more like a death trap – and that creeping barrage that seemed intent on seeking him out. He wanted to give into his fear, just like the pig, to leap to his feet and run away and never come near a war ever again. However, he still possessed just enough sense to realise that to rise above that shallow declivity would almost certainly be the death of him. His one and only hope was to remain where he was and pray that an errant round didn't land in the hollow. Yes, that was certainly the wisest course of action under the circumstances, but it still didn't address his fear. Instead, it was what his fear triggered that saved them both.

It has often been said that, whenever faced with death, one's life passes before one's eyes and so it was now, reminding Yuri of a time long ago.

Turning to the pig still trembling beside him, he asked, "Have I ever told you about Daryna?"

The simple conversational tone he used was so completely incongruent with the situation that it caused the pig to momentarily slip free from the clutches of his own fear.

"She was my wife," Yuri informed him. "We were married for an entire year."

The pig adjusted his snout to better see Yuri and offered an interrogative grunt. At the same time an artillery shell landed close by, shaking the ground and covering them both with debris. With his singularity of purpose, Yuri ignored the close call and pressed on with his tale.

He recalled, "She was the oldest daughter from a farm down the road. I chose her because she was strong and would be a good help about the farm. Also, she could cook. Oh, but she could cook! Her salo was without equal, and even Mother Oksana's vereniki paled in comparison."

Apparently enthralled by Yuri's story (perhaps because it included food), the pig gave a little wriggle to make himself more comfortable, temporarily forgetting about the thundering barrage.

"She was a good girl and went to church every Sunday. In fact, that's where I first met her. It was Easter and she was wearing a dress of multiple colours and a garland of wild poppies in her hair. I took one look at those strong shoulders and knew straight away that she was the one for me."

As the story evolved, the tone of Yuri's voice began to change, taking on a softness and depth the pig had never heard from the squire before.

"We were married in that same church six months later, just after the harvest. There were turnips in the east field that year, and the price was reasonable for a change, so there was enough money to pay for the priest and even for a supper and a musician afterward." Leaning closer to the pig, he confided, "Although, of course, I had never danced a step before in my life.

"The dress she wore was as golden as the sunflowers and blue to match her eyes. Of course, being a woman, she *could* dance – for it is well known that they are gifted in such things – and with her help, I was able to participate without disgracing myself."

Unheeded, the ground continued to tremble as the barrage crept ever closer.

Fondly reflecting, Yuri said, "That was a good year, the best one in my entire life. My parents had already passed away, so the farm was mine to do with as I pleased. We grew barley in the south field, wheat in the east, cabbages in the north and left the west field to go fallow. At the beginning of August, I was overjoyed when she told me that she was pregnant but insisted that she could still help with the harvest." Filled with wonder even after all this time, Yuri gave an appreciative shake of his head. "What a woman she was," he said. Then, perhaps because the memories became too real, he grimaced and looked away.

The pig gave another interrogative grunt, urging him to go on.

"You must pardon me, pig," Yuri said, "for I have not been completely truthful with you. It's been such a long time."

Another shell burst close by, followed by yet another, dislodging more and more branches from the trees, causing them to tumble down all around.

"It wasn't the strength of her shoulders that first attracted me or even the gossip from the neighbours of what a good cook she was." Glancing shyly at the pig, Yuri confessed, "It was her smile." With his own expression softening with the memory, he said, "When she smiled, it was like the sun coming out on a cloudy day. When she smiled at me, it was like ..." Frustrated, Yuri searched and searched for the correct word, then, lost in memory he sighed, "Heaven."

With his eyelids half closed, the pig exhaled a long, wistful sigh.

Reflecting, Yuri parroted the sigh. "She smiled at me often that year." Then his tone changed yet again, this time to something darker and more foreboding.

Unsettled by the squire's change in mood, the pig uttered a concerned grunt while Yuri took a deep breath and forced himself to let it out slowly.

"I was in the south field harvesting barley. Daryna's belly had grown huge by then, but she had been helping me as she had promised she would, in spite of my protestations that she rest. When it came to be late afternoon, she had returned to the cottage to make supper, just like she always had." His voice was little more than a low groan when he said, "That was the last time I saw her alive."

The pig was regarding him intensely, but Yuri never noticed, nor did he notice the 'crump' of exploding shells. All was lost in the pain of memory.

Gasping now, as if struggling to breathe, he said, "I was told that she had gone into labour a full week before she was due ... and that there were complications with the birth." Here Yuri hesitated briefly before forcing himself to continue. "It was what they call a breech birth, where the baby is born backwards. I was told that it is a very dangerous condition for both mother and child." A single tear meandered down Yuri's cheek, reflecting the pain that still endured over the years. "If only I had insisted that she not work so hard. If only I had been with her at the time, I would have been able to run for help." He shook his head, reliving the torment. "So many 'if onlys,' so many regrets that I've carried in my heart ever since, even when knowing that a thousand 'if onlys' and a million regrets would not make one bit of difference. As it was, I found both of them dead when I came in from the fields." Looking at the pig he said, "Ever since that day I no longer speak of such fanciful things as love, nor do Mother Oksana or I ever speak of Daryna. It's simply too painful for the both of us. We tell ourselves that there is the farm and only the farm." Yuri's gaze strayed past the pig to fixate on a memory. "But sometimes unspoken words are the loudest. Every day they speak of our loss, and every day we ignore it because to acknowledge the pain is more than we can bear."

Yuri fell silent, unable to continue. The pig was also silent, as if in reflection. They lay concealed in the hollow, staring at one another, while the moment dragged.

That's when the shell burst directly above them and everything went dark.

*

The pig squealed in surprise, terror, and pain all combined. A white-hot sliver of shrapnel grazed his haunch, spurring him out from the cover the squire had so laboriously constructed for them; and he was running blindly through the forest, trying with all his might to outdistance the pain, all the while squealing at the top of his lungs.

As luck would have it, the round that had found them was the last of the barrage, although it took several minutes for the pig to notice. All he was aware of was the fright he'd had and, of course, the pain.

However, although it had bled freely, his was a slight wound. Soon the pain began to recede and – as is the way with pigs – his memory of the explosion began to fade with it. Then – as is also the way with pigs – finding himself alone for the first time he could ever remember, he began to root inquisitively through the rich moss of the forest floor. Before long he found himself in hog heaven (so to speak) when he came upon a large cluster of mushrooms close to a dried-up pond. Red with white spots, they looked different from any mushroom he'd ever seen before, but the pig was famished and not inclined to be discerning. So, with the merest sniff by way of a passing nod to caution, he began devouring one mushroom after the other.

The pig found comfort in grazing. It was an occupation he was well used to and just the repetitiveness of it eased the tension of that terrible day from his weary mind. When at last he had rooted around and found every last one of those tasty treats and gobbled it down, he thought that a nice nap was in order. A brief inspection revealed that the bed of the pond wasn't as dry as he'd first thought. There was perhaps an inch of rainwater at the lowest point and, after supping his fill, he settled in for a good wallow. Soon he was happily covered in dark green slime from the tip of his snout to the tassel on the end of his tail.

Closing his eyes, he exhaled the most contented of sighs and prepared to slip off into the Land of Nod ... and to dream. What happened next was something of a mystery.

When the explosions began anew, it seemed very real and not like a dream at all. Deafening crescendos mixed with brilliant flashes of yellow and orange flames erupting all around again, causing the ground to tremble and shake as it had before. But then, this time, the ghosts appeared, hordes of them, horribly disfigured, writhing in agony, crying out in pain, covered in a veritable ocean of blood.

In all his life, the pig had never been afraid of the ghosts, but this time was different. Whether it was the terrifying explosions, or whether it was the bone-chilling screams of all those tormented souls, the pig took fright, possibly because now it was all too easy to visualise himself included in their number. By and large, the pig was an easy going fellow, but imagining his own death had shaken him very badly, for pigs seldom cared about such things. They didn't plan for the future or dwell in the past but were ever-present in the moment. Rarely did they stop *to consider what might happen, but now the pig's confused mind was faced with that very thing, and he didn't take it at all well.*

A mistake had been made, that much seemed obvious. Someone, somewhere, had decreed that he had not survived the recent terror, and instead of leaving him in peace, these spectres had risen from a dark place intent on returning there with him in their grasp. It was an extraordinary vision, but the pig was just an ordinary pig and reacted in the way any ordinary pig would.

Gripped with panic, he sprang to his feet and blundered off blindly into the woods, squealing with fright, intent only on escaping those fiends howling at his heels.

Chapter Fourteen

Yuri could only have been unconscious for a short period of time, for the first thing he was aware of was the unmistakeable smell of spent ordinance. It continued to linger in the air even though the bombardment itself had subsided.

Opening his eyes, he noticed immediately that the pig was gone, but when he tried to leap to his feet, a sickening pain washed over him, sending him back to his knees. Confused, he brought his hand to his forehead, and when he brought it away again, saw that his fingers were covered in blood. He remained very still, waiting for the nausea to leave, but ended up vomiting, instead. What was worse, each time his stomach convulsed another wave of pain washed over him until he thought his head must burst.

Under so much distress, you might be forgiven for thinking that there was no room in Yuri's mind for anything else, but then you've never known a true Homstooder.

"My pig," Yuri muttered to himself. "I must find my pig."

Dazed and confused, struggling with the aftereffects of his injury, somehow Yuri found his strength, and gritting his teeth against the pain, forced himself to his feet, the accumulated detritus of branches and leaves tumbling away from him in the process.

Searching, he turned this way and that, fighting to ignore fresh waves of nausea and the insistent pounding in his head. With more deliberation, he slowly turned, searching, fearing the worst – that he would discover the pig dead amongst the moss and ferns – but instead he found nothing at all.

Struggling against the first tendrils of fear, Yuri murmured to himself, "I must find him! I must! Without the pig, everything I have endured to this point will be meaningless. I must find him at once!"

Starting off, he blundered blindly into the forest, much as the pig had himself only moments earlier, and would have stumbled headlong to the ground again had he not caught hold of the trunk of a young birch. Standing there, swaying, gripping the tree for all he was worth, at the same time, willing his knees not to buckle, it soon became apparent to Yuri that his condition was such that he wouldn't be able to do much of anything 'at once.'

Long moments passed while he stood, leaning his forehead against the smooth bark of the tree, hoping and praying for his equilibrium to return. At length, he tentatively released his grip on the trunk, one hand at a time. He continued standing for another long moment, swaying like a ship on an angry sea, but when he attempted to move his feet, he soon found himself embracing the young birch again as if it was a long-lost lover. Five minutes passed before the procedure was repeated with the same result. Ten minutes more and he was finally able to stagger drunkenly out of the declivity, gingerly searching for a clue as to what had become of the pig. Sadly, in his confused state of mind, it was a fruitless endeavour.

Growing more and more frantic, Yuri's search progressed in an ever-widening circle, but with no result. Then, just when his eye caught something that may or may not have been a drop of blood on a blade of grass, he heard voices. They were too far away to comprehend exactly what was being said, but it was obvious that they were very angry. Yuri cared rather less about that than the fact that those detached voices must belong to humans who, presumably, had eyes.

Had he been in his right mind, Yuri almost certainly would have taken all due precautions in such a perilous place. As it was, with the wound to his head coupled with his overwhelming concern for his property, he reacted on instinct.

"Perhaps they have seen my pig," he said and blundered off in the direction from where the angry voices continued to fill the air.

On and on Yuri struggled, mindless of the thorns and brambles as they lacerated his face and hands, with only one identifiable thought cosseted in the fog of his confused mind.

"They *must* have seen the pig," he said feverishly, without any definable reason why that might be so. "For a certainty they have." His foot caught on a vine, causing him to stumble to the ground, further lacerating his hands on some brambles. Not noticing, he struggled back to his feet without so much as a wince. Tarrying only long enough to steady himself, he said, "I'm coming for you, pig! I'm coming! Don't lose hope!" Grimly, he continued on his erratic journey toward the sound of the angry voices.

Eventually he drew close enough to where he could identify the words being spoken (or angrily shouted) but he paid no heed. He only hoped that they would continue speaking until he found them.

At last, he stumbled across an old overgrown trail with a clearing ahead. It was from there that the shouting was emanating. Fighting against a sickening spell of vertigo, he forced himself on, desperate to be reunited with his pig.

In time, he arrived at the clearing, absently noting three soldiers with the red, white, and blue shoulders patches on their sleeves identifying them as Zlaimperians. Behind them, burning furiously, was a scout vehicle with a body of an Xorainian soldier lying beside it; but the Zlaimperians paid neither the vehicle nor the dead soldier any heed. Instead, they were all concentrating on the single Xorainian soldier kneeling before them.

Absently, Yuri noted that the man had been ill used. His face was covered with bruises and both eyes had been blackened. Whether that had been a result of the destruction of his vehicle or from the fists of the Zlaimperians he couldn't say; but regardless of the fact that it held no priority for him, it was a question that was soon answered.

Even as he watched, one of the Zlaimperians, with a sergeant's stripes on his sleeve, shouted an obscenity at the Xorainian soldier, and demanded, "Where is it, you Nazi bastard?" When no answer was forthcoming, he lashed out with his boot, catching the prisoner on the side of his head, sending him sprawling into the grass.

Yuri blinked, vaguely surprised at the cruelty, then he impatiently put it aside and called out. "Have any of you seen my pig?" Under different circumstance, the response to his query might have been gratifying, in that it was so immediate.

As one, the Zlaimperians spun towards him, rifles raised and at the ready.

Holding his hands some distance apart, Yuri said, "He's about this big and might be trailing his leash."

"Keep your hands where they are!' the sergeant barked, glaring at him through the sights of his Kalashnikov. "Come closer and don't try any funny business!"

Obeying, Yuri explained further.

"It's not like him to run off but he was frightened of the bombardment. Still, he can't have gone far."

One of the Zlaimperians, intent upon Yuri, cast an aside to his comrade. "What's he on about?"

"Dunno," came the reply. "Something about a pig."

Unsettled, the first soldier looked over his sights so that he could better see what manner of being they were faced with. Apparently not finding anything untoward, he shook his head in a wondering sort of way before returning to glare at him down the barrel of his rifle.

When Yuri had halved the distance between them, the Zlaimperian sergeant shouted, "That's far enough!" And stepped forward to make a closer inspection.

"Careful, Sergeant," one of the two remaining soldiers warned, "he could be armed."

"Just you keep him in your sights," the sergeant growled. "And if he so much as scratches his nose, fill him full of lead."

Drawing cautiously nearer, the sergeant barked at Yuri, "Turn around! But let me see those hands!"

Still obeying, Yuri explained, "I'm taking him to the Capital to get the shipping tax repealed – it's quite unjust, you know. Then I can send him to market and grow sunflowers in the east field."

"Shut your god damned mouth about your god damned pig!" the sergeant snarled. Then, shouldering his rifle, he covered the remaining distance between them. Relieving Yuri of his knapsack, he tossed it to his men. "One of you search through that. I can smell a spy a mile away and this fellow reeks to high Heaven."

"And when I sell the sunflower seeds, I might use some of the proceeds to purchase a real boar with papers."

"I told you to shut up about the fucking pig!"

"Oh, but I wasn't referring to *that* pig," Yuri assured the sergeant while he went through his pockets. "I was speaking of a different pig, one with a pedigree. He's going to make me rich one day, you'll see. Then maybe I can afford to repair the barn and mend the roof of my cottage."

Ignoring him, the sergeant found Yuri's wallet and thumbed through the contents. Discovering his driver's licence, he studied the photo and then, frowning, Yuri's face.

"I was quite a bit younger when that was taken," Yuri explained.

Still frowning, the sergeant continued to study the document, and said, "This licence expired twenty years ago."

"That's what I just told you," Yuri said. "Well," he amended, "in so many words."

The sergeant continued to peruse the licence with scepticism, but aside from being drastically outdated, he could find no fault with it. Frustrated on that front, he turned to the soldier who had rifled through his knapsack and received a shrug and headshake in return.

"What did you expect, sergeant?" the third soldier asked. "Did you think you'd find something obvious, like a paper, perhaps, that said, 'I AM A SPY'?"

"Shut your fucking mouth, smart ass," the sergeant growled.

"I'm just saying that he could still be a spy," the soldier retorted defensively.

"I'm not a spy," Yuri volunteered, but, of course, no one listened.

"Do you think I don't know that?" the sergeant challenged the soldier in a threatening tone. When no reply was immediately forthcoming, he said, "I'm well aware that he's probably a spy. I was simply looking for proof."

"They want proof to ease their conscience when they execute you."

Yuri turned at the sound of this new voice and saw that the Xorainian soldier had recovered to the extent where he could make his opinion known, albeit through cracked and bleeding lips.

Studying him, Yuri saw that he was a captain in his mid-twenties. Further study revealed that, were it not for the bruises covering his face, he might possibly be handsome.

Finally, the penny dropped as to his meaning.

"What do you mean 'executed?'" he asked, both genuinely curious and suddenly nervous at the same time.

"It's simple," the captain explained. "They won't have any problem killing me because I'm in uniform, so they can blaze away to their hearts' content; but with you, well, you're a civilian, aren't you? So, the issue's not so clear."

"Quiet, you!" snarled one of the Zlaimperian soldiers, threatening him with the butt of his rifle; but the captain was unquelled.

"Oh, please," he scoffed, "don't pretend that that wasn't your plan all along."

"As you wish," the sergeant replied. "That *is* our plan." Gesturing to Yuri, he said, "Spy or not, lack of evidence won't save him."

"Well, what do you know," the captain's face transformed into a painful sneer. "Honesty from a Zlaimperian. Who would've thought?"

"But I'm *not* a spy," Yuri repeated, and was again ignored.

"Save your breath, Father," the captain advised. "It's all one to them. They just don't care."

"This is also true," the sergeant agreed amiably, cocking his rifle.

"But I'm not a spy," Yuri repeated a third time. "I'm just looking for my pig."

"I'm not going to tell you again," said the sergeant, suddenly furious, "shut up about your pig, you fucking Nazi!"

Yuri protested, "But I'm not a Nazi, either." Then, gesturing to the captain, he added, "And neither is he."

"Of course I'm not," the captain agreed. "And do you want to know the bitter irony of it all?"

"What's that?" Yuri asked.

"I'm Jewish!" The captain cackled laughter, but then winced when that simple action caused his bruised lips to split anew.

"Another likely story," one of the Zlaimperians said, cocking his own rifle in turn.

"There, do you see, Father?" the captain asked. "They simply don't care."

"The only good Xorainian is a fucking dead one," the sergeant observed, before taking Yuri by the scruff of the neck and forcing him to the ground beside the captain.

"What," the captain asked, "you're not going to force us to dig our own graves first?"

"You can rot where you fall for all I care," the sergeant replied as he took careful aim at point blank range.

Parroting the move, one of the Zlaimperians levelled his rifle at Yuri. "Let's get it over with," he said. "This forest is giving me the creeps."

The second soldier guffawed. "Fine woodsman you are." But he, too, sounded nervous, regardless of how much he tried to show otherwise.

The first soldier retorted, "Look who's talking. The closest you ever came to a forest was when you were mugging tourists in Gorky Park!"

"Enough!" cried the sergeant. "In a minute you two can carry on like frightened little girls for as long as you like, but first we have to put these Nazi bastards out of their misery."

The two soldiers exchanged sour glances but lacked the nerve to argue with the sergeant. Instead, they returned their attention to Yuri and the captain as ordered.

"Ready?" asked the sergeant.

"Shouldn't we blindfold them first," asked one of the soldiers.

Wonderingly, the captain taunted, "Don't tell me you don't have the guts to shoot an unarmed man when he's looking you in the eye."

"He's right," the sergeant agreed, delivering a vexed look at the soldier. "Fuck the blindfolds." For the second time he asked, "Ready?"

Both soldiers cocked their rifles.

Yuri, now fully sensible of his predicament, and how close he was to death, was too shocked for words, but he heard the captain mutter under his breath. "Bastards!"

"Aim!"

Yuri found himself staring down the muzzle of the Kalashnikov, wanting to spit in the man's face, but his mouth had gone completely dry. Then, just as he closed his eyes, anticipating the order to fire, there came an eldritch scream some distance away, sending a shiver down his spine, in spite of the fact that he had more pressing problems to deal with.

One of the soldiers – the one who had suggested blindfolds – darted a worried glance at the sergeant. "What, in the name of all that's holy, was that?"

The second soldier, equally as nervous – so nervous, in fact, that he completely forgot to taunt his comrade – said, "It sounded like a fucking witch!"

"Shut up!" cried the sergeant. Training his rifle toward the surrounding forest, he demanded, "Did either of you fools happen to notice where that came from?"

Before they could answer, the cry came again, but closer than before.

"S-k-r-e-e-e-e-e-e-e-e-e-e-e-e-e-e!"

Still the sergeant was uncertain, the muzzle of his rifle playing across the trees.

"What about now?" he demanded, but evidently neither of the soldiers could pinpoint the source of the horrible cry that time, either.

Instead, the first soldier almost whimpered, "Back home, they often spoke of demons in the woods near our village."

"It was the same in our village," the second soldier nervously concurred, insinuating without actually saying that it stood to reason they might expect demons to inhabit this forest, as well.

"Belay that talk," snapped the sergeant. He was gripping his rifle so tight that his knuckles had grown pale. "Just tell me which direction that cunting noise is coming from!"

Once more they heard it, this time much closer.

"S-k-r-e-e-e-e-e-e-e-e-e-e-e-e-e-e!"

Now they could hear the sounds of the undergrowth being disturbed, so violently that the first soldier couldn't withhold an actual whimper this time, but still they lacked any specific direction to train their guns.

The sound of the mysterious intruder blundering through the undergrowth was rapidly growing louder and louder. Whatever was out there was approaching with considerable speed.

Unable to wait any longer, and past caring about such ridiculous things as orders, the first soldier let loose a long burst of automatic fire into the trees. His example was instantly followed by his comrades, each burst longer than the one before.

The noise was deafening as three rifles raked the treeline, clipping branch after branch and generally adding to the chaos. Then, just when they were forced to stop and reload, the demon burst out of the trees directly in front of Yuri.

It came upon them so suddenly that all the naked eye could see was a blur of black and green slime, and blood-red, satanic eyes. Charging headlong, the fiend came straight for them, obviously intent on murder and mayhem, shrieking its battle cry as it came.

"S-K-R-E-E-E-E-E-E-E-E-E-E-E-E!"

It was too much for the privates. Just one look at the fearsome creature and they turned tail and ran for their lives, screaming almost as loudly as their nemesis. Only the sergeant lingered long enough to squeeze off a short, wildly aimed burst before his own nerve gave out, and he was running pell-mell after them.

    Dazed by the suddenness of it all, both Yuri and the captain remained motionless, with eyes bulging and jaws wide open, as Yuri's pig sped by, apparently in hot pursuit.

*

*   The ghosts, the rapid explosions, the thunderous din of the salvos repeatedly burst in the pig's mind, driving him onward in a blind panic. He had no knowledge of breaking into the clearing, nor did he see the people there, or even the squire. The only thing he was certain of was that he mustn't stop, not for anything, because the fiends of Hell were hard on his heels.*

Chapter Fifteen

Against the captain's protests that they were unarmed in the middle of no man's land, Yuri insisted on giving chase ... to the pig, not the Zlaimperians, and set off without a backward glance. The captain, having shouted himself hoarse that it was far too dangerous, watched him go until he was almost out of sight; then, heaving the most exasperated of all exasperated sighs, he called out for Yuri to wait before running to join him.

They caught up with the pig an hour later, having run himself to the ground. A pitiful sight, he lay on his side, ribs heaving like a bellows, covered with slime, and the pupils of his eyes dilated to the point where his irises had all but disappeared. Thankfully, the nerve-shredding squeals had come to an end, leaving in their place a low, doleful groan.

"Is this your pig?" asked the captain.

After a careful study, Yuri affirmed, "It is."

"What's wrong with him?" the captain asked, clearly perplexed.

"God only knows," Yuri replied, shaking his head.

"Let's get him back to the clearing," the captain said. "I have to see to my comrade."

"Yes, of course," said Yuri, then gesturing helplessly at the exhausted pig, he asked, "But how? Clearly, he's not capable of traveling on his own."

The problem was solved when, after a cautious search, they fortuitously discovered an abandoned cottage close by. A quick exploration of one of the outbuildings produced a rickety old wheelbarrow, upon which they were able to load the pig with some difficulty.

"Christ, the brute's heavy," the captain complained.

"Fifty point four three kilos," Yuri proudly replied. "But remember, he saved our lives."

"That's true," the captain agreed, and they both spared a moment to gaze with varying degrees of fondness at the pig, lying hungover on the wheelbarrow's bed. "But the truth of the matter is that you both saved my life." Extending his hand, he said, "It compels me to ask your name, Father, for my life holds some value to me. I am Captain Olesky of the Armed Forces of Xoraina, Captain *Marko* Olesky, at your service." Accepting his hand, Yuri completed the introduction by giving Olesky his own name, after which, predictably, the captain enquired, "If you don't mind my saying, your accent isn't a local one. Where are you from?" and upon being told let out a low, appreciative whistle. "You've come a long way, my friend, through some very dangerous territory."

"None more dangerous than where we are now," Yuri observed. Glancing at the lengthening shadows of the trees, he added, "We'd better be on our way if we don't wish to be caught in the open when the sun goes down."

In response, Captain Olesky gestured in the direction from which they had just come. "Lead on, Father, I was born and raised in the city, so I have no doubt that your woods craft is superior to mine."

With that, the trio set off, the two men keeping a wary eye out for any further Zlaimperian patrols and maintaining an avid, if subdued, conversation, while the pig snored on in a martyred sort of way.

Even though he was disposed to be friendly (as was typical of any true Homstooder), the captain's mentioning of being a city dweller had awoken a long-held distrust from Yuri, for it was well known that there were pickpockets and vagabonds in such places, aye and certain women of ill-repute, as well. Hans Gromp had once made the long journey to visit his sister in Lofstov, and when meeting Yuri later in the market square back in Homstood, often related lurid tales of what he had been told there. So, mindful of such warnings, as surreptitiously as possible, he checked that his wallet was safe and secure from the clutches of the captain's potentially larcenous, city-dwelling fingers.

"What are you doing?" Captain Olesky enquired with mild impatience, for Yuri had set down the wheelbarrow, removed his knapsack, and was currently checking the contents of one of the side pockets.

"Oh, nothing, nothing at all," Yuri replied airily. "I was just adjusting an uncomfortable lump in my pack."

To which Captain Olesky frowned, for the side pocket could hardly interfere with the pack's comfort; but he decided to say nothing, for even though this Homstooder had saved his life, it was well known that, to a man, those living in the region between the Carpathians and the forest were completely *nevcheniy*. Besides, the very fact that he *had* saved his life reassured the captain that, while the rugged-looking old fellow might be somewhat eccentric, he surely meant him no harm. Instead, he muttered something about the need to make haste, but by then Yuri had already donned his knapsack once more and taken up the handles of the wheelbarrow.

The sun was hovering just above the highest limbs of the trees by the time they made their way back to the destroyed reconnaissance vehicle, the dying flames having long since reduced it to a smouldering ruin. Captain Olesky peered inside where he knew there was a shovel, and sourly observed that the handle had been reduced to ashes.

Cursing under his breath, he said, "I don't know how I'm going to bury him now."

Meanwhile, Yuri had covered the unfortunate driver with a blanket and had taken station over him, hands clasped in a sign of respect.

He pondered the question for a moment, and said, "It shouldn't be too difficult, Captain. With all the artillery fire hereabout, at least one of the shells must have struck close by."

The captain considered this proposal and, seeing as how he didn't have a better one to put forward, it was decided that they would conduct a search, proceeding with caution, as neither man wished to be subjected to another Zlaimperian interrogation.

The sun was just a murky glimmer through the trees when they came upon a hole blown into the earth a mere hundred metres from the clearing. It must have been a sizable artillery shell that made it, for a giant oak, blasted free from its roots, lay over the excavation.

Nodding approval, Captain Olesky said, "A fitting marker. Stas was fond of trees. Although I could never tell one from the other myself."

Bending low, Yuri observed, "There's just enough room under the branches for us to manage. What do you think?"

Casting worried looks at their lengthening shadows, Captain Olesky replied, "We'd better hurry before it becomes too dark to see."

Carrying the body to the gravesite proved more difficult than either of them had imagined, for the forest, overgrown in places, left insufficient room. However, when Yuri gently nudged the captain aside and hefted the driver's body over his own shoulder, they made the gravesite just as the sun was going down.

Laying the hapless Stas beside the excavation, the two men crawled through the gap left by the limbs of the oak, dragging the body after them.

Yuri had intended on retrieving his blanket before the burial, but Captain Olesky, lost in his own thoughts, began covering the body with loose earth straight away. Instead of objecting, Yuri decided to hold his peace. Under the circumstances, sacrificing a blanket seemed a small price to pay. He would just have to shiver through the night without it, and so thinking, dropped to his knees and began to help the captain cover the body.

The darkness was very nearly complete by the time they had finished, to the point where they had to feel their way out from the grave.

Standing over it now, it only seemed right to say a few words in recognition of the sacrifice that had been made. Yuri tried to think of a fitting passage from the Bible, but Captain Olesky simply said, "He was a good soldier," before snapping a salute, while Yuri stood respectfully at his side until the captain lowered his arm. After which he ventured a solemn, "Rest in peace."

Replacing his service cap, the captain said, "At least it was quick."

Quietly, Yuri asked, "How did it happen?"

Equally laconic, the captain replied, "A missile," correctly assuming that no further explanation was required.

Arriving back in the clearing, for the first time since setting out, Yuri was hesitant about what his next step should be. Making camp out here in no man's land wasn't a very inviting notion, as a fire was out of the question. A pity that, for after all that he had been through that day, a fire would have been soothing. However, making camp seemed to be the last thing on Captain Olesky's mind.

Retrieving a cell phone from his pocket, he turned it to the compass feature, and said, "Best get your pig, Father."

"Why?" Yuri asked, bewildered. "Where are we going?"

"You wanted to get to the Capital, didn't you?" Olesky asked. Pointing due north, he said, "Our lines are right over there, less than ten kilometres away. If we hurry, we might just make it there before dawn."

*

But of course, they didn't hurry. Blundering about in a forest in the dead of night, with or without a drunken pig on a wheelbarrow, would have been inviting disaster. Nor did they make it to the Xorainian lines that morning. Each time they tried to creep out into the open a Zlaimperian patrol foiled their plans. Therefore, temporarily accepting defeat, they had retreated back into the forest and took refuge in an old shell hole.

They remained cloistered there for the entirety of the next day, Olesky noting acidly that only the pig seemed comfortable with the situation and wondered aloud for the second time what had caused the beast to behave as he had when saving them from the Zlaimperian soldiers.

Yuri regarded the beast with a strange feeling that, if he didn't know any better, was something akin to affection … which was obviously ridiculous, for no true Homstooder ever felt affection for something that could only be regarded as chattel. Still sound asleep, thankfully, the pig in question had ceased his snoring. Instead, a long string of drool descended from his lax jaws to the ground.

Peering closer, the captain noticed crumbs of an unknown substance intermingled with the drool. Extending his finger, he scooped up a sample of the pig's saliva and inspected the fragments floating in the revolting mess. Yuri watched as the captain brought the sample to his nose and was preparing to look away if he showed the least sign of tasting it. That was a spectacle he was spared, however, for after another moment had passed, the captain wiped his finger on his battle dress and knowingly said, "Mushrooms."

Unimpressed, Yuri replied, "But of course, he's very partial to them," and spared another affectionate smile for the dormant pig.

"Not like these," said the captain, grinning. Holding up the red flecked specimen on his thumbnail, he said, "See this? I'll bet a month's wages that this is from the cap and there, you see? That's the rim of a white dot. These particular mushrooms contain a strong hallucinogenic." Gesturing all around, he said, "You'll find an abundance of them growing in these woods. In happier times, I'd come out here with my friends to pick them." Delivering a playful slap to the pig's corpulent haunch, he said, "Beyond a doubt, our friend here came across a prodigious cluster and ate his fill, to the point where he became delusional. That would explain his behaviour, and why he's still suffering from the effects."

Yuri was caught between wanting to know more about the effect these terrible mushrooms would have on his pig and being appalled that Captain Olesky knew so much about them. Apart from vagabonds and pickpockets and ladies of ill-repute, Hans Gromp had also told lurid tales from the city that included drug addicts which, of course, were inestimably worse than all of the other three combined. Unconsciously, he reached around to reassure himself that his wallet was still safe in the side pocket of his knapsack before enquiring further.

"Will he recover?"

"Oh yes," the captain couldn't refrain from chuckling. "He'll be fine, but most likely still be a bit groggy when he wakes up."

"When will that be?" Yuri enquired, feeling anxious.

"God only knows," Olesky replied. "It depends on how much is in his system."

"If I know that pig," Yuri said with some confidence, "his system will be filled to the brim."

It appeared that Yuri *did* know his pig, after all, for he didn't waken until the sun was just beginning to set that evening.

"He must have found the motherlode of all clusters," Olesky wryly observed.

"You're sure he'll be okay?" Yuri asked dubiously, while the pig staggered this way and that.

"Well, the mushrooms didn't kill him so I'm guessing he'll be fine," the captain reasserted. "In fact, a little exercise will do him good."

"I wish I had some water to give him," Yuri fretted. "The poor fellow must be parched."

"Well, we don't," Olesky replied, "and unless you're willing to risk another encounter with those Zlaimperian bastards, we had best be on our way."

Moments later found them creeping out into no man's land again. The sky was clear, and the broken ground was dimly illuminated under a quarter-moon. Once again progress was necessarily slow as Yuri and the captain stole forward with their heads on swivels, alert to every sound. Still not quite himself, the pig seemed inclined to stand and stare at the stars as if still dreaming, requiring several tugs on his leash to convince him to follow along.

They had scarcely covered a hundred metres when the captain held up his hand, cautioning them to the ground.

Peering into the darkness, Yuri saw yet another Zlaimperian patrol approaching a hundred metres away. Turning, Captain Olesky made a circular motion with his finger, the signal for them to return to the forest's edge. Once that had been accomplished, he gestured to the east; they would try again further down the line.

Eventually, they arrived at a declivity leading out to unoccupied territory. Too shallow to be called a trench, what was of immediate interest was that it ran north and south, straight as an arrow, toward the heart of where the captain said lay the Xorainian lines. Lowering himself to his hands and knees, Captain Olesky proceeded forward, hidden from sight by all but the most inquisitive eyes. Yuri followed with the pig stumbling along after.

Presently, they arrived at where a cluster of trees bordered the declivity to the right, the moon casting long, skeletal shadows from the denuded limbs. They were just proceeding past when Captain Olesky suddenly froze, signalling caution. Carefully placing his hand over the pig's snout to keep him quiet, Yuri peered over the lip of the sunken ground ... and almost gave birth.

The approach of the Zlaimperians must have been hidden by the trees, but now they had breasted them and were coming on in single file, the nearest one scant metres away.

Yuri scarcely dared to breathe, too gripped by panic to turn and run. Perhaps that was just as well, for he would have been shot down before he had covered half the distance to the trees. As it was, though, the approaching soldiers were so close they could hardly fail to see where they lay hidden in their shallow trench.

For a wonder, however, they didn't.

One by one they passed over where they lay, virtually on top of Captain Olesky. Tired and bedraggled, every one of them walked at a crouch, carefully placing one foot in front of the other, taking pains not to make a sound.

They were only half a dozen in number, but their passing seemed to take an eternity. One of them actually stopped at the lip of the declivity, his head turning this way and that, searching for signs of danger. If he happened to look down, he couldn't fail to see them, but presently he moved on when the man behind urged him forward with a whispered curse. Finally, the last man was past so, naturally, that was when the pig decided to let out a long, inebriated grunt.

Muzzled as he was by Yuri's hand, it came out as a muffled groan, scarcely noticeable, but it was enough for the last soldier in line to stop and turn. If he looked down, which he was bound to do, all would be lost.

It wouldn't be fair to say that Yuri reacted out of panic, only that he reacted without thinking. One moment he was motionless on the ground, the next he was standing in front of the soldier, whose eyes were growing wider by the instant. When he opened his mouth to cry out, Yuri struck.

Street brawling was frowned upon in Homstood and that particularly pertained to a man close to fifty, so Yuri was woefully unprepared for the encounter. All he knew was that on no account could the soldier be allowed to shout a warning. Thus it was that his fist flashed out, connecting with the Zlaimperian's jaw.

The man dropped like a stone without uttering a word of warning to his fellows, but the rattle of his kit as he hit the ground was enough.

"Halt!" someone cried, and a shot rang out, the bullet buzzing past Yuri's ear.

That was all the encouragement the captain needed. He was off like a shot, his boots drumming over the broken ground in a rapid staccato, with Yuri hard on his heels, and the pig trundling along in tow.

By now, a veritable fusillade shattered the night as the Zlaimperians opened fire. Several bullets buzzed past Yuri's head while several more kicked up the earth at his feet, but still he forged on, expecting every moment to be his last.

The captain was scarcely ten metres ahead when Yuri saw him stagger. With no time to think, he scooped him up as he fled past.

Aggrieved, Olesky cried, "The bastards shot me in the ass!" even as he clung to Yuri's sleeve. "Don't stop," he ordered. "Help is just ahead."

That was when the night lit up with an even more deafening fusillade from where Olesky claimed the Xorainian lines were situated.

Without slowing, Olesky shouted at the top of his lungs, "Comrade! Comrade! Cease fire, damn you! We're Xorainian you trigger happy bastards! Let us in!"

And with that, Yuri tumbled into the waiting trench, with Captain Olesky in his grip.

The pig landed on top of both of them, made a disgruntled moan, and promptly fell asleep.

*

The pig remembered running in terror from the loud explosions filling the air and the cries of a horde of ghosts dogging his heels. They continued on in his dreams and again when he awoke until the squire finally dragged him into the trench. It wasn't like the pig to complain, but it had been quite an unsettling few days. What wouldn't he give right now for some delicious swill followed by a nice relaxing wallow? In lieu of that, however, he closed his eyes and, this time, dreamed of better days, and the sweetest, kindest sow in all the world waiting for him at home.

PART TWO
Chapter Sixteen

The Capital was a sprawling city of three million people, straddling a lazy bend of the Dnapro River, in the north-eastern region of Xoraina. Surrounded by a belt of thickly forested hills, to Yuri (who had never seen a city before), it seemed like something right out of the Enchanted Kingdom.

As they drove through the narrow, winding streets, his neck craned this way and that, while he stared, unabashedly amazed. The vast, neatly trimmed parks, the sprawling department stores, the bustling traffic (which was a mere fraction of what it had been before the invasion), all were as foreign to him as the dark side of the moon.

When they turned onto Mariinsky Prospekt on their way to Parliament, the modest apartment buildings (even the damaged ones) lining both sides of the avenue, seemed to tower in the sky. But the glaring difference between here and the demolished village he had passed through earlier were the people.

Yuri had never seen so many people in his life, not even if he added them all together since the day he was born. There must have been hundreds of them, maybe even thousands, possibly even tens of thousands, passing by on the streets as they went about their business.

For that was the real difference between the Capital and the village. The village was dead, crushed beneath the heel of a ruthless invader. The Capital, although now only a shadow of its former self, was a functioning metropolis and the still-beating heart of Xoraina.

However, even the Capital showed the scars of war. A closer inspection revealed a damaged building here, a cratered street there, and of course, burnt out hulks of vehicles dotted throughout the course of their journey.

Some of the buildings showed recent signs of damage. One or two still had smoke roiling from gaping scars where a missile had struck, for ironically, just as they had been running for their lives to reach the Xorainian lines in the southern sector, a major attack had been driven back north of the city. The battle had not been won without a cost, however, as the wailing sirens of emergency vehicles was a sobering reminder.

Even as he watched, mouth gaping with amazement, Yuri could see firemen and other rescue workers scurrying over the blasted remains of a building like so many ants over a disturbed hill, searching for survivors.

As they continued on their way, carefully skirting around the odd crater, it seemed to Yuri that the trauma of the destruction must be enormous, but the people he saw on the street, while unanimously wearing the same grim expression, showed no signs whatsoever of defeat.

By great good fortune, Captain Olesky's wound had been a mere graze across his left buttock. After a doctor had stitched it up, he was pronounced fit for travel, although a pillow was advised for sitting on. With a minimum of fuss, they had been given transport to the city once the Xorainian commander, a full colonel, had verified Captain Olesky's identity, which didn't take long, for it was he who had sent him on his mission in the first place.

"I congratulate you on your safe return, Captain," he had said, diplomatically ignoring the bloodstained tear in the seat of Olesky's pants or the fact that he was leaning on a cane. Then, more soberly, he added, "It's a pity about Private Melnyk, however."

The conversation lagged, transforming into a moment of silence, which all three men observed with bowed heads. Then the moment was past and it was time to get down to business, such as it was. When the captain had shared what little intelligence he had been able to glean, the commander sighed, and said, "I'm afraid it will have to do. We should be able to hold them off for the time being, provided they don't come at us with too much armour. In the meantime, I'm sending you on convalescent leave. The doctor tells me that three weeks should suffice." Then, before the captain could argue (which he appeared to be on the verge of doing) the colonel turned to Yuri, and demanded, "And just who are you?" When Olesky vouched for him, adding some detail in the bargain, he added, "Good gracious, a pig did you say?" And when this had been confirmed, much to Yuri's confusion, they'd been dismissed in a gale of laughter.

They spent the night in barracks on the outskirts of the city. The sergeant in charge had looked upon Yuri, a civilian, with some scepticism, and his pig with total disbelief. An argument might have ensued had Captain Olesky not vouched for them both a second time and hinted that he might pull rank if the sergeant decided to cause any trouble. Early the next morning, Olesky had requisitioned a truck and told Yuri to get in.

Puzzled, Yuri had enquired, "Why? Where are you taking me?"

Sitting behind the wheel, the captain looked at Yuri, and explained. "You said that you wanted to have that shipping tax rescinded, didn't you? Well, I'm giving you a golden opportunity to do just that."

"To what? Meet the President?" Even to Yuri's simplistic vision of the workings of governments this seemed highly improbable.

"And why not?" Olesky asked. "The old boy's my cousin!" When Yuri continued to remain sceptical, the captain said, "Look, you've saved my life twice now, okay? So, I figure I owe you that much, at least. I can't promise you what the president's answer will be but at least I can give you the opportunity to state your case." Then, with a matter-of-fact look, he asked, "Okay?" When Yuri had continued to hesitate, fearing that this might be a trick city people played on honest farmers, Olesky grinned, and said, "I wasn't joking about his being my cousin, you know?" So, hiding his misgivings, Yuri had relented and allowed himself to be persuaded to get in the back of the truck with his pig.

"Here we are," Olesky called, pulling up in front of the Parliament Building – a vast neo-classical limestone monstrosity, fronted by Doric columns and a massive dome for a roof. In the otherwise immaculate garden, the ugly muzzles of two anti-aircraft guns pointed skyward from a nest of sandbags – an ominous sign of a country at war. As Yuri jumped down from the bed of the truck, hoisting the pig down after him, a uniformed guard stepped forward and saluted before hopping in and driving their truck away.

Yuri watched it go with some trepidation, for he was completely at sea in this strange city with their strange ways. Noting this with wry humour, Olesky assured him, "Don't worry, he's only taking it to the vehicle compound. We'll get it back."

Although unconvinced, Yuri realised that he was helpless to control circumstances in this strange new world and, whether he liked it or not, he would just have to take Olesky at his word. Therefore, he dismissed his misgivings and filed them away in his mind under '*just the way things were.*' Then, with leash in hand, he took in the Parliament Building with a long, pensive glance – knowing that the success or failure of his mission might be only moments away – and followed Captain Olesky inside.

*

Two soldiers stood guard at the main entrance. Stamping to attention, they brought their rifles to salute as Captain Olesky hobbled by. Yuri, feeling self-conscious, tried to hide his embarrassment as he followed along in his wake, their bootsteps (and the pig's hooves) resonating on the marble floor throughout the cavernous interior.

With the captain leaning only slightly on his cane, they stepped along at a brisk pace down a long colonnade. Well used to the building, the captain looked neither to the left nor the right but continued forward, exchanging salutes with a steady stream of generals coming from the opposite direction, or a clipped greeting if the person happened to be a civilian. All who they encountered, whether military or otherwise, seemed preoccupied and in a desperate hurry that was, perhaps, the most foreign thing of all for any true denizen of Homstood. Indeed, so preoccupied were they that not one of them paid the slightest attention to the pig.

Of all that teeming mass only Yuri and his charge seemed to notice the opulent grandeur they encountered with every step, from the fine carpets to the marble statues, to the many paintings on the walls depicting the country's past leaders, each arranged in a heroic pose.

Resplendent in their dress uniforms, guards stood at every door, alert for any danger. This brought home to Yuri more than anything – more than the bombed-out villages or charred caravans of vehicles, even more than the stench of decaying bodies or the brutal presence of Zlaimperian occupiers – that this was not only a country at war, but a country fighting for its very survival.

Any Homstooder worth their salt would swear that such opulence amidst the grimness of war would have left them unimpressed but, to a man or woman, they would have been lying. It wasn't that Homstooders made a habit of speaking untruths, but faced with choosing between a harmless fib or admitting that they were intimidated by such surroundings, a true Homstooder would always choose the former, if for nothing else, for the honour of their village. Thankfully, this was a question that no one thought to ask of Yuri, for the further they travelled into the interior of the vast building, the more intimidated he felt.

Eventually, they passed through an arched doorway and entered a vast room with royal blue carpet bordered in gold. The room's centrepiece was a wide stairway leading up to the second floor. It was to this stairway that Captain Olesky led them without hesitation.

At the top of the stairs, lined with a balustrade, was a long oblong-shaped promenade. The civil servants bustling about their business, disappearing in and out of various offices, were even more evident here than on the ground floor.

They hadn't gone very far, however, before Captain Olesky drew Yuri aside, out of the stream of traffic, and pointed. "There he is."

Following the direction the captain was indicating, Yuri saw two men, both somewhat older than he was himself. One, tall and slender in a general's uniform bedecked with gold braid and medals, was in agitated conversation with his companion, a squat, bow-legged figure in a rumpled suit who Yuri recognised as the president of Xoraina. As the two men drew nearer, he could plainly hear what they were saying.

"You misunderstand me, my dear general," the president was saying in a restrained tone. "It's not that I don't care about our casualties – such a statement is clearly ridiculous – it's just that our lines must hold at all costs."

"And I'm telling you, Mr President," the general replied sourly, "that such a feat may not be possible for much longer. While it's true that our boys inflicted heavy casualties on the invaders, we lost too many in return. The Zlaimperian numbers can be replaced, ours cannot. I can't answer for our effectiveness if they come at us again, which they surely will."

"Now is not the time for weakness, General. As my Minister of Defence, I expect you to … well, would you look at what the cat dragged in, if it isn't my cousin Marko!"

Spying Captain Olesky, the president grasped him by the shoulders, offering him an affectionate smile. "How does it go at the front?" Then noting Olesky's cane, he frowned. "I heard you'd been wounded. I hope it's not serious?"

While the captain took a moment to provide his kinsman with an update, and assure him of his wellbeing, Yuri took the opportunity to study the President, as well as the Minister of Defence, more closely.

He noted the grey at the President's temples and the deep lines around his eyes. His smile, although genuine as he listened to Olesky relate his news, was weary. His ill-fitting suit had hidden much of his physique from a distance but up close, he could see his vest bulging from a sizeable paunch. Heavily jowled with bags under his eyes, to Yuri, he bore a distinct resemblance to a morose beagle. However, upon further inspection, the clear set to his eyes showed promise of intelligence and compassion.

In contrast, the defence minister was everyone's idea of a dashing military man. Towering over the president by a good eight inches, a haughty expression of the socially privileged was affixed to his handsome face. Standing straight as a ramrod with shoulders well back, his chest was thrust out the better to exhibit his medals. While there was no grey in his hair, Yuri noted a slight smear of dye behind one ear. Confidence was in every inch of his bearing, although, judging by the snippet of conversation Yuri had overheard, that confidence was reserved for himself and not for the forces under his command.

At some point, before Captain Olesky was finished with his tale, the President's eyes strayed toward Yuri standing patiently a few steps behind. His smile grew quizzical when he noted his simple homespun clothing, stained and dirty from long weeks on the road; but then it grew to somewhere between disbelief and wryly amused when he noticed the pig, waiting just as patiently at Yuri's heel.

"I'm happy that you're safe and sound, Cousin, and I imagine that your mother will be even more so," he told the captain. "You must come by the palace for dinner this evening so that I might hear about how things fair at the front in greater detail." Then, turning fully to Yuri, he said, "But first you must introduce me to your friend and tell me what brings you here when you should be taking your ease."

Gesturing to his companion, Captain Olesky made the introduction, adding, "I thought he deserved an audience, as he has gone to a great deal of trouble to get here."

"Is that so?" the President said, offering Yuri his hand. Addressing him directly this time, he asked, "And where have you come from, Brother?" Upon hearing Yuri's halting reply, he frowned and darted a querying glance at his cousin, as if to ascertain that this wasn't all some elaborate joke. The captain, understanding the cause of the president's confusion, merely nodded his assurance, adding, "He saved my life, by the way."

This time it was the president who let out a long, low whistle of appreciation.

"You must tell me more about it this evening," he said. Then, to Yuri, "I thank you for my cousin's life, Brother." With a wink at Olesky, he said, "He's not much but he's all that his mother has. Now, you have come far and endured a great deal to get here. I can appreciate such determination. Tell me, how can I be of service to you?"

However, having gone to such lengths for this opportunity, now that it had finally arrived, Yuri's nerve threatened to desert him. It was all well and good to gather in the marketplace after church and criticise the great and powerful, but it was quite another matter to do so face to face. The intimidating surroundings only added to the problem.

Still halting, Yuri managed to stammer, "It ... it's the tax, Your Honour."

Frowning, the president asked, "The tax?"

At which point the captain briefly intervened. "He means the new shipping tax for livestock, Mr President. He thinks it's unfair, as he can't afford to send his pig to market."

While the pig and the President exchanged glances, Yuri nodded vigorously in agreement with Captain Olesky but otherwise held his peace ... which was more than could be said for the Minister for Defence.

"Oh, what nonsense!" he cried. Rounding on Yuri, he barked, "Fool, what is the meaning of this? Haven't you heard we're at war?"

That was enough to spur Yuri out of his catatonic state. As would any true Homstooder, his jaw jutted out pugnaciously when he said, "The war is no business of mine, Excellency. All I want is to send my pig to market so that I can grow sunflowers in the east field and finish the repairs to my barn and perhaps mend the roof of my cottage. So, you see, I have no need of your war. You can take it to the devil for all I care!"

Taken aback by the outburst, the general growled, "Your President has far more important things to attend to than such a paltry issue! You should fall to your knees and beg his forgiveness for having wasted so much of his time!" Then, in a much more restrained tone, he turned to the president, and stared meaningfully at his wristwatch. "Which reminds me, sir, our meeting with the Cabinet will begin shortly."

The president, who had been listening to the exchange with bemused detachment, said, "Don't be so hard on the man, General. He has suffered enough just to be here and saved the life of my cousin in the bargain. Besides, what is my duty if not to our people, eh? Why else are we fighting if not to serve them?" Then, turning apologetically back to Yuri, he said, "But the Minister of Defence is correct, we do have a meeting to attend, and it is of some urgency. So, I regret that I cannot address your grievance right this minute." Half turning, he stopped for a moment in indecision. Then, squaring his shoulders, he turned back again. "However, in light of all that you have gone through to see me, I wish to extend to you an invitation to stay at the palace for the duration of your visit." After a pause, just in case Yuri entertained any thoughts of bringing the beast to the palace as well, he added, "And we'll find some suitable accommodation for your pig, too." Turning to the captain, he said, "See to it, Marko," and left, ignoring the defence minister's disapproving frown.

*

It had been an interesting day for the pig. Although there were far too many humans about in this great building for comfort, it was reassuring to have the squire close by. Many points caught his interest, along with many smells, but there was a vague feeling of disappointment that such a grand place contained neither a decent wallow or even a shred of toothsome swill.

Chapter Seventeen

While it can be said with some accuracy that a true Homstooder doesn't shock easily, Yuri had been deeply shocked by the president's invitation to stay at the palace. After all, here he was, a simple farmer, suddenly an honoured guest of the most powerful minister in all the land, merely because he had managed to make it to the Capital without getting himself killed. It seemed a meagre qualification, especially when one considered that there must be many others who were equally qualified, and quite frankly, it made him uneasy to be treated with such consideration. Even his attempt to voice his troubled feelings to Captain Olesky didn't entirely serve to erase his misgivings.

"Oh, that," the captain had said, "I wouldn't worry about it if I were you. I can vouch for the president. He was impressed by your ordeal, and this is his attempt at honouring you for it, nothing more. Of that I'm certain." But then, as an afterthought, he added, "Although, he is also a consummate politician, and never misses a trick." Considering briefly, he shrugged, and said, "Anyway, if he has anything up his sleeve, you'll know about it soon enough."

After dropping the pig off at a facility for holding livestock at the city's fairground, Yuri presented himself at the palace dressed in his finest homespun along with Captain Olesky, looking smart and very martial in his dress uniform.

As at the Parliament Building, the Presidential Palace – another stone monstrosity, heavily decorated with columns and cupolas, with twin towers on either wing – was also heavily guarded, with anti-aircraft batteries positioned in the gardens while heavily armed soldiers patrolled the perimeter of the grounds, as well as inside the palace itself.

At the door, an usher bowed them into an anteroom before relieving Yuri of his knapsack (which he held pinched between thumb and forefinger as he carried it away) and informed them that their host would arrive presently. In the meantime, could he offer them a refreshment?

Olesky asked for vodka, but when Yuri asked, hopefully, for nalivka – the homemade brandy every true Homstooder cut his teeth on almost as soon as he was weaned from his mother's milk – the poor man had frowned, looked uncertainly at the sideboard heavily laden with bottles and decanters containing the finest spirits from all over the world, and said that he would see what he could do before exiting the room. In the ensuing silence, although he couldn't understand what was being said, Yuri thought he could hear a hurried conversation, interspersed with the odd muffled expletive, coming from just beyond the door where the usher had retreated. After a rather lengthy pause, the man re-entered the room armed with a leather flask, and in due course the nalivka was presented to Yuri in a cutglass snifter resting on a heavily ornate silver platter. The man seemed reluctant to divulge anything more on the subject, but when pressed, admitted to sending a boy to the market, where it was known that some of the less exalted shops had a plentiful supply of the fiery spirit.

That so much trouble had been gone to on his behalf only made Yuri feel more uncomfortable than ever, but as soon as he took a sip, the heady aroma took him back to pleasant memories of Homstood and the green fields at the foot of the Carpathian Mountains. It almost felt as if he was home again.

Yuri wished this was so in fact as well as fancy. He wished that very much, indeed.

"Why so glum?" Olesky asked with untypical solicitousness.

Frowning, Yuri said, "This is, by far, the furthest in distance and time I have ever been away from Homstood in my entire life, and I feel the lack of the old place."

The captain, who found it hard to imagine yearning for some country hovel in the midst of all the finery of the palace, gestured around, and said, "This should help deal with your homesickness."

"But that's just it," Yuri wagged his shaggy head, "I feel the lack so keenly that I would trade all of this to be back there again. It has taken hold of my mind, until it has eclipsed even my unease with all this big city finery."

The captain studied Yuri for a long moment, making an honest attempt to understand, but in the end, he simply shrugged and said, "You'll get used to it." It was a statement he plainly believed, for he seemed entirely at ease himself, in a way that Yuri could only envy.

Just then, the grand double doors to the room swung open and a liveried manservant stepped into the room. Bowing, he said, "Gentlemen, the President of Xoraina," and in walked the ugly little dwarf with a resigned, apologetic smile.

"You must forgive the formality," he said. "I try to tell the staff that I'm perfectly capable of walking into a room unannounced, but they won't hear of it. They tell me that it's for the prestige of our nation and who am I to argue with that?" Approaching, he said confidentially, "Just between ourselves, they order me about the place so much I'm not entirely sure who's in charge, them or me." Then he laughed at his own joke, and it was such honest laughter that Yuri instinctively found himself warming to the funny-looking little man.

Meanwhile, ever courteous, the president continued.

"Please, gentlemen, do be seated and make yourselves comfortable." Offering Olesky a playful frown, he said, "I expected more from you, Marko. You should know better by now." Turning to Yuri, he explained, "I simply cannot abide my guests not feeling as comfortable as if they were in their own home. Isn't that right, Marko?"

Dipping Yuri a wink, Captain Olesky said, "It is, Mr President. In fact, our mutual friend and I were discussing that very thing."

The president looked pained. Turning to Yuri, he said, "What nonsense is this, Yuri Yurivich?" Gesturing around the richly appointed room, he said, "Am I to understand that all these baubles are making you feel ill at ease? I won't hear of it!" Plonking himself down in the nearest chair, he swung himself sideways until his legs were draped comfortably over the arm. "You must remember that these are all just things, Yuri. It's true that there are many pieces of art among what I so cavalierly refer to as 'baubles' and there are some that are very fine, indeed, but never forget, Yuri, in this house it is you, a Xorainian citizen, who is the true work of art. Now come," he said sternly, "make yourself comfortable. I insist!"

Once all were seated and reasonably at their ease, the president, ascertaining that his guests had been supplied with refreshments, and paying special attention to Yuri's glass, called to the manservant, "My palate craves something different this evening, Oleg. I believe I'll have some nalivka, as well."

After this had been supplied, Yuri, emboldened by the president's urging to feel at home, summoned the courage to ask, "About the new shipping tax, Your Excellency, have you given any thought about my request?" In answer to that worthy's blank stare, he added, "It's quite unfair, you know."

By then the president's memory had made the connection. Carefully assuming a solemn politician's mask, he said, "Ah yes, the new shipping tax. Thank you for bringing it up. I was just about to do so myself." Then, frowning, he said, "I can sympathise that this must be a burden for you, Yuri Yurivich ..."

"I can't afford to send my pig to market," Yuri interrupted.

"... But you must be aware that the country is at war," the president continued smoothly. "Wars are very expensive enterprises."

Downcast, Yuri asked, "So your answer to my request is no?"

Too accomplished a politician to ever speak so directly to a potential voter, the president frowned, and said, "I did not say any such thing, Yuri. I'm merely pointing out that there are two sides to consider. As president, it is my duty to see to the wellbeing of all Xorainians. The solution is not always so easy to find. Do you understand?"

Soberly, Yuri replied, "I do, Excellency." Then, in a sudden fit of pique, he said, "Damn Zlaimperia for invading our country!"

At which point, Captain Olesky interjected, "That's something I can drink to." Raising his glass, he said, "Gentlemen, I propose a toast, damnation to Zlaimperia!"

"Hear! Hear!" the president cried, downing his nalivka.

Just as all the glasses were being drained, Oleg, the manservant, re-entered the room. Bowing, he said, "Dinner is served, gentlemen. If you will accompany me to the dining room, please."

*

In deference to Yuri, the president had instructed that dinner should consist of plain traditional Xorainian fare, but never in his life had Yuri ever tasted anything so delicious.

The meal began with *rosolnyk*, a vegetable soup made with potatoes, pickled cucumbers, barley, carrots and onions. The president and Captain Olesky ate theirs in cultured silence all the while politely ignoring the voracious slurps coming from Yuri's quarter as he, armed with a spoon firmly wedged in his fist, devoured the concoction with much lip-smacking and grunts of pleasure. Indeed, he was only prevented from taking the bowl and licking it clean by Captain Olesky tactfully clearing his throat.

Next came *vinigret*, a salad consisting of beets, sauerkraut, potatoes, onions and carrots. It was a dish Yuri often had in the past, only this time he was delighted to note that it also included pickles mixed with salted sunflower oil.

After the servants cleared the table, each of the diners was presented with a dish of *zavyantsi*: beef rolls stuffed with mushrooms, onions, eggs, cheese, sauerkraut, and carrots. Neither the president nor Captain Olesky so much as batted an eye when Yuri asked for a second helping.

Taking this as his cue, when the time came for dessert, the chef made sure that a mountain of *syrnyky* – fried milk curds with raisins, served with a choice of sour cream, jam, or apple sauce – was presented on a giant platter. Yuri's eyes grew wide at the sight of all that bounty, and while the president and captain ate sparingly, Yuri, who had been subsisting on the plainest of fare for weeks on end, took it as a personal challenge; but after a lengthy episode of gorging, even he finally had to admit that he couldn't eat another bite.

When the brandy and cigars were brought out, Yuri declined both, preferring instead his nalivka and a cigarette which he rolled at the table.

When all three were puffing away contentedly, Yuri renewed his case against the new shipping tax.

"Excellency, while I concede that the government needs money to pursue its war, I don't agree that they are going about it in the correct way."

"Oh?" the president asked, "And how is that, my friend?"

"Well, you see, sir," Yuri began seriously, "while the shipping tax may supply the government with *some* money, if the tax is excessive the pigs won't be shipped. Then the government gets no money at all."

"He has a point, sir," Captain Olesky said. "An excessive tax could actually hurt the economy."

While Yuri made his case, aided occasionally by some input by Captain Olesky, the president sat and listened. Ordinarily a quiet, soft-spoken man, one might be mistaken for thinking that listening was his greatest asset. It was only when the wellbeing of the nation was discussed that he insisted upon being heard. Then his voice assumed a timbre and richness that had previously been lacking, exhibiting a power of oratory that had carried him to office the previous year. Listening as he weighed the pros and cons of the new shipping tax, Yuri could sense his deep love for their country, which puzzled him, although, of course, he was too polite to say so.

After having presented his argument, the president thanked Yuri, declaring that it was rare to have such valuable input from ordinary citizens. "Not that I think you are an ordinary man, Yuri Yurivich," he hastened to add, "quite the contrary, your exploit continues to astonish me. I merely acknowledge that you are closer to the issue than I am."

Yuri accepted the compliment by growing red in the face and stammering his thanks. After which, the president promised that he would certainly take his views under advisement, and before Yuri could interject further, he turned to his cousin.

"Now then, Marko, of course the Minister of Defence keeps me informed as to how the war is proceeding in an overall picture, which, Heaven knows, is quite serious, with Zlaimperian forces making gains in the south and threatening to surround the Capital here in the north, but perhaps you would be good enough to lend some meat to those bones and apprise me of what life is like at the front? Tell me, how is the morale of the troops? Are they still willing to fight?"

"Morale is not all that could be hoped for, cousin," Captain Olesky confessed. "The men *want* to fight, even in the face of heavy casualties, but we are vastly outnumbered and lack the tools to push the enemy back. If things continue as they are, I can't answer for how long we can hold out." Frustrated, he said, "Give us the tools, sir, and we'll send these Zlaimperian bastards straight to Hell. As it is, however ..." He shrugged and left the rest of the sentence unfinished.

"Oh dear," said the president, "as bad as that?" When no reply was forthcoming, he said, "All hope rests with the United States and her allies. As you know, Marko, they have already sent us some munitions, but they are antiquated and insufficient in number."

"What I wouldn't give to get my hands on some of their modern weapons," Olesky sighed.

"They are hesitant because they aren't sure the country will survive," said the president.

"Antiquated or not," Olesky said, "we will give them their victory," but his voice sounded hollow, lacking conviction.

"Until then we must hang on at all costs, Marko. Do you understand? At all costs."

Yuri, who had been surprised and a little unsettled to find himself privy to such a conversation – where matters of high import were being discussed freely in front of him – asked if he should leave the room.

"What?" the president cried, before offering Yuri his most winning smile ... which rather resembled a grimacing orangutan. "After all that you have been through, Brother, I highly doubt that you are a Zlaimperian agent, and besides, we are not discussing anything that isn't already being discussed in every household in Xoraina. The situation is as grave as can possibly be imagined. Very well, we freely admit it, but not for one instant are we suggesting surrender. Xoraina has tasted freedom and we will never again submit to the yoke of a tyrant!"

Yuri, who, as you know, had his own thoughts on the matter, opened his mouth to speak, but he noticed that the president was suddenly regarding him with speculative interest.

"What?" he asked.

The president continued to study Yuri for another moment, making him feel the same as he had many years ago, as a child at school, under the unsmiling scrutiny of the headmaster. He was beginning to squirm uncomfortably in his chair when the president seemed to reach a decision.

"Your country has need of you, Yuri Yurivich," he said.

Yuri, who, as a good Homstooder, was willing to do anything within reason, provided it wasn't dangerous and didn't require too much exertion on his part, guardedly said, "Oh?"

Still speculative, the president asked, "How would you feel about appearing on television?"

Captain Olesky, who had remained silent to this point, asked, "What are you driving at, cousin? What trick do you have up that sleeve of yours?"

To which the president said, "Think, Marko. What does the country need?"

"Victory," was the unhesitant reply.

"True," the president admitted, "and it will have it in due course; this I firmly believe. But, until then, what Xoraina needs is a hero." At this point both men turned to Yuri, one with an air of satisfaction, the other with unfettered amazement.

Unsettled more than ever, Yuri again asked, "What?"

Having overcome his amazement, with growing enthusiasm, Captain Olesky said, "Yes, this could work!"

Leaning forward, the president stabbed the air with his cigar, again and again, as he continued in his most persuasive tone.

"Think of it, Brother. Forgive me, I don't mean to belittle, but you are a simple man of the people, yes?"

Mystified, Yuri had never considered himself to be anything else.

"Why, yes, of course."

"And you came from the foothills of the Carpathians all the way to the Capital, just to protest the new shipping tax."

"It's really quite unfair," Yuri insisted.

"The ability to protest is the right of every Xorainian," the president continued. "But to do so, you risked your life crossing not one war zone but two. Isn't that correct?"

"Why, yes," Yuri frowned, "but …"

Stabbing with his cigar, the president said, "That took courage and resilience and, yes, dogged determination, and you won through in the end, didn't you?" Without waiting for Yuri to reply, he said, "Yes, you did, and in point of fact, it was nothing short of heroic."

As the president's words slowly sank in, the penny finally dropped. Staring, mouth agape, Yuri thought, '*Hero? Me? Preposterous!*" But then he thought, "*But if His Excellency thinks it will help …*" And even further, "*And if I do this for him, perhaps he will do something for me … like rescind the shipping tax, for instance.*"

Collecting himself, he managed to say, "Excellency, I am at your service."

*

The pig was despondent. He had been placed in this strange pen by himself and the time passed ever so slowly. He couldn't complain about not being properly cared for as his pen was swept clean regularly; but there was no mud for a decent wallow. The food was adequate, although not the swill that an honest pig could really sink his teeth into. But most of all, as well as missing the sweetest, kindest sow in all the world, he missed the squire and missed him badly.

Dejected, he sank into boredom and idly began to chew at the wooden boards of his enclosure.

Chapter Eighteen

Early the next morning found Yuri strolling around the palace grounds feeling troubled and uncertain about the president's offer. In his entire life, he had scarcely even *watched* television let alone appeared on a program. A growing certainty that he would be making a fool of himself had taken hold in his thoughts, so much so that he would have gone to the president, if he had been available, informing him that he'd changed his mind; but that worthy was currently attending parliament and would not be returning to the palace until much later that evening.

As far as Yuri was aware, no one from Homstood had ever been on television before, not even the village administrator. What would they think if they saw him there, speaking of his journey through war torn Xoraina and giving his opinion about this or that when any one of them had more right to do so and would manage far better?

"After all," he muttered to himself, "I'm just a simple farmer, not some worldly diplomat with more than one suit of clothing. Clearly, the president drank too much nalivka the previous evening and it had muddled his wits for him to even consider such a thing. Just as clearly, I myself had imbibed too much, as well, which caused me to agree. Yes," he thought with some finality, "when the president returns, I will definitely inform him that I must decline his invitation and swear to never drink nalivka again for the duration of my stay in the Capital."

It was thoughts along this vein that were occupying Yuri's mind when he saw a young man approaching, dressed in the uniform of a lieutenant of the Xorainian army. As the soldier drew nearer, Yuri could see the braid of an equerry looped over one shoulder. In due course the lieutenant stamped to attention in front of Yuri, whereupon he threw an immaculate salute. After some hesitation, Yuri returned it, sure that his sorry attempt was completely laughable.

"Do I have the honour of addressing Mr Yuri Zavlov of Homstood?" the young man asked politely. In reply to Yuri's hesitant nod, he said, "I am Lieutenant Shevchenko, on the staff of the Ministry of Defence."

At the mere mention of the Ministry of Defence, Yuri was reminded of yesterday's unfortunate encounter, causing him to dart furtive glances to the left and right, searching for a bolthole. Of all the people he wished to put from his mind it was the all-powerful Minister of Defence.

Stammering, he managed to ask, "Wh-what does His Excellency want with me? I am only a simple farmer."

Ever so correctly, the lieutenant replied, "The minister wishes to convey his regrets over yesterday's unpleasantness and seeks to make amends. Further, he wishes to convey that he would consider it an honour if you would attend him for morning tea, so that the unfortunate rift might be repaired." Then, murmuring, he advised, "There's just enough time to freshen up if you hurry."

Suddenly, all thoughts of a television appearance were banished from Yuri's mind. What business did the Minister of Defence have with him of all people, and why would he care about a few harsh words spoken in the heat of the moment? The man had a war to conduct, after all. Surely a peasant from Homstood must be the furthest thing from his mind.

However, the invitation (which was, no doubt, tantamount to a command) was from the second most powerful man in the land and not to be taken lightly. If there was enmity between them, then surely the best course of action would be to accept the olive branch the minister was offering, in spite of the fact that he would almost certainly not be able to help him get his pig to the market in Lofstov.

To the lieutenant, he said, "I will be happy to accept the Minister's invitation. Just give me a minute to change my shirt."

However, as Yuri hurried off, it was not without grave misgivings.

*

Built of concrete and glass, the building for the Ministry of Defence was a product of the 21st Century. The Minister of Defence was not.

Yuri was ushered into an office decorated in a minimalist's ultra-modern style. As he rose to greet him, the perpetually dissatisfied twist to the defence minister's mouth gave him the sense that he would have preferred décor from a bygone time – the Victorian era for example, or possibly from the days when Xoraina was still under the bootheel of the old Zlaimperian Empire.

As previously mentioned, tall and handsome in a uniform bedecked with gold braid and medals, the minister positively oozed old school elegance as he offered Yuri his hand.

"Ah," he said, attempting a smile, "Mr Zavlov. Thank you for coming." Gesturing to a chair made of chromed tubing with red leather cushions, he said, "Please be seated."

Yuri did as invited, trying his best not to fidget.

The defence minister resumed his own seat behind a matching desk with chromed legs and a glass top that must have been five centimetres thick. Devoid of clutter, or even papers of any kind, the sole occupants of its surface were a decorative pen set and the minister's elbows.

Twisting his lips into a grimace that Yuri supposed was intended as a smile, the minister said, "Now then, you must be wondering what this is all about, isn't that so?"

Cautiously, Yuri inclined his head to the affirmative.

"Just as I thought," the minister said with a triumphant air. "Listen, Mr Zavlov, I am not only wise in the ways of war, you see. I am also wise in the ways of government. I can see that our president has taken a liking to you – even made you a guest at his palace. So, in the interests of cooperation between our two offices, it behoves me to extend my hand, as well. Do you understand?"

Yuri didn't, of course. The ways of governments were as foreign to him as everything else outside of Homstood, but he replied, "Yes, certainly, sir," all the same. If the minister was going to take the trouble to make peace between them, then far be it from him to stand in his way.

Tall and elegant though he may be, sadly, the defence minister was not as gifted with the easy flow of words as the president. They sounded as though they were forced from his mouth when he said, "First, allow me to … apologise for my … ah … boorish behaviour the other day." When he was finished, his grimace was so pronounced it seemed as though he had spent the entire morning sucking on lemons.

"That's quite all right, Excellency," Yuri replied quickly, bewildered that such an exalted person would bring himself to voice his regrets, especially over such a paltry matter, but clearly, that must be why he had been invited here in the first place. Beginning to rise from his chair, he said, "Well then, if that is all, I'll leave you to get back to your work."

"Please remain seated," the minister said, with only the faintest touch of annoyance. "I thought we might become better acquainted."

The word was out of Yuri's mouth before he had time to think.

"Why?"

The minister's eyes widened with surprise, before he could force a hollow laugh.

"Bold and to the point, I like that Mr Zavlov. You're a man after my own heart. But considering that unfortunate episode yesterday, it's a fair question. I hope we will be able to put it in the past, eh?"

"Assuredly, Excellency, I would like nothing more."

Nodding approvingly, the minister said, "Good." Then eyeing Yuri critically, he said, "As you may imagine, Mr Zavlov, as Minister of Defence, I have many duties of grave import, none more so than now, when the enemy is at our very gates. With the wellbeing of the country at heart, the stress is tremendous and, unfortunately, my temper may become somewhat frayed in the process. I do hope you can understand?"

"Oh, absolutely, Excellency," Yuri hastened to assure him, and to his horror, began to do what he ordinarily did when he was nervous, which was to run on with his mouth. "I have many weighty decisions of my own to make. For instance, I must decide whether or not to leave the west field fallow, or whether I should try to squeeze another crop out of it for one more year. Of course, I must decide, if that is to be the case, what that crop should be. Then, naturally, the decision to grow sunflowers in the east field is a great risk, especially if I'm unable to send my pig to market. If I should fail, then I might lose both the pig and the sunflower seeds, and where would I be then? In the poor house, that's where, and Mother Oksana will be forced to beg in the streets. So, yes, Minister, I understand completely when you speak of grave responsibilities."

"Ah … *yes*," the minister replied in a distracted sort of way. "Quite." Then, attempting to get the conversation back on track, he said, "Now then, Mr Zavlov, I'm sure that you are aware of the situation around the Capital. We are heavily outnumbered and surrounded, or soon will be. The enemy has control of the skies and for every artillery piece we can bring to bear, they can bring ten. They have more artillery, more tanks, more and better aircraft, more men – more everything. Every day they press forward, and though our heroic army resists as well as it can, we are being forced to retreat, one step at a time. Any day now the enemy is expected to breach our defences. At which point they will come pouring through the gap, and then it will be all over for us. Men will be shot on sight, women will be raped, and children will be sent to Zlaimperia to become indoctrinated into learning their culture and forgetting our own." Pausing to consider, bitterly, he said, "Perhaps that's as it should be because by the time they are grown, Xorainian culture will have disappeared, blasted to oblivion by Zlaimperian artillery."

"Oh, Your Excellency," Yuri cried, "that sounds terrible!"

"I am being truthful with you, you see."

"Yes," Yuri replied. "You make it sound as though the situation is hopeless."

The minister didn't deign to reply, the consequence of which caused Yuri to become unnerved and blurt out, "But this is not my war!"

The minister levelled a gaze at Yuri, and said, "Forgive me, Mr Zavlov. But it is now."

Growing desperate, Yuri protested. "This is the government's war, not the people's. I want nothing to do with the government."

"And yet you want the shipping tax repealed," the minister mused aloud. "That has a great deal to do with the government."

Frustrated, Yuri demanded, "Why are you telling me this?"

"I told you, Mr Zavlov," the minister replied. "I wanted to have a frank and honest conversation so that you can see there are matters superseding your pig, a great deal of them, in fact." Notable by what Yuri thought was a lack of emotion, the minister continued. "Now is the time for all Xorainians to rally around the flag, to put aside their selfish interests, and do what is best for the country. Which brings me to the next subject." Placing both hands flat on the surface of his desk, he said, "It has come to my attention that the president wishes you to submit to an interview on national television."

Frowning, Yuri asked, "How did you know that?"

"We in the Ministry of Defence have our ways, Mr Zavlov."

"Do you mean spies? You do, don't you?"

Again, the minister refused to reply, although his silence spoke volumes.

"You have spies in the Presidential Palace?" It was intended as a question but came out more as an accusation.

The minister, however, was unapologetic.

"We have spies everywhere," offhand, he added, "in the interests of national security, of course."

"Yes, but in the *palace*?" Yuri demanded. "Why would you do such a thing? Surely, the president is above suspicion?"

Unsmiling, the minister said, "No one is above suspicion, Mr Zavlov, not even the president. I reiterate, we are at war, and war causes strange bedfellows. Don't you agree?"

"Are you trying to suggest that the president is colluding with the Zlaimperian dictator? That makes no sense."

Airily, the minister replied, "In times of war, very little seems to make sense, until one digs deeper."

"But, if what you are suggesting is true, why go to all the trouble?" Yuri pressed. "Why this charade? Any fool can see that Zlaimperia must prevail in the end. Why not just surrender and have done with it? Think of all the lives that would be saved! Think of all the damage that could be prevented!"

The minister did not immediately agree. Instead, leaning forward, in a tone that could only be described as dangerous, he asked, "What did you just say, Mr Zavlov?"

Yuri offered him a quizzical expression, and said, "Think of all the lives …"

"No," the minister interrupted. "Before that. You said that Zlaimperia would prevail." In the blink of an eye the elegant gentleman from the old school was gone to be replaced by something far more menacing. Looking every inch a predator – in fact, looking as if he had just heard exactly what he had hoped to hear – he sprang his trap. "That is dangerous talk, Mr Zavlov. Some might say it is treasonous. Do you know what happens to traitors in times of war?"

Yuri opened his mouth to protest, then stopped. Wondering, he thought, was it true? Were all his thoughts about the war treasonous? But wait …

Still believing that reason must prevail, he said, "I was merely voicing my thoughts, Excellency. How is that treason?"

"Maybe you were, and maybe you weren't," the minister replied, the danger still evident in his voice. "In times of peace, the line between patriot and traitor can become blurred, I grant you, but in times of war, that line becomes more clearly defined. Possibly yours was just an ill-advised remark, but it is equally possible that it had seditious intent. The courts will have to decide."

Close to panic, Yuri cried, "No! That's not true! I am innocent!"

"I'm relieved to hear it," the minister replied smoothly. Then, leaning forward again, he asked, "But how can I believe you?"

If there had been a moment to collect his wits, Yuri might have said otherwise, but unfortunately that moment didn't exist. In a single breath, he blurted, "Ask anything of me! Anything, and I will do it to prove my innocence!"

"Anything?"

"Yes, anything!"

The minister studied Yuri for a very long time through narrowed eyes. Finally, reaching a decision, he said, "You will report your conversations with the president to me, every day, is that clear?" Raising a warning finger, he said, "But have a care. You are already aware that we have spies in the palace. If you choose to tell me an untruth I'll know about it, understand?"

Struck dumb by the madness of it all, Yuri could only nod.

"Good," the minister replied. "Convince me that you are a true patriot and that will go a long way toward pleading your case of innocence."

Feeling sick to his stomach, Yuri whispered, "But I *am* innocent."

"That remains to be seen," the minister replied without meeting his eyes. Then assuming an air of heavy responsibility, he said, "Now, if you'll excuse me, I have much work to attend to."

Yuri rose, uncertain what to say. Then, realising there was nothing he *could* say, he took his leave. Walking to the door, his legs felt foreign to him, as if they might collapse at any minute. At the threshold, the minister called out.

"Until tomorrow, Mr Zavlov."

Closing the door behind him, Yuri raced to the men's room, arriving just in time to prevent the contents of his stomach from spewing onto the floor.

*

Absently working at the boards of his pen with his incisors, the pig reflected that life had become an endless stretch of time in this windowless place. Impossible to tell night from day, he slept when he was tired and returned to chewing the boards of his pen when he was not. The only sounds that penetrated was the occasional lowing of a cow at the far end of the building, the war in the distance that was more subtle vibrations than actual sound, and, of course, his chewing.

Perplexed that the squire had abandoned him, his mind was reduced to a state of profound depression. For as long as he could remember he had been devoted to the squire. Without him there was nothing.

Deeply saddened, he chewed on.

Chapter Nineteen

"Yuri! Wait!"

Yuri looked up from his doleful musings and saw Captain Olesky hailing him from across the street. His intention had been to return to the palace after his meeting with the defence minister, but an hour later found him wandering aimlessly throughout the Capital, wondering how everything had so suddenly spiralled out of control. Whatever he had expected from that meeting, in no way was spying on the president part of it, and he, like any true Homstooder, found the prospect unsettling.

Olesky didn't bother with a crosswalk but sprinted across the busy thoroughfare amidst a cacophony of blaring horns, screeching brakes, and curses from annoyed motorists. Laughing, he ran up to Yuri, and asked, "What are your plans for the day?"

Yuri, who hadn't thought that far ahead, merely shrugged. "Nothing special. Why? What did you have in mind?"

"Actually, it's not what I have in mind, this is the president's idea." Explaining, Olesky said, "He thought that, due to your upcoming television appearance, it would be in the best interest of the country if you had a well-rounded view of the current situation and by that, of course, he means the war. In order to help you achieve that, he thought it might be a good idea for you to meet some of the people who are doing the actual fighting. I happen to agree, and considering that my unit just came off the line and is currently in a support position, I thought you might like to come with me for a visit?"

Yuri pondered Olesky's (or rather, the president's) suggestion. If the truth were to be told, he'd rather be left alone to ruminate further on the difficult situation he now found himself. However, such a luxury didn't seem to be in the cards. After all, if one did not simply say no to an invitation from the Minister of Defence, he supposed that would go double to a 'suggestion' from the president. But then further rumination told him that taking a trip with Olesky might not be all bad; if nothing else, it should take his mind off his troubles.

He asked, "When do we leave?"

*

The journey was distressingly short – a mere thirty minutes from the perimeter of the Capital. As Yuri jounced along in the scout car over the broken roads, he remembered that the journey had been significantly longer that night when, with the captain leaning on his shoulder, and the pig squealing in panic, they had all tumbled into the Xorainian trench and relative safety.

Driving with what Yuri considered to be reckless speed, Captain Olesky wove through the heavy traffic with all the careless skill of youth, where quickness of eye and reflexes were taken for granted. Tapping his horn at the lorry ahead of them, he pulled out into the oncoming lane to pass, and said, "The Zlaimperians constantly pressure our boys day and night. Sometimes we are able to hold them, other times we're forced to fall back. Slowly, bit by bit, the perimeter around the Capital is shrinking. Soon, in a week, maybe two, it will be in the suburbs."

Although sobering, the captain's tone wasn't doom-laden; in fact, he seemed rather cheerful, which puzzled Yuri until he realised that Olesky wasn't anticipating the outcome of the war so much as he was excited about being reunited with his comrades, which puzzled him even more. It wasn't that he didn't understand friendship – in Homstood, virtually everyone was his friend, to a greater or lesser degree. What interested him was the camaraderie that existed among those who risked life and limb together, day after day. He'd got an inkling of that during the firefight that night in the trench when he had patched up that soldier's arm, but only enough to be intrigued by it. In that regard he wasn't really surprised by Olesky's excitement, but in another aspect, it troubled him; for it didn't fit into his own personal narrative of Xoraina's inevitable defeat.

They entered the compound early in the afternoon, the scout car splashing through a puddle, sending water cascading over soldiers who were alternately cleaning kit or weapons, or simply loafing around, enjoying the watery rays of the sun. This was greeted by a rain of profanities which the captain cheerfully returned in kind before braking to a stop in front of the bombed-out shell of a cottage the battalion was currently using as its headquarters.

One might imagine that a unit posted to the rear would be in relative safety and, to a point, that would be true. However, by its very definition 'relative safety' is a relative term as Yuri discovered when Olesky informed him that they had been subjected to a rocket attack earlier in the day.

As they careened through rank after rank of sodden tents, Yuri could see evidence of it everywhere – burning buildings, mounds of blasted earth, and the twisted metal that was once a vehicle. He saw it again when he leaped down from the car, where the tail fin of a rocket protruded from the ground, the grass around it burnt to ash. A burly soldier, wearing the stripes of a corporal, hunkered down next to a remnant of that fire, roasting a sausage on a stick. Looking up at all the curses and shouts of protest that erupted upon the newcomers' arrival, his face split into a grin of pure joy when he recognised the driver.

Rising to his feet, he caused Yuri's eyes to bulge in disbelief as his body uncoiled to a gigantic height.

"Captain!" he bellowed.

"Illya!" Olesky cried, and the two men embraced, roaring with laughter.

Then, holding one another at arm's length, still grinning, the corporal looked down at his friend, and exclaimed, "We thought you were dead!"

Olesky laughed. "As you can see, that rumour has been greatly exaggerated."

"So we were told," rumbled the corporal, nodding toward the burnt out hulk that was now their headquarters. "The old man said something about your being rescued by a pig of all things. It can't be true, of course, but the story has kept us in stitches for days!"

"The story *is* true," Olesky said, explaining, "the pig was intoxicated with mushrooms at the time." Then, turning to Yuri, he added, "Here is its owner. Yuri Zavlov, I would like to introduce you to this reprobate, Corporal Illya Kovalenko."

Caught between being apprised of the truth of the 'pig story,' as it was referred to by their comrades, and the quasi-formal introduction, the corporal was at a loss, which was precisely what Olesky had been aiming for all along.

Grinning, he asked, "Cat got your tongue, Kovalenko?"

Sputtering, the corporal burst into laughter. Reaching for Yuri's hand, he enveloped it in his massive paw, and politely said, "I'm very pleased to meet you, Father." Then, to Olesky, "I should have known that the story was true! It suits you, Captain!" Then, after bellowing more laughter, he said, "Listen, I have a bottle of vodka I liberated from a Zlaimperian soldier." Offhandedly, he added, "He had no further use for it in any case. Why don't you come to my tent, and we'll talk of the old days?"

Grinning, Olesky said, "By the old days, you mean last week. Don't forget, Corporal, we haven't known one another that long."

"Not in days, perhaps," Kovalenko admitted, "but what is that to brothers in arms, eh? Already we have enough stories to last into our dotage!" Then, with a nod to Olesky's cane, he sobered and asked, "How is the wound?"

The captain shrugged, and said, "It's just a scratch. I'll be back before you know it. As for your invitation, we'll be happy to accept, isn't that so, Yuri?"

Left with little choice, Yuri managed a facsimile of a smile and gave a nod. "Yes, of course."

Returning the nod, Olesky said, "Good. But first, Illya, I have to check in with the old man. I'll find you later, yes?"

"Of course," was the reply, "but don't take too long, eh?" Wagging his impaled meal at Olesky, he said, "Vodka goes well with sausage, or so I am told!" and bellowed even more laughter. He was laughing still when Yuri and the captain entered the cottage, closing the door behind them.

*

They found the corporal comfortably settled in his tent accompanied by a private with a cynical face and about half the height and girth of Kovalenko. He seemed happy to see his captain, however, and gave Yuri a friendly nod. A half-empty bottle of vodka rested on his lap.

"I see they haven't killed you yet, Captain," he said, grinning an evil grin.

Neither of the two soldiers bothered to rise to their feet or otherwise come to attention, let alone salute their superior officer. Later, Olesky informed Yuri this was because he chose to relax discipline when his men came off the front line.

"The bullet that will get me hasn't been moulded yet," Olesky boasted. "How are you, Kuzma?"

Spreading his arms as if to invite inspection, Kuzma replied, "As you see, sir, sucking air and pumping blood."

Glancing around with an expectant smile, Olesky asked, "Where are the others, Sasha and Dimitri?"

The atmosphere in the tent immediately grew more sober and the two men uncomfortably looked away.

Noting their meaning, Olesky's brow furrowed when he asked, "When?"

"Two days ago," Illya replied, "just before we pulled out of the line."

"Artillery got them," Kuzma added quietly.

Olesky swore, and said, "Damn Zlaimperia to Hell. They were good soldiers."

"We heard about Stas," Illya said, referring to Olesky's deceased driver.

Nodding, Olesky said, "Anti-tank missile. He never knew what hit him."

"At least it was quick," Kuzma observed. Then, holding up the bottle in a toast, he said, "To the fallen," and took a swig before offering it to Olesky.

"The fallen," Olesky agreed, taking his own swig before passing the bottle to Yuri.

Yuri accepted it uncertainly, a fact that was not lost on the others.

"Is there a problem?" Kuzma asked, and the way he asked sounded less like a question than a challenge.

Not meeting their eyes, Yuri said, "They were your comrades. They fought alongside each of you, not with me. I'm not sure if I'm worthy."

Unsmiling, Illya demanded, "You're Xorainian, aren't you?"

"Yes, of course."

"Then they were your comrades, too. So, drink up!"

After another brief hesitation, Yuri decided to comply. It wasn't that the reason for his hesitation had been a falsehood – it was true, compared to these men, he did have doubts about his worthiness – but it wasn't the whole truth. They were fighting a war that, in his heart of hearts, he believed couldn't be won. Sharing a drink with them made him feel like he was being deceitful.

The spirit was strong, burning its way to his stomach, making him cough. The others laughed derisively, which was their curious way of acceptance.

"More potent than nalivka, eh, Father?" Olesky asked.

It wasn't, but Yuri nodded anyway. The reason for his grimace was because the taste was sour.

"What were their names again?" he asked.

"Sasha and Dimitri," Kuzma told him.

"To Sasha and Dimitri then and," with a glance at Captain Olesky, "of course, Stas."

The second sip tasted just as bad as the first, but Yuri managed to swallow without another coughing fit. He recognised their laughter for what it was, and for a reason he couldn't quite define, placed a high value on it.

With the formalities seen to, Olesky deemed that it was time to get down to business. He introduced Yuri, mentioning that he came from a village at the foothills of the Carpathians (here Kuzma interrupted with a good-natured jibe, that it was known all such inhabitants were *nevcheniy,* which got a laugh from everyone). However, when the captain mentioned that Yuri had passed through not one but two war zones to reach the

Capital, their smiles began to fade. When Olesky told them that Yuri had saved his life and helped put Stas to rest, this was greeted with definite signs of respect. But, of course, when he mentioned the episode with the pig, their laughter erupted all the stronger. Both Illya and Kuzma claimed that such an unbelievable story must be true and that it could only happen to their captain, at which point the bottle was passed around again.

"All right," Olesky said. "Quiet you reprobates, I'm not finished." When they were prepared to listen, he said, "I didn't relate that story for your edification."

"Ooo," Kuzma taunted, "such a big word!" but found himself ignored.

"I told you because the president has asked Yuri to relate his experiences on the *Stinislav Berkos Show*."

Although this meant very little to Yuri, who had never heard of Stinislav Berkos, the news was greeted with respectful gasps by the others.

Meanwhile, Olesky continued.

"He believes that our friend is an example for all Xoraina to admire, and I agree. His is a story of courage and a stubborn will to resist. In short, his story is Xoraina's story. Are you with me so far?" After everyone had nodded, he said, "Good. Now, if you are wondering why I brought him here to grace your presence, it's because the president wants him to hear first-hand what it's like at the front. You know as well as I do that the *Stinislav Berkos Show* will be widely watched, and this is an opportunity to relate our own stories to the people."

To Yuri's ears the captain sounded trite, possibly even ridiculous. After all, who was he, Yuri Zavlov, to relate such stories? But his men listened without so much as a smile.

"Well, then," Olesky said in conclusion, "is it agreed?"

"Yes," Illya said without hesitation.

Kuzma shrugged, and said, "What do we have to lose?"

At which point the captain turned to Yuri, and gesturing to his men, said, "Ask them anything, anything you like."

Once again Yuri hesitated, as this approach to the subject was unexpected and something he wasn't prepared for.

After all, who was he to ask anything of these men? But the stage had been set, so he felt he had to ask them *something*. The most obvious question seemed like the best place to start.

"What's it like?" he asked.

"It's Hell," Kuzma replied, to which Illya readily agreed.

"I see," Yuri nodded slowly, "but perhaps you could expand on that a little? Why is it Hell?"

"Because we're cattle being brought to the slaughter," Kuzma said, with a trace of bitterness. "Every day those bastard Zlaimperians pound us with artillery. For every one of our guns they have ten, and airplanes and helicopters and missiles besides, not to mention an endless supply of ammunition. So, day after day they bombard our positions, and day after day we die. Then, when enough of us are dead, they send in their tanks and infantry and more of us die. Those of us who are left are forced back, always back, closer and closer to the Capital, and the next day it starts all over again."

"Retreat, always retreat," Illya said bitterly. "Make no mistake, it is the correct course of action, but we leave behind settlements that depended upon us for their safery as our perimeter continues to shrink." Staring straight ahead at nothing in particular, he said, "The villagers beg us not to abandon them, but we have no choice. If we don't retreat, we will be destroyed." His voice grew soft, almost a whisper. "But I still see their faces, terrified, with the last vestiges of hope dissipating from their eyes." Looking at Yuri, he asked, "Have you ever seen anyone left without hope, Father? Everything is written on their faces, nothing hidden, and none of it good." Looking away, he said, "I still see those faces in my dreams."

"Nightmares," Kuzma said.

"Call them what you like," Illya retorted irritably. "Dream or nightmare, they haunt me, and I can't help wondering how they fare."

Olesky said, "We had no choice, just as you said, Illya. When we first entered the line, there were two hundred well-trained soldiers in our company. Now there are less than half that number."

"Kuzma is right," Illya said, "cattle to the slaughter."

"What's it like to be under bombardment day after day?" Yuri asked.

"Terrifying," all three said at once.

"Definitely at first," Illya clarified. "There's nothing you can do but huddle in your trench and hope that nothing they're throwing at you has your name on it."

"Or that you don't shit your pants," Kuzma said. Yuri thought that he was joking, but not so much as a trace of a smile creased his lips.

"It's like you've been placed there as a sacrifice," Illya continued. "It's like all that you were before the war, all you've become, no longer matters. Now you're just a pawn on a chess board, or rather a meatgrinder, without the means to fight back. As I said, a sacrifice to the Gods of War."

Kuzma said. "It was far more terrifying at first, when every moment I was convinced that I was going to die. Fearing for your life is a terrible thing, Father. It paralyzes you, making it impossible to do your job, which, of course, is to resist."

Yuri listened, lost for words. Finally, he admitted, "I can't imagine what that must be like."

"Be thankful that you can't, Father," Illya said, but without rancour.

"But …" Yuri stammered, "but how do you manage? How do you do that, I mean suffer through that day after day? And, more important, why?"

"Many didn't, Illya replied frankly, "especially at first. The fools jumped out of their trenches and tried to run away and got caught out in the open when the shells came raining down."

Kuzma nodded. "There wasn't enough left of some of them to fit in a tablespoon."

"Fools," Illya reiterated.

"Bloody amateurs," Kuzma agreed.

"We lost half of our total casualties during those first few days," Olesky said.

Yuri struggled with the vision of swaths of men being cut down by artillery, simply disappearing in the explosions or sliced to shreds in a hail of shrapnel, and couldn't prevent himself from shuddering.

"But God be praised, you survived," he said.

They all regarded him blandly.

"We don't mention God out here," Olesky said.

"And we sure as hell don't praise the son of a bitch," Kuzma said bitterly.

"One day at the front, and you won't either, Father," Illya said.

Not overly religious to begin with, Yuri shook his head. "I can understand that, but what I mean is that those of you who survive, how do you manage to overcome your fear, day after day?"

Kuzma shrugged. "For me it was simple. One day I just accepted that I wasn't going to survive, that sooner or later one of those fucking shells was going to get me and that would be it. Once I accepted that it was possible for me to do my job."

Yuri looked around and saw that both Illya and Olesky were nodding in agreement.

Troubled, he said, "But you still haven't answered my other question. You say that you accept that you won't survive so that you can continue to fight. I'm not sure you understand just how disconcerting that is to my ears. You are young and alive, with everything to live for. Why do you continue to fight when all seems hopeless? You could just walk away and no one could blame you. Why don't you? Why do you stay and continue to subject yourselves to this madness?"

All three men regarded Yuri as if it was *he* who had lost his mind, not them. It was Illya who replied first.

"Zlaimperia is ruled by a cruel and iron-fisted dictator who will not suffer any challenge to his grip on power. But having his bootheel on the necks of his own people isn't enough for him, he wants his boot on our necks, as well. Zlaimperians have no say about their own country. If he wins, we wouldn't have any say about Xoraina, either. Many of his people live in poverty and must bow to his bidding. In contrast, Xorainians do not bow so easily. Life is much better here. We have everything they have in the West, and can take part in choosing who will lead us into the future. This is our birthright, and the Zlaimperian dictator means to take it away from us. That can never be allowed to happen."

"Such an idealist," Kuzma scoffed at his comrade, although with a modicum of affection. To Yuri, he said, "Look, Father, this is our land. Those Zlaimperian bastards are trying to take it from us. For me, that is enough."

"A fine sentiment," Yuri allowed. "But really, is it worth dying for?"

Illya scowled, and rumbled, "Far better those Zlaimperian vermin die for *their* cause, but yes, some things are worth dying for." Looking at Yuri, he said, "I scarcely know you, Father, but I would die to protect you and all those others who cannot protect themselves."

"Even those who are *nevcheniy,*" Kuzma grinned and winked.

At that moment the tent flap was swept aside to reveal a corporal stooping through the entrance. Yuri couldn't help a surprised gasp for this soldier was a woman. In fact, she was quite a pretty one, in spite of her face being so grim. He had heard of such things before, of course – women fighting in the Great Patriotic War had been quite common – but he, personally, had never witnessed such a thing.

Possibly the corporal was used to this sort of reaction, for apart from her eyes flicking to Yuri in a hard gaze, she made no sign of noticing his surprise.

In contrast, the other men greeted her easily as one of their own,

"Valla!" Corporal Kovalenko rumbled. "Come join us for a drink!"

However, the woman neither acknowledged Illya's greeting, nor his invitation. Instead, her eyes fixed on Olesky.

"I heard you were back," she said.

"Just for a brief visit for now, I'm afraid," said Olesky, indicating his cane. "Doctor's orders."

After all due solicitations had been made, along with assurances that he was rapidly on the mend, Valla said, "In that case, I'll leave you to continue with your visit," and turned to leave.

"Stay a moment," Olesky said. Gesturing to Yuri, he made the introductions, and added, "The president wishes for him to learn more about those of us who are fighting at the front." Turning to Yuri, he invited, "Perhaps, Father, you might ask our little Valla the same question you just asked us."

Yuri regarded the woman uncertainly. She regarded him with no visible emotion at all, not even curiosity. She simply waited patiently (or impatiently, it was difficult to tell) for Yuri to ask his question.

Suddenly nervous for no reason he could fathom, Yuri swallowed hard, and said, "I was just asking these men why they choose to fight, so I will ask the same of you, why are you here?"

Over the previous discourse, it had soon become apparent that Valla wasn't one to waste words – when asked a question, she answered, and as laconically as possible – so Yuri was mildly surprised when, this time, she chose to be somewhat more forthcoming.

"I come from a village in the north-eastern region of the country," she began. "I lived there with my parents and younger sister." Without any visible emotion, she said, "All three of them are dead now, killed when a Zlaimperian missile struck our home during the first days of the war. They died and I lived. Now you ask why I fight?" She fixed Yuri with an ice-hard gaze. "I fight to kill Zlaimperians, as many as I can." With that she glanced at Olesky, seeking permission to leave. In response to his nod, she turned and exited the tent, leaving Yuri with much to consider.

*

All day those terrible explosions had been growing closer and closer, just as they had that day when he had been separated from the squire in the woods. The pig wanted to think about home and the sweetest sow in all the world. He wanted to think about wallowing in the mud and savoury swill, but the explosions wouldn't let him. 'So loud,' he thought. 'So frightening! Surely a world such as this was never intended for a quiet, peace-loving pig like me!'

With such unrelenting thoughts coursing through his mind, he continued to worry away at the boards of his pen, without ever really noticing while he was doing it.

And the barrage continued to creep nearer and nearer.

Chapter Twenty

Outside, Zlaimperian artillery rounds had begun creeping into the outlying suburbs of the Capital. Inside the Ministry of Defence, the barrage was reduced to a low rumble, although every so often the windowpanes in the minister's office would vibrate from an explosion less distant than the others.

The minister himself ignored the distraction and regarded Yuri with a less-than-satisfied frown.

"You have nothing to report?" he demanded, echoing that very assertion Yuri had just made. "How do you expect me to believe that, Mr Zavlov?"

Yuri's mouth was dry, but he attempted to swallow anyway, his throat producing an audible 'click' as he did so.

"But it's the truth, Excellency, I have not been in conversation with the president since we last met."

"You've been saying that every day for weeks now!"

"Because it's the truth!" Yuri retorted, but he couldn't prevent his voice from wavering. It was damned unnerving standing up to the minister, and the fact that he actually was only speaking truth to power wasn't as much help as he thought it ought to have been. It was true, that with a war to run the president had very little time for his guest, but it was also true that Yuri was now convinced that the president was, not only innocent of the minister's dark suspicions, but, on the contrary, had displayed nothing but conduct of the highest order, and was deserving of his country's admiration. As a result, while he continued to be reluctant to support the president's policy of resistance, he was even more loath to continue to be the minister's creature. However, having reached that decision, Yuri also had to accept the fact that he couldn't simply tell the second most powerful man in the country to go to the devil, not when his own neck was on the line.

"But you are his prize possession, his pet project, you might say. Don't you find it odd that he wouldn't make time for you?"

"In all honesty, Excellency, I would find it odd if he did. Whatever you may think, I am still just a simple farmer."

Frustrated, the minister swore. "He's up to something, I know it!"

"Excellency?"

"The president, you fool! He's an enemy of the people!"

Still none the wiser, Yuri could only offer the minister a blank stare.

"He insists on this foolish adventure, placing the country in harm's way just to ingratiate himself to the Americans!"

Even now, when he had yet to see the Minister of Defence for what he was, this struck Yuri as an especially foolish comment.

"From what I have seen with my own two eyes, sir, it is the will of the populace to resist the invaders."

"Bah!" the minister scoffed. "The people are fools who require strong leadership. They need to understand that the situation is hopeless. Every day they are dying. Every day, the Zlaimperian noose slowly tightens around our necks and there's nothing we can do about it. They need to understand that their will counts for nothing. The country needs a leader who will tell them what to think, who is willing to make the difficult decisions for them." The minister continued, as if reading from a well-worn script. "What *isn't* needed is an idealistic fool like the president. He spoils them by catering to what they *think* they want, when what they *really* want is to be told what to do!"

Yuri sat, listening with growing unease. It was clear that the minister saw himself as the strong leader he was referring to – the saviour of Xoraina, a national hero. Truth be told, that while the minister's ideas aligned with his own, Yuri wasn't about to lift a finger to help the invaders. He wasn't sure which camp that put him in, but what was setting off alarm bells in his mind was the fact that it was becoming increasingly clear that, if given the chance, the Minister of Defence was prepared to hand the country over to the Zlaimperian tyrant on a silver platter. He was being disloyal, not only to the president but to the will of the country; and in that moment, he wondered if every government was really the same as he had so often claimed to his friends back in Homstood? He saw now that his cynicism made him appear more worldly to the unworldly and more educated to the uneducated; but it was a cynicism based on his knowledge of the past, dating back to the old empire. While much of that may have been grounded in fact, however, to assume all those in power were equally deserving of scorn was a flawed concept. Sometimes a leader actually cared.

Meanwhile, the minister was speaking.

"I'm very disappointed in you, Mr Zavlov, and completely out of patience. Tomorrow when you report, I will expect something more substantial. I need evidence against the president, some sort of dirt I can use to bring about his downfall, or as God is my witness, I will invent something, and you will swear on the Bible as to its veracity."

Yuri gulped. "Do you mean lie, Excellency?"

The minister's voice had a dangerous edge when he said, "I don't care what you call it. Just remember that your freedom is subject to my will." Leaning closer, his voice as smooth as a cobra's, he said, "These are chaotic times, Mr Zavlov, people disappear every day. Fail to do as you're told and you will find yourself tossed into the Dnapro with a heavy chain fastened to your ankles. Do I make myself clear?"

Yuri stared at the minister, thinking that any true Homstooder would have told him to go to the devil, but of course he didn't say that. He couldn't. The minister had caught him out at a careless moment and now here he was, a prisoner to his wants, with the threat of exposure hanging over his head. He was angry with the minister but even more angry with himself. He thought that he had been on guard against the nefarious ways of the city, but he had fallen into this Machiavellian trap so easily, before he was aware what was happening. One thing was for sure, if he ever made it back to

Homstood again, wild horses wouldn't be able to drag him back to the Capital, or, for that matter, any other city on the planet.

"Yes, Excellency," he said, "perfectly clear."

*

To say that Yuri was deeply troubled when he left the Ministry of Defence would have been an understatement of gargantuan proportions. Instinct told him that he wasn't dealing with the kind of man who was prone to making idle threats.

"But what can I tell him?" he muttered to himself. "I refuse to invent some nonsense to incriminate the president who, from what I can tell, is a good and decent man." It was such an unsolvable tangle and seemed grotesquely unfair, when all he had ever wanted was to grow some sunflowers. Again and again, he found himself wishing that he was back in his cottage at Homstood so he could voice his troubles to Mother Oksana. She would know what to do. She always did.

The mere thought caused him to recall those nights on his journey when the pig had been a substitute for that wise old woman who had always been so adept at listening. He recalled how the mere act of putting his troubles into words had brought him comfort and wondered if that might be so again?

"Of course, it is foolish to believe that the pig can help," he continued to mutter, so deep in thought that he failed to notice the worried glances he received from people he met on the street. "However, it would be equally foolish to ignore the fact that our conversations never failed to ease my mind, and if my mind ever needed easing it is now. Besides," he said uncomfortably, "under the circumstances, I cannot return to the palace and risk facing the president." Vexed, he scoffed, and said, "What a silly thing for a true Homstooder to say! A true Homstooder would not be afraid to meet anyone, anytime, or anywhere!" Then, miserable, he admitted, "But I have never felt less like a true Homstooder in all my life."

*

The fairgrounds were all but deserted at that time of day. The odd worker could be seen hefting bales of either straw or hay into various barns, but they were too engrossed in their work to pay any attention to Yuri as he made his way along to the barn at the far end of the grounds. In the distance, the night sky glimmered from the same artillery barrage that had shaken the windows in the defence minister's office. Clearly it was heralding some serious development for the very near future.

The main door was open, so Yuri slipped inside and made his way to the isolated pen in the back. Once or twice, he had to retrace his steps as his memory failed him, but eventually he was able to find his way to his faithful travelling companion, and when he did, what he saw was enough to illicit a gasp of shock.

At first, he thought he must be at the wrong pen, for surely *this* could not be his pig, but a closer inspection revealed the truth, but not in a way that brought him any comfort.

The pig had lost a great deal of weight and no longer resembled the healthy animal that Yuri had left in the care of the workers. His tail, once curled into a jaunty corkscrew of vibrant health, now hung limp with dejection. The once curious eyes were now clouded over with apathy in a lustreless head that drooped with disinterest.

Alarmed, he raced outside, and finding the nearest worker, took hold of his arm.

"Quick," he said, "I must see a veterinarian immediately!"

The worker, a tow-headed youth with freckles, frowned as he considered, but then brightened immediately.

"You're in luck, Grandfather," he said. "A veterinarian just arrived less than an hour ago to deliver a foal. I'll track him down and send him to you, yes?"

Too anxious to care about the grandfather remark, Yuri thanked the boy and returned to his pig. Illogically, he hoped that the pathetic creature he had discovered had only been a figment of his imagination, and that, when he came upon his pen this time, he would find him as hale and hearty as he always had in the past. That was not to be, however, for when he arrived, he saw that the pig's condition hadn't changed. Not knowing what else he could do, he stood wringing his hands until the veterinarian arrived some minutes later.

"Now then, what seems to be the problem?" asked the doctor, an old grey hair with a stoop and bushy eyebrows.

Gesturing to the pig, Yuri groaned. "As you can see, Doctor. When I left my pig two weeks ago, he was the most healthy animal you could ask for. Now look at him. He's dying! Please, sir, you must save him!"

The veterinarian frowned when he beheld his patient for, at a glance, the pig appeared to be very sick, indeed. He didn't comment, however, but with black bag in hand, he opened the gate to the pen and went inside. Half an hour later, he stood up from his examination and scratched his head.

"Everything appears to be normal," he said. "His temperature seems fine, as well as his heartbeat. His respiration is a little fast but not alarmingly so."

"But that can't be!" Yuri cried. "You can see for yourself something's wrong."

Still frowning, the veterinarian said, "I'm not disagreeing with you, but my examination has revealed nothing useful. He looks quite thin. Has he been eating?"

Yuri gestured to the trough filled with ground oats. "I have already mentioned that I have been away, but by the look of him, I would say not very well, and that's quite telling for a pig who has always lived to eat."

"Hmm," the vet mused, once more scratching his head, "ordinarily, I would suggest that we take him to my clinic for an x-ray, but it was destroyed in a missile attack last week." Ruefully he grimaced and said, "Who knew my little clinic was so strategically important to Zlaimperian imperial interests?"

Ignoring (or not hearing) the comment, Yuri pleaded, "Please, Doctor, is there nothing you can do?"

Folding his arms over his chest, the veterinarian regarded his patient. "I have seen this sort of thing before," he said. "And while I can't say with any certainty without an x-ray or having a laboratory examine a blood or stool sample, my years of experience tell me that this is a case beyond medicine."

"This is a catastrophe!" Yuri cried and was about to launch into his story about planting sunflowers in the east field when the good doctor held up his hand, commanding silence.

"I merely said that it was beyond medicine," he said. "I didn't say that it was beyond hope. Look, friend, what I'm saying is that your pig is sad."

Blinking rapidly, Yuri stared at the good doctor, and asked, "Sad?"

"Not just sad," the vet allowed, "he's very sad, perhaps even traumatised, to the point where he's losing the will to live." Packing his medical instruments back into his black bag, he said, "If I were you, I would approach the problem from that aspect. Now, I really must go, I have a cow with colic in another barn." As an afterthought, he added, "Good luck to you," and left, taking a hurried glance at his wristwatch as he went.

Yuri watched him go before turning back to see his pig lie down on trembling legs. He might not know much about medicine, but he knew enough about pigs to know when they lay down like that they seldom got up again. Alarmed, he entered the pen and sat down beside him. Without thinking, he gently began to stroke his flank. It was a very un-Homstood-like thing to do.

"Poor fellow," he crooned. "We have been through so much together since we left the farm all those weeks ago, or has it been months now? I enjoyed talking with you over the campfire. You have given me companionship and helped ease my troubles; what have I given you in return? Abandonment, that's what. I am unworthy of such a noble creature." Overcome with remorse, Yuri asked, "How can you ever forgive me?"

The pig did not move other than a single twitch of one ear, that might have meant that he was shooing away a fly or might mean nothing at all … or it *might* mean that he was acknowledging Yuri's presence.

"I came to you hoping to return to those times," Yuri continued, "for there has been much troubling me since we've been apart; but I can see that there is even more troubling you." On impulse, he leaned forward, and carefully lifting the pig's head, placed it on his lap. Gently stroking his jowls, he said, "It's difficult to know what treatment to provide when you're unable tell me what the problem is." Then, again without thinking, he said something even more remarkably un-Homstood-like. "You deserve better, my friend."

This time both ears twitched.

Noticing, Yuri caught his breath, scarcely daring to hope, but in lieu of any better idea, he decided to continue talking.

"By now, you are well aware of my thoughts about this stupid war," he said. "But I wanted to speak with you about the brave young people I've met and also about the Minister of Defence, who I fear is neither brave nor noble. In fact, he has threatened my life if I don't do his bidding. He wants to bring down the President who, I feel, is a good and honest man who wants what is best for the country. It is all such a mess that I can scarcely begin to describe it."

The pig opened his eyes and stared at Yuri. His flanks rose and fell as he heaved a long, weary sigh.

"I thought the war was hopeless," Yuri continued, "and I think that still; but those young people," he said, reflecting, "you should have seen them, pig. They were inspiring! They have put themselves between us and those murderous Zlaimperian swine, willing to give their lives so that we can continue to live in peace." Remembering the burned-out convoys, the destroyed villages, all the destruction they had witnessed after setting out on their journey and, of course, the body of the woman hanging from the tree, he said, "And we know what will happen if those young people fail, don't we, pig? Yes, I think we do." Scoffing, he said, "Listen to me, I said 'if' they fail, not 'when.' What do you make of that, eh?"

Listening intently, the tip of the pig's snout slowly waggled up and down as if he could smell the meaning of Yuri's words.

Still scoffing, Yuri admitted, "Of course, it's foolish to hope, just as it's foolish to think that I can stand up to such a powerful man as the Minister of Defence. Xoraina is bound to lose this war in any case, and the president will fall regardless of what I do." Now, his voice grew wistful. "But it's tempting to give into the idea, though, isn't it? To hope, I mean."

By way of an answer, the pig wriggled his ears and uttered a low (definitely contented) grunt.

*

The pig could hardly believe that the squire had returned and was speaking to him as he had in the past. All was not well with him; he could smell it. Something was terribly, terribly wrong. But for the moment that didn't signify. All that mattered was that the squire had returned to him. Whatever the problem was, they would address it together in their own good time.

He was surprised at how much of a struggle it was to regain his feet, and how much his legs trembled as he walked over to the trough.

'Very curious,' he thought, then put it from his mind as he began to feed.

Chapter Twenty-one

Yuri had just entered the palace when he was accosted by Captain Olesky.

"Where on earth have you been?" he demanded. "We've been looking all over for you." Then, belatedly taking note of Yuri's demeanor, he asked, "Here, what's wrong?"

Visibly agitated, Yuri said, "I want an audience with the president."

Taken aback, Olesky arched an eyebrow and said, "An audience with the president, eh? Well, well, you've certainly come up in the world, haven't you?"

Ignoring Olesky's gentle sarcasm, Yuri said, "I must see him at once, Marko. You must arrange it."

"Must I?" Olesky asked, unable to suppress a smile. Then, more amiably, he asked, "Come, Yuri Yurivich, what's this all about?"

Irritably, Yuri replied, "My pig, of course. I must see the president immediately."

"Ah, I see," Olesky replied sagely. "You want to speak to the president about your pig." Struggling to keep a straight face, he said, "And here I thought that it might be for some ridiculous reason." Pausing as if to consider, he added, "He's rather busy, you know?"

"I don't care!" Yuri replied with feeling. "I want to see the president at once!"

Startled by the outburst, Olesky held up his hands placatingly. "Calm yourself, Yuri Yurivich, I beg you. Now, ordinarily, I would laugh in your face at such a request, and if you had your wits about you, you would see that it would be richly deserved." Snorting derisively, he muttered, "Demand to see the president, is it? Of all the bone-headed notions this one has to be the most bone-headed of all." As Yuri opened his mouth to protest, Olesky interrupted, "But before you get yourself wound up again, you should know that the president wants to see you, too."

The storm of invective that Yuri was about to deliver died on his lips as his mouth closed with a 'clop.'

Then, "He does?"

"Yes, of course," Olesky replied, as if the answer was plain. "He wants to speak with you about your appearing on the *Stinislav Berkos Show* tomorrow. In fact, he was somewhat annoyed when you were nowhere to be found."

Suddenly fretful, Yuri asked, "Annoyed?"

"He actually frowned ... well, almost anyway. He said I was to take you to him as soon as you walked through the door."

"In that case," Yuri said, "lead on."

*

If he was, in fact, annoyed, the president did a good job of hiding it when Yuri was ushered into his office. Rising from behind his desk, he approached him like the happiest gargoyle in the world.

Extending his hand, warmly, he said, "Yuri Yurivich, how good of you to come."

Disarmed as always by the president's charm, Yuri replied, "I was told that you wanted to see me, Excellency."

"Yes, of course," the president said, gesturing for him to take a seat. "I wanted to speak with you about your television appearance tomorrow." Settling himself behind his desk again, he leaned forward. "Now then," he said, "do you think you're ready?"

Confused, Yuri asked, "Ready, Excellency? Ready for what? I was under the impression that I was only to relate my journey."

"And that's what will be asked of you," the president assured him, "but the interviewer *may* ask a few other questions, too."

"Questions? What sort of questions?"

"Oh, I don't know," the president replied smoothly. "I won't be interviewing you, so it isn't my business, you see. But, as you are aware, I asked Captain Olesky to take you to speak with some front-line soldiers to give you their impressions of the war." The president shrugged innocently, and said, "You may be asked about your own impressions, but then again, you may not. Still, it's best to be prepared, wouldn't you agree?"

Like any true Homstooder wary of city folk, Yuri's eyes narrowed suspiciously.

"What you're saying then, is that such questions are certain to be asked."

Smiling that he had been caught out, the president cheerfully admitted, "Yes, exactly, but let me assure you that you may speak as you see fit. We live in a democracy, after all, where everyone is free to speak their mind."

"In that case, Excellency," Yuri replied, "you may not want to have those questions asked."

The smile faded from the president's lips as he leaned back in his chair, studying Yuri quizzically.

"Is that so?" he asked.

"It is, Excellency."

"May I ask why? Aren't you in favour of our resistance?"

Miserable, Yuri replied, "I don't know, sir. I just don't know."

Leaning forward again, the president simply said, "Tell me."

Slowly, Yuri began.

"When I first heard about the invasion, I thought that it had nothing to do with me. Governments fight governments over high ideals that mean little to me or my village. All I cared about was getting my pig to market so that I could sow the east field with sunflowers. Then I could repair my barn and perhaps even mend the roof of my cottage. What did I care what the great and powerful thought or did? They make peace or wage war with equal disregard for my opinion."

If he was stung by the inference, the president kept it carefully concealed. His expression remained impassive, and for all intents and purposes, he still appeared ready to listen.

"To tell you the truth, Excellency, I wouldn't have started out on my journey if I thought otherwise."

"Go on," the president urged.

Even less comfortably, Yuri continued.

"I am of sufficient years to remember the days of the old empire, when we were still part of Zlaimperia."

"As am I," the president pointed out.

"Yes, of course, sir. But what I mean to say is that life wasn't much different for my village then than it is now. Of course, we had a commissar to keep us on the straight and narrow, but he was a harmless old soul who merely wanted to be liked, so he let us say and do whatever we wished."

"You were indeed fortunate," the president pointed out dryly, just as the unfortunate Hanna Gorchenko had done a lifetime ago.

Yuri allowed, "I have heard that before, Excellency, so what you say may be true, but the point is, that when the old empire collapsed and Xoraina gained its independence, nothing much changed for us in Homstood. We were left alone to work our fields and generally do as we wished. Then we were told that democracy had arrived and still nothing changed, that is," he said eyeing the president slyly, "until I tried sending my pig to market and discovered that I couldn't because a new shipping tax had been imposed."

"Yes, well," the president replied brusquely, "I'm still giving that some thought."

"So, when I heard about the invasion," Yuri pressed on, "and that the Zlaimperian dictator had vowed to return us to the old days, it still meant nothing to me. My life hadn't changed under the new regime, so I couldn't see that it mattered if we returned to the old one."

"I see," said the president, nodding slowly.

Yuri shrugged, "Zlaimperian or Xorainian, what did it matter what others called us? In Homstood, we know who we are."

"And we know who *we* are," the president replied levelly. "We are you and you are us, one and the same, we are all Xorainians."

"Your pardon, Excellency," Yuri replied gently, "but if the president I was talking to right now was a Zlaimperian, he would say the same thing."

For the first time since Yuri had known him, a flash of anger sparked in the president's eyes, but then was gone again, so quickly that, later, he couldn't be sure that he had ever seen it. Eventually, he smiled, albeit a forced one.

"Your point is well-taken, Yuri," he said. "Now I ask you to take *this* point: If I was a Zlaimperian president, you wouldn't be sitting across from me at the moment, now would you?"

Yuri considered, then slowly wagged his head.

"No, you wouldn't," said the president. "You would still be on your farm in Homstood, and by now, would have put all thoughts of planting sunflowers aside, because the very idea of complaining to your president would have been unthinkable."

"But tell me, Excellency, will it do me any good that I *do* have this right?"

"Let me put it this way, Yuri," said the president, ever the politician, ""it would do you no good at all if you didn't."

Contemplating, Yuri nodded as the president's meaning became clear.

With Yuri showing doubt, the president might have pressed his point harder, but instead he appeared to change the subject.

"Tell me, what was it like at the front? How were the men's spirits?"

Striving to keep pace, Yuri frowned and admitted, "After all that they've been through, their spirits seemed to be very high, Excellency."

"No signs of giving up?"

"Why, no, Excellency, none at all."

"Did you ask them why they fight, when all seems so hopeless?"

"I never heard anyone admit that the situation was hopeless, sir, not in so many words, but yes, I did ask them that question."

"And what was their answer?"

"One of them argued for democracy, claiming it was better than having to live with a Zlaimperian boot on our neck, and another said he fought simply because the Zlaimperians were here uninvited, and it was up to Xoraina to see them off."

The president laughed. "Both are right in my view."

Not sharing in the laughter, Yuri's mien remained serious. "There was a third soldier, Excellency, this one a woman. When asked, she told me that, having lost her family early in the war, her only reason for living was to kill as many Zlaimperians as possible."

Nodding soberly, the president said, "I fear that the ranks of our armed forces are filled with those with similar stories." Then, regarding Yuri, he asked, "Tell me, what did you think of them?"

"I thought they were magnificent," Yuri said, eyes aglow. "They encompass the best this country has to offer: bold and brave, they bow to no man and are confident in their strength. One of them also said that he fought to protect *me*," hesitating, he blushed and added, "even if I was *nevcheniy.*"

Again, the president laughed, but that quickly died when he noted that Yuri's serious expression remained.

"But ...?" he asked. "There is a 'but,' isn't there, Yuri?"

Spreading his hands helplessly, the president noted the tears in Yuri's eyes when he said, "They are *dying*, Excellency. Every day, more and more of them are lost in the face of overwhelming odds. This angers and frustrates them, even though they accept that they will die fighting to save the Capital. They are willing to give their lives, sir, it's just that ..."

"It's just that what?"

"Well, Excellency, it's like one of them said just as I was leaving: 'We are not afraid to fight for our country. We are not even afraid to die." Looking directly at the president, Yuri said, "'but we are afraid of not being allowed to win.'"

The silence that followed was filled only by the ticking of a Queen Anne clock on the mantlepiece. Finally, the president said, "I see."

"An entire generation of our soldiers, the flower of our country, are dying fighting a war they cannot win."

The president's eyes narrowed. "Is that what you think?"

Yuri couldn't look at him. "It is, sir."

"And what do you think I should do?"

Evasive now, Yuri replied, "Your Excellency, I'm just a simple farmer."

"That's not an acceptable answer, Yuri," the president pointed out, not unkindly. "You are Xorainian, you have a say in the fate of your country."

Unable to reply, Yuri's head remained bowed.

"You think that I should surrender, don't you, even though you've seen with your own eyes what the Zlaimperians will do to helpless Xorainian citizens?"

At last Yuri looked up again, his face deeply troubled, and once again said something very unHomstood-like.

"I don't know, Excellency. I just don't know."

The president studied Yuri at some length. Finally, he admitted, "That's a more honest answer than I've received from anyone else at the Capital." Then, addressing some papers on his desk, he said, "That will be all. But please make sure that you're ready for tomorrow."

Confused, Yuri asked, "Tomorrow, Excellency?"

"Yes, for your interview. Have you forgotten already?"

"Why, no, Excellency, but do you still want me to be on national television, in light of what I've just told you?" No matter how Yuri looked at it it seemed unlikely.

"Yes, of course," the president said, and setting aside his papers, added, "Regardless of your feelings about the war, yours is still an inspiring story, Yuri. It shows heroism and courage and a stubborn refusal to back down in the face of a tyrant. These are attributes that all Xorainians must have as we continue to resist."

"Yes," Yuri said, although he didn't necessarily agree with the president's assessment, "but that was for my pig."

"That," the president assured him, "is the best part."

Still confused, it was sufficient for Yuri to know that he was still expected to appear on national television in the morning.

"I'll do my best, sir," he said uncertainly.

The president failed to conceal a heavy sigh. The conversation was taxing his patience.

"There's another 'but,' isn't there?"

"As a matter of fact, sir, there is. I had meant to mention it when I first came to see you."

Even less patiently, the president heaved another sigh.

"Yes? What is it?"

"I meant to tell you that I'm leaving the palace."

The furrows on the president's forehead knit together. One could almost say that they *violently* knit together. "Leaving the palace? Whatever for?"

"To be with my pig, Excellency. He hasn't been doing too well without me."

"You want to be with your pig?"

"Why, yes, Excellency. After all, he's the reason why I'm here."

Yuri wasn't sure of the reason why, but he felt relieved to see the president's good nature return. Scribbling something on a sheet of paper, he handed it to Yuri, and said, "Here, give this to Olesky. He will see to all the arrangements."

Accepting the paper with a puzzled frown, Yuri asked, "Arrangements, sir?"

A third heavy sigh.

"Yes, Yuri, arrangements." Then, seeing that this offered no enlightenment, he relented, and said, "Look, like it or not you are still a national hero, or soon will be, and we can't have our heroes sleeping in pigsties without a comfortable bed, now can we?" Then, throwing up his hands, he said, "Now leave before I change my mind and have the pig brought to the palace, instead!"

Rising from his chair, Yuri turned to leave, less sure of anything than ever before, only that the president made no effort, whatsoever, to conceal his laughter.

*

The pig chomped happily away at his second supper, feeling stronger by the minute. Before he had left, the squire had had a word with the workmen – he had seen it for himself – and although they had been fairly attentive before, they were even more so now.

With his tail curled up once again into a tight corkscrew, he allowed that, while the food they gave him wasn't swill, it was passable fare under the circumstances. And while he wasn't quite sure what those circumstances were, he was content knowing that the squire would return. Then all the problems would be resolved.

Really, barring the absence of a good wallow and the kindest, most beautiful sow in all the world, what else could a simple pig ask for?

Chapter Twenty-two

Olesky was waiting when Yuri stepped outside the office. The sound of the president's laughter caused his forehead to furrow into a quizzical frown.

"How did it go?" he asked.

Yuri shrugged, but Olesky could see he looked troubled. "What is it?"

Yuri waited for his thoughts to formulate more clearly before he could even attempt to put them into words.

Hesitantly, he began. "When I met your comrades all those weeks ago, I thought they were very brave, but even more, I thought they were magnificent, ready to lay down their lives to protect our country. They are a true inspiration." Gesturing with a tilt of his head to where the president's laughter could still be heard through the door, he said, "Then, when I spoke to him, I thought he was even more inspiring, but ..."

This time Yuri's hesitation grew so long that Olesky gestured toward a sofa. "Here," he said, inviting Yuri to be seated. Let's make ourselves comfortable. I sense this might take a while." When both were settled, he said, "Now then, Yuri, tell me what's on your mind."

But seated or otherwise, Yuri was still far from comfortable when he said, "Every day the perimeter around the Capital grows smaller and the Zlaimperian siege grows stronger. Our casualties continue to mount, day by day, and still we retreat. To me, the situation appears to be hopeless. So, by what right does the president inspire the people to resist? He's only ensuring that more of those brave men and women will die before events reach their inevitable conclusion."

Again, the silence grew long, this time on Olesky's side. Then, quietly, the captain said, "So, you think the conclusion is inevitable, do you?"

Miserable, Yuri shrugged. "The Xorainian forces around the Capital are vastly outnumbered. Zlaimperia has more men, more tanks, more guns, more everything." He looked at the captain and shrugged. "Inevitable? How could it be otherwise?"

After a thought-filled pause, Olesky said, "I see. It is your opinion that, far from being a hero for inspiring our country to resist, the president is, in fact, a criminal for doing just that. Is that so?"

Yuri remained silent, eyes downcast, which was an answer in itself. Belatedly, he murmured, "Otherwise, I think he's a very good man." Looking at the floor as he was, he didn't see the captain's wounded expression.

"Perhaps," he began slowly, "being from such a remote area of the country, you're unaware of the feelings of the rest of Xoraina."

"Perhaps," Yuri allowed, although he didn't sound convinced.

"What I mean," Olesky continued, "is that the president hasn't tricked the country into resisting, as I believe you are suggesting. He, at least, is aware of the mood of the people."

Yuri flushed as Olesky's inference became clear.

"If he hadn't chosen to resist, the country would have risen against him and found someone who would."

At this, Yuri raised his head to look at the captain. Clearly baffled, he half-suspected that he was speaking in jest, but if he was, he couldn't see it on Olesky's face.

"But how is that possible?" he asked.

"My poor provincial friend," Olesky said. "That is how democracy works. Don't you see? The leader is merely an echo of the will of the country. Oh, I'm aware that this is not always the case – all too often the people *are* tricked by an unscrupulous politician – but not in this instance, not when the national mood is so united." Seized with an idea, he said, "Here, let me give you some examples. Have you heard of either Stefan Bondarenko or Ivan Kovalchuk?"

Yuri dredged through his memory, but finally conceded that he hadn't.

"Just as I thought," Olesky said, "although that's really quite remarkable that you haven't."

Feeling every bit as provincial as Olesky accused him of being, Yuri asked, "Who are they?"

"The correct way to ask that question," the captain said, "is who *were* they. They're both dead now."

"Ah," Yuri replied, "I see. That's unfortunate."

"Yes," Olesky agreed, "very unfortunate. They were both soldiers in the Xorainian Army. Bondarenko died on the first day of the invasion, Kovalchuk a week later, both hundreds of kilometres from each other. In fact, Kovalchuk died a few miles from here." Quietly, he added, "I knew him."

Afraid to ask, Yuri forced himself to anyway. "How did they die?"

"Bondarenko was a wireless operator posted to a small coastal defence station south of Lofstov – no more than twelve soldiers altogether, without any heavy weapons for support. They had barely received word about the invasion when a Zlaimperian cruiser was sighted on the horizon. Minutes later, word came over the radio from the ship's commander, demanding their surrender or face immediate destruction."

Guessing accurately, Yuri said, "But they didn't surrender, did they?" even as he felt the skin shrink on his scalp.

Instead of answering, Olesky said, "Just imagine, Yuri, a modern cruiser, armed with missiles and heavy guns of every description, the smallest of which would have dwarfed the single light machinegun at the station's disposal. Surrendering would have been the sensible option to take. Indeed, it would seem to be the only option available, and who could blame them if they had?" Placing his hand against his chest, he said, "Not me, that's for sure. I believe that I possess a certain amount of courage, but not enough to stand in defiance of a cruiser. However, Bondarenko and his comrades *did*. Remember, they had just received word of the invasion, and all was confusion. They could have surrendered, and no one would have blamed them or even accused them of dishonour. They would have been swept aside and scarcely anyone would have noticed. But you are right, Yuri Yurivich, they didn't surrender. Remember, they were still in a state of shock by the news, as was the rest of the country, and until Bondarenko gave the Zlaimperians their answer, they couldn't have had time to express their feelings about it even to themselves."

Impressed by the imagery of it all, Yuri asked, "Do you know what he said?"

Olesky laughed a bitter laugh. "Do I know what he said? Why, everyone in the country knows." Amending slightly, he said, "At least outside that mountain village of yours. He said, 'Zlaimperian ship, go fuck yourself.'"

Gasping, Yuri said, "He didn't!"

Nodding grimly, Olesky said, "He did."

"What happened then?"

Olesky shrugged. "The cruiser bombarded their position, killing many, Bondarenko among them. Those who survived were taken prisoner."

Crestfallen, Yuri merely replied, "Oh."

"But don't you see?" Olesky urged, "The message had been sent, not just to the warship, but to the Zlaimperian dictator himself, as well as to the people of Xoraina. In fact, I have heard that it has become famous throughout the world. Instead of surrendering, Bondarenko gave voice to our people's indignation. It was as if that small garrison were a microcosm of Xoraina as a whole, and spoke for all of us, inspiring the nation to stand up and resist."

"But, if you want to continue with the metaphor of that little station representing Xoraina as a whole," Yuri said meaningfully, "allow me to point out that Bondarenko and his comrades are still dead."

Olesky replied without hesitation. "So might the same be said of Achilles, or of Leonidas of Sparta. They recognised that some things are worth fighting for – yes, even dying for – for the glory of a nation."

Yuri shook his head. "What use is glory?"

"Glory is freedom," Olesky replied quietly.

Taken by surprise, Yuri was unable to answer. Instead, he asked, "What about the other one?"

"Kovalchuk?"

"Yes, the one you knew. What happened to him?"

Olesky grew sombre as the memory returned. It wasn't a slow transformation but something that was instantaneous, betraying an emotion that was never far from his consciousness.

"It was just a week into the conflict," he said. "We were still reeling from the suddenness of the invasion and falling back on all fronts. The enemy was threatening the very outskirts of the Capital.

"There were three bridges spanning the Dnapro in our sector, and the order had been given to destroy them to slow the enemy's advance. Two were successfully brought down with explosives, but with the enemy just minutes away, when Ivan cranked the magneto to demolish the third bridge, nothing happened."

"My god," Yuri gasped. "What did he do?" Although he thought he could guess.

Olesky wouldn't look at Yuri. Instead, his eyes were fastened on the opposite wall, but it was plain that it wasn't the decorative furnishings that he was seeing.

"I was with him at the time. After he triggered the wire we waited a moment – a few seconds, nothing more. He cranked the magneto a second time, and again we waited, but still nothing happened.

"By now the enemy was close enough that we could hear the squeal of their tank tracks, and see the muzzle flashes of their rifles, both steadily approaching. In those few minutes hung the fate of our nation. If they reached the bridge before it could be destroyed there was nothing to stop them from taking the Capital."

Still staring into the past, Olesky said, "I remember Ivan turning to me. We both knew what had happened – the wire had been cut somewhere, whether deliberate or by a piece of shrapnel, it made no difference. The bridge was still standing, and if something wasn't done immediately, the country would be lost. The question for me was what could be done in so little time?

"With Kovalchuk the answer was clear. He wasn't plagued by doubts or lack of courage as I was. In that moment when he looked at me, all he said was, "Tell my wife I love her," and then he was racing across the bridge before I could stop him. Minutes later, there was a powerful explosion, knocking me to my knees, and the bridge collapsed into the Dnapro. Naturally, I never saw Kovalchuk again."

Feeling for his friend, Yuri said truthfully, "I can't imagine what it must have been like at that terrible moment."

Olesky said, "I called out for him to stop but, of course, he didn't listen." In anguish, he turned away from the wall, eyes glistening with tears. "Truth be told I didn't call out as loudly as I could have because, deep down, I knew what needed to be done as well as he did. The only difference was that I lacked the courage to act, and he didn't. The same can be said for both Kovalchuk and Bondarenko: when their moment arrived, they were not found wanting."

"They must have been very brave," Yuri agreed.

By way of a reply, Olesky said, "I've relived that moment over and over again in my mind. If I had been with someone else that day, and if that someone had lacked the courage, would I have been able to act so bravely in his place?" Shrugging, he said, "The answer eluded me then and it eludes me still."

"Such courage must be rare," Yuri said, but to his surprise, Olesky didn't agree.

"Our president has been lauded the world over as a champion for freedom. Do you know how he answers?" When Yuri shook his head, Olesky said, "He says, 'I'm just an ordinary man caught up in extraordinary times.' Meaning, of course, that we are all of us ordinary people during this, the most extraordinary time of our lives. Until we are faced with our own moment, who knows how we will respond?"

"That was very well put," Yuri conceded.

Olesky explained. "He was faced with his own moment of truth the minute the first enemy tank crossed the border. The Zlaimperian tyrant made no secret that he wanted our president dead – not only him but all his family, as well. The risk couldn't have been more dire because, at the time, no one knew if the army would fight against such overwhelming odds. You must understand that, for a father, the choice was clear: leave the country, escape with his wife and children, and place them beyond the reach of that vengeful despot. But the president knew that the office he held was more than just one father, more than just one husband. He represented *all* the fathers, *all* the husbands …all Xoraina. So, when the United States of America offered him refuge, his reply was immediate."

Leaning forward, Yuri asked, "What did he tell them?"

Olesky looked at him, and replied, "He said, 'Don't offer me an escape. Offer me weapons, instead.'"

Yuri thought of the unassuming little man and the kindness and dignity with which he carried himself. Who would have thought that he harboured the spirit of a lion beneath his insignificant breast?

"Truly inspiring," he said. Olesky agreed.

"Yes," he said. "When he and his family refused to leave, it put strength in the backbone of our country, and so we fight on."

"You've given me much to think about," Yuri admitted, and in the silence that followed, gradually recalled the slip of paper in his hand. It had been all but forgotten during their conversation.

Offering it to Olesky, he said, "Here, the president wrote this for you."

Frowning, Olesky accepted the note. After he read it the furrows on his brow only deepened.

"It says here that you're leaving the palace."

"I am," Yuri confirmed.

"So that you can be with your pig."

"That is also true."

Olesky looked up from the sheet of paper and stared at Yuri as if he had just arrived from Mars.

"Whatever for?"

Yuri hesitated, unwilling to share his innermost feelings on the matter; when the truth was he was scarcely able to share them with himself. On his way to the palace, he had been governed by one overruling thought: that he needed to be more attentive to the pig. There hadn't been time to delve into the why of it, merely that it was a step that he would just have to take. However, with the urgency of the situation slowly fading, he was coming to see the reason on a level any true Homstooder would understand, even though he had an uncomfortable feeling that there might be something more to it than that.

Instead of trying to plumb the depths to a deeper truth, he merely replied, "The pig has shown signs of wasting. If you'll recall, I have a vested interest in his health. A great deal depends upon it for the prosperity of my farm."

Olesky arched a dubious eyebrow, and though he didn't reply, Yuri could almost see a cartoon thought cloud floating over his head bearing a single word: *nevcheniy*. He refrained from rising to his own defence, however, mainly on account of the fact that he wasn't sure he didn't secretly agree.

Finally, Olesky shrugged in an exasperated sort of way, and with a level of dismay difficult to put into words, he said, "Very well, I'll see to your damned sleeping arrangements. Now go, you impossible man!"

*

The pig was happy that the squire had returned, especially so now that he was sleeping on a cot next to his pen. Workmen had brought it in before he arrived. Even then the pig had sensed that this portended a big change, and what could be bigger than this? Now, who could doubt that all would be well?

Resting his chin on the bottom rail of the enclosure, he closed his eyes, and with his anxiety vanquished, allowed himself to dream of home and the kindest, most beautiful sow in all the world.

Chapter Twenty-three

The Minister of Defence stood with his back to Yuri, facing the window, staring at, but not seeing, the busy pedestrian traffic on Mariinsky Prospekt.

"I've been thinking," he said. "This is precisely the opportunity we've been waiting for."

Sitting opposite, across the minister's desk, confused as ever, Yuri asked, "Excellency?"

"Your appearance on national television this evening, you fool!" Suddenly turning on him, the defence minister said, "This is our opportunity to tell the people what a disaster the president has brought the country to. Then we can be done with him, once and for all."

"Oh," Yuri replied doubtfully. Then, remembering his conversation with Captain Olesky the previous evening, he said, "Do you think that's wise?" In response to the minister's glare, he added lamely, "The people rather like him. What I mean to say, Excellency, is that they regard him as a hero."

"Bah!" The minister swore and demanded, "Ridiculous! Where did you hear such rubbish?"

"Oh, here and there," Yuri replied evasively.

While having determined not to report to the minister about his conversations with the president, Yuri was equally evasive about his conversations with Captain Olesky or anyone else. But he was finding all this subterfuge to be extremely nerve-racking, and not at all what a true Homstooder was cut out for. In that light, it was inevitable that he began to fidget.

At that moment, a mechanical 'ting' sound came from a flat, rectangular object on the minister's desk. Not being as provincial as some might think, Yuri recognised this as one of those new-fangled telephones he'd seen all over the Capital ever since he'd arrived.

Glancing down at the instrument, the minister picked it up, read what was on the display, and typed a reply with his thumbs. Then, replacing the phone on his desk, he turned back to the window.

"It is preposterous to regard the president as anything other than what he really is," he said, "a fool and a traitor. As for the people," he scoffed, "they will believe what we tell them to believe, don't you worry about that, Mr Zavlov. No, this is too good a chance to miss. He must be exposed."

Well out of his depth, Yuri continued to fidget. Exposing the president, someone he continued to see as a good, honest man, seemed unthinkable, but on the other hand, Yuri's own position on the futility of resistance hadn't changed, regardless of the heroism of the people. More to the point, he entertained doubts that those same people would be ready to believe whatever the minister chose to tell them, either. But what did he know? He was just a simple farmer, after all.

Verging on panic, with the minister's back still turned to him, Yuri's eyes happened to light upon the phone resting on the minister's desk. Without thinking, he reached out to pick it up. A small, insignificant part of his mind realised that he'd never held one before, and while he hadn't the least inclination to learn how to actually use it, he was curious as to how it would feel in his hand. Meanwhile, the vast majority of his mind had other, far more important things to consider, to the point where getting his pig to market never even registered.

"If I may be so bold, Excellency," he said, "how do you propose to, as you say, expose him?"

The telephone was surprisingly heavy for its size, and he gave it an appreciative heft in an attempt to guess how much it weighed.

"Not I, you fool!" the minister cried. "You! *You* will be the instrument of his downfall!"

Of course, Yuri should have seen this coming, but the minister's reply so shocked him that his grip on the telephone tightened involuntarily, causing the screen to light up. Gasping in panic, he had barely enough presence of mind not to make a sound when, with his palms slick with nervous perspiration, it leapt from his grasp.

To his horror, he watched it turn over and over in the air, a mere split-second from crashing to the floor. Desperately, he lunged out with his hand, and by the greatest of miracles, just managed to catch it in a pincer between two fingers.

"Me, Excellency?" he stammered, and given the state of his funk, he added, "You can't be serious!"

"Oh, but I am, Mr Zavlov, I am!" And, suddenly feeling affable at the thought of the possibilities that had been presented, he turned to Yuri with a triumphant smile.

Much later, when there was time to reflect, Yuri would wonder how he had been able to react so quickly, but faced with the unenviable prospect of being caught in the possession of something so personal as the minister's phone, he reacted on instinct. Obviously, replacing it on the desk would take too long so, in a fit of panic, he stuffed it inside his shirt.

Stuttering, he asked, "A-and just how am I to expose the president?"

The Minister of Defence regarded Yuri with disappointment, his affable smile beginning to fade.

His face suddenly engorged with rage, he cried, "You defame the bastard! You tell the country that he's leading them down the road to destruction, that the situation is hopeless, and that he alone is responsible! You bury him with lies if you have to. I don't give a damn. After that, you can leave the rest to me. Do I make myself clear?"

Yuri was so transfixed with terror that he wasn't capable of anything more than a simple nod by way of a reply.

"Good!" the minister fumed, "Be sure that you do," now his voice did become softer, dangerously so, and rich with menace, "otherwise it will go hard for you, Mr Zavlov, very hard, indeed. Never forget that." Then, once more wheeling around to face the window, he snapped, "Now, get out, I have much to see to."

His mind numb with fear, Yuri rose from his chair and fled the room.

*

"Can you not do anything about the bags under his eyes?" Olesky demanded testily.

The makeup artist, a thickset woman in her forties with a single eyebrow spanning the breadth of her forehead, equally as testily replied, "I'm an artist, Captain, not a fucking miracle worker."

Yuri sat in a chair in the makeup department of the national television studio, painfully aware they he was being discussed as if he was a prize poodle about to be exhibited at a dog show.

"I'm right here," he said pointedly but, of course, was ignored.

"At least you could have given him a shave," Olesky accused, clearly unsatisfied with Yuri's appearance.

Not to be outdone, the woman in charge of said appearance was giving as good as she got.

"Then he should have seen a barber, shouldn't he?" she snapped, and added in a voice dripping with sarcasm, "Or, oh, I don't know, bought a *razor*?" Then, returning to a more professional tone, she said, "As for the bags under his eyes, I've already applied two coats of concealer. If you want me to do a better job, I'll need a wheelbarrow and a trowel."

Blushing furiously, Yuri explained, "I didn't sleep well last night."

"Imagine that," Olesky replied just as sarcastically as the makeup artist, "and in a pigsty of all places. Under such conditions one might have thought you would have slept like a baby."

Her application brush poised over Yuri's face, the makeup artist asked, "Did you just say he slept in a pigsty?"

"Where else?" Olesky shrugged in an exasperated sort of way.

"My pig has been ill," Yuri explained.

Strangely reluctant to explore the conversation any further, the makeup artist frowned and also shrugged. She had already learned that Yuri was from that remote region between the forest and the Carpathians, so she was ready to believe the worst. Applying herself once more to her task, after a few more brush strokes, she stood back, hands on hips.

"It's not my best work," she conceded, her single eyebrow performing a rolling wave, "but I defy anyone else to do better."

Running a critical eye over Yuri's face, Olesky allowed, "At least you were able to cover up most of the grime."

Eyes narrowed, Yuri pointed out, "I can hear you, you know." But he was once again ignored.

Just then, there came a knock on the door and a stagehand stuck his head inside.

"Five minutes!" he called cheerfully and vanished again.

"Oh crumbs," squeaked Yuri, doing his best to vanish as well.

"Don't worry, my friend," Olesky said, suddenly all business-like, "you've got this." Then, to the makeup artist, he asked, "Is there anything you can do to deepen his complexion? He's pale as a ghost."

Shaking her head, the makeup artist replied, "I told you, I don't perform miracles."

Deciding he would have to do, Olesky assisted Yuri from his chair. Removing the protective bib from around his neck, he frowned and said, "It's a pity he's not shaved. Ah well, it can't be helped."

"Do you really think so?" the makeup artist asked, "A shadow is all the rage in Hollywood these days, or so they tell me. Personally, I think it gives him a rakish air."

"If you say so," Olesky agreed doubtfully. "Anyway, it's too late for that now. Right," he said, taking Yuri by the shoulders, "it's time. Remember, just tell the truth. Let the country know what a hero you are and show them some of that stout Xorainian courage!" Then, taking him firmly by the elbow, he guided Yuri out the door and onto the set reserved for the *Stinislav Berkos Show*.

*

The set itself was not particularly impressive, resembling a small lecture theatre one might find in universities all over the world. It was the lights that Yuri found unnerving; they didn't shine so much as glared on the two lonely chairs situated on a modest stage at the bottom of an equally modest amphitheatre. Those two chairs were unnerving, too, accompanied by a low table, on top of which sat a bowl of plastic fruit in a sad attempt at decoration. Waiting patiently, a crew stood by two large television cameras which, in Yuri's elevated state of panic, more resembled some sort of futuristic monsters bent on his utter destruction. But it was the chairs that put him in a funk most of all. He would be expected to sit in one of them and be mercilessly grilled by this Stinislav Berkos fellow, in front of a live audience that was, even now, beginning to find their way to their seats in the amphitheatre. Who Stinislav was Yuri had no clear idea, but he was in no doubt that he was the very epitome of a city person which, of course, meant that he couldn't be trusted one iota.

At present, the only person showing any real animation was the show's producer. When Yuri appeared, he ran up to him with a flurry of comments, none of which settled Yuri in the least.

"Ah, Mr Zavlov!" he cried. "Welcome, welcome! Now, if you'll follow me, please, we'll just get you seated. Mr Berkos will be with us shortly." As soon as Yuri's bottom touched the negligible cushion of the chair, the producer said, "Good, excellent," and then went off to hector a crewman who was smoking a cigarette and holding the sound boom.

Squinting, Yuri was just able to peer past the glare of the lights and saw that the amphitheatre was filling up quite rapidly now. Frantically, he twisted in his chair, searching for a friendly face, and saw Olesky standing in the wings. The captain offered him a ghastly smile, but if anything, he looked even more nervous than Yuri did himself. Thankfully, they didn't have long to wait.

Just as Yuri turned back to study the bowl of fruit on the table, the audience burst into applause. Looking up, he saw a man who he took to be Stinislav Berkos himself stride majestically onto the stage, waving to the audience in a way that reminded Yuri of the Pope blessing the faithful.

Whereas Stinislav was close to the same age as Yuri, the resemblance ended there. Where Yuri was rough and ruggedly stolid, Stinislav was lithe and elegant, with perfectly coifed silver-grey hair, a mouthful of gleaming dental caps, and, it should be added, a pink face that was freshly shaved.

"Thank you! Thank you! Oh, you're too kind! You're too kind!" he grinned, blowing kisses to the audience, all which, of course, caused the applause to increase tenfold. When it was thundering, he gave them a final wave before turning his attention to the poor wretch perched on the edge of his chair like a doomed man awaiting all the pleasures of the Spanish Inquisition.

Holding out his hand, Stinislav said, "Ah, Mr ..." he peered down at a flashcard in his hand, "Zavlov, good to see you, sir. Good to see you."

Accepting his hand, Yuri belatedly thought to stand and gave it a firm shake, as was befitting any true Homstooder, and Stinislav's professional mask slipped considerably.

Grimacing in pain, he hissed a curse through his teeth, and said, "Whoa there, fella! Say, that's quite a grip you've got!" and yanked his hand away. Massaging his mangled digits, he forced a smile and turned to the crowd. "They grow them strong out in the back of beyond!" which was answered with appreciative laughter. Then, gesturing for Yuri to regain his seat, Stinislav settled into the one opposite.

"Thirty seconds!" cried the producer.

"I'm sorry, Mr Berkos, sir," Yuri whispered miserably. "I'm very nervous."

"Yeah, well, never mind that now," Stinislav said, continuing to massage his hand. "Okay, so I'm sure you've seen the show before, so you know how this goes?"

"Actually, sir," Yuri confessed, "I've never watched it before in my life."

Although Stinislav's professional mask remained intact, his eyes seemed to be doing their level best at imitating a ruptured goose. Hissing another curse, he said, "Never seen my show?" then muttered to himself, "Just what the hell have they got me into this time? I wanted the Minister of Defence, but oh no, the president had to insist!" Then, regrouping, he said, "Okay, okay, that's fine," although it clearly wasn't. "Just follow my lead and we might just get through this, *capisce*?"

Unnerved as never before, Yuri stared back at Stinislav in abject terror.

"Five seconds!" cried the producer.

Stinislav managed to hold up a placating hand. "Don't worry," he said, "I've got this," although he didn't sound very convincing.

Now the producer was holding up his hand, fingers extended. Five ... four ... three ... two ... and then he pointed at Stinislav, indicating that they were live. At the same time the 'Applause' light came on and the audience dutifully obliged.

"Ah!" Stinislav cried out to them, "Welcome to the *Stinislav Berkos Show*!" Then, into the camera, "And welcome to our viewers at home. I am your host, Stinislav Berkos!"

The applause rose to a tumultuous din.

After waiting patiently for it to die down, he read from the teleprompter, "We've got a great show for you tonight, broadcasting live from the Capital! A man who's been through Hell and back just to be with us, who is an example of the bravery and courage that exemplifies the spirit of the country. This is a story that you're not going to want to miss. Ladies and gentlemen, from a small village on the foothills of the Carpathian Mountains, I give you Mr Yuri Zavlov!"

To Yuri, the roar of applause that followed sounded more like the knell of doom.

*

In the distance, the pig could hear the low 'crump' of the artillery barrage drawing nearer, making him increasingly agitated. His sense of well-being from the previous evening now forgotten, he'd give anything to have the squire with him right now.

His ears, finely tuned instruments of detection, told him that the explosions had been coming closer and closer for days. How long would it be before they burst into this very enclosure? Trembling, he recalled that day in the forest when he had feasted on the mushrooms – the blinding flashes, the deafening mayhem ... and the fear. Oh, Great Pig in Heaven, the fear!

And always, **always** *the wails of the ghosts.*

Chapter Twenty-four

"So, Mr Zavlov ..." Stinislav paused, "Or Yuri, you don't mind if I call you Yuri, do you? Yes," he said brusquely, hurrying on from Yuri's voiceless stare. "Now, your village of ..." Stinislav glances at his notes, "Homstood, is pretty isolated, isn't it?"

This time, Yuri actually managed a nod.

A few nervous titters from the audience.

Stinislav, doing a masterful job of hiding his impatience, quipped, "I realise this is television, my friend, but speaking is also allowed. In fact, it's even encouraged!"

Robust laughter from the audience.

This seemed to have the desired effect, for Yuri, blinking owlishly, managed to stammer, "Y-yes. Yes, it is, very isolated."

"In fact," Stinislav said, "it's over five hundred kilometres from the Capital, isn't that so?"

"Y-yes, five hundred kilometres, that is correct."

"And yet you decided to make the journey here with a war raging all around, and," here he paused for dramatic effect, turning to the audience, "on foot!"

Gasps of amazement.

Yuri swallowed nervously, and nodded. "Yes."

Stinislav might have feigned his own amazement, in fact, he had done so several times in the past, but this time it was genuine.

"Whatever for?"

"Well, you see," Yuri began, "the Kamaz needed a radiator hose and there was no one in the Homstood dealership to order it for me. And also," he added sheepishly, "my driver's licence had expired."

"Oh, dear me," Stinislav said for the benefit of the audience, "you shouldn't let your licence expire." Then, smoothly moving on, he said, "But why is it that there was no one at the dealership to order you a new radiator hose?"

"At first I wasn't sure," Yuri conceded, "but I've since come to the conclusion that they were trying to escape the bombing. You see, the Zlaimperians had destroyed the railway station. So, everyone left before they started bombing the village itself."

In a voice filled with revulsion, Stinislav said, "The Zlaimperian warmongers bombed the railroad!"

Angry murmurs from the audience.

"And there was no one left to give you a ride, so you set off on foot, is that it?"

"Yes."

His voice rising, Stinislav faced the camera. "And you made it!" Then, to the audience, he invited their response with, "Isn't that incredible?"

Thunderous applause.

"Yes, quite incredible, I must say. And you travelled through a war zone to get here!"

"Two war zones, actually," Yuri managed to point out.

"Indeed," Stinislav said appreciatively. "You must have seen some terrible things."

"Yes, I did."

Turning back to the camera, in a voice filled with fatherly concern, Stinislav said, "I must caution our viewing audience, what they hear next might be disturbing to some of you. So, if there are young children watching, you might want to ask them to leave the room. Then, turning back to Yuri, he said, "Perhaps you could tell us more about that?"

Fidgeting, Yuri looked up to the ceiling as if to assist his memory.

"Helicopters with rockets, people charred to ashes, hundreds of them. Villages in ruins, bodies lying in the streets, bodies everywhere. Destruction everywhere. Our once green and fruitful country is being turned into a graveyard. There was a dog ..." Suddenly, he stopped, unwilling to go on.

Sensing that it would not be wise to press Yuri about the dog, Stinislav asked, "Anything else?"

"A girl took her own life," Yuri said, then nervously corrected himself. "No, there were two, or possibly two, I'm not sure. One hung herself and the other slit her wrists, or at least I think she may have. Her name was Hanna, that is to say the one who may have slit her wrists – after I left her, she had a knife. It was very sharp. I forget the other one's name. That one had been …" leaning forward, he whispered to Stinislav, but loud enough for the microphone to pick up, "Can I say 'raped' on television?"

"Yes," Stinislav replied, without any hint of rancour.

"She had been raped several times by Zlaimperian soldiers before she could escape. I don't know why she hung herself. Perhaps she couldn't live with the shame, which makes no sense, because the shame wasn't hers. It belongs to those soldiers who violated her."

Angry growls of assent from the audience.

"I'm not sure why Hanna took her own life, either," Yuri shrugged. "She had also been raped, so perhaps it was that. Or perhaps it was hunger, but I think she had just lost hope." Reflecting, he said, "Hunger can do that, of course. And she had lost her husband in the fighting; that may have had something to do with it, too." Spreading his hands helplessly, he said, "It all seems very confusing."

"I'm sure it does," Stinislav said, not unkindly. From the audience there wasn't a murmur.

Recalling in imperfect order, Yuri said, "I spoke to a guard once, at a crossroads. He was Xorainian. I wanted to pass but he wouldn't let me. When he discovered that I intended on going to the Capital, he said that I was *nevcheniy*."

Nervous laughter from the audience.

"In fact, both times I met Xorainian soldiers, they called me that." Twisting in his chair, Yuri pointed an accusing finger at Olesky. "Captain Olesky – he's right over there, standing in the wings – he said that I was *nevcheniy*, too."

Hearty laughter from the audience.

Seeking to change the tone of the conversation, Stinislav quipped, "Is it possible that both are wrong?"

More hearty laughter.

Frowning stubbornly, Yuri avowed, I am *not nevcheniy*, I am from Homstood!" At which the studio's roof fairly shook from the laughter, which only increased in volume at Yuri's obvious incomprehension.

Sensing that it was time to change direction again, Stinislav said, "That's very interesting, Yuri. Now, those were Xorainians, as you said. In your travels, did you happen to run into any Zlaimperian soldiers?"

Recalling, Yuri replied, "Yes, twice. Well, maybe three times, if you count when they were shooting at me …"

Laughter mixed with gasps of amazement.

"… But that would mean that I would have to count a third time I talked with a Xorainian soldier, possibly a hundred of them, but I remember one in particular." Explaining, he said, "We were in a trench and the Zlaimperians were attacking."

"What did this one say?" Stinislav asked.

"He wanted me to pass him some ammunition." Pause. "Actually, I think he wanted to call me *nevcheniy*, too!"

More laughter, one or two hysterically so.

"It seems to be unanimous then," Stinislav said to some appreciative chuckles. "But getting back to your encounters with the Zlaimperian soldiers, what happened there?"

"The first time they were travelling in a huge tank," Yuri recalled. "I was walking along the road. They stopped to question me." Indignantly he said, "They called me 'grandfather' and accused me of being a Nazi!" Finally, warming to the subject, heatedly, he said, "Let me tell you this: I'm no one's grandfather, *or* a Nazi. What nonsense that is! My own grandfather fought against the likes of *those* people in the Great Patriotic War!"

Dry chuckles from the audience along with more than a few angry scowls.

Amused, Stinislav asked, "Is that what you told them?"

"You're god damned right that's what I told them!" Yuri replied heatedly, then stopped, dismayed by the look on Stinislav's face. He was about to apologise when the audience erupted into raucous laughter that went on for more than a minute, regardless of the producers' frantic attempts to persuade them to stop.

Finally, when the interruption died down amidst happy groans and several people wiping mirthful tears from their eyes, Stinislav decided to join the bandwagon, and said, "That's telling the bastards!" and grinned at the appreciative laughter from the audience, adding, "My goodness, I certainly hope the censor caught that. Judging by our producer's complexion, we may have stirred the pot a little, eh?" Which, of course, set them off again. After a lengthy pause, while those in the crowd attempted to get themselves under control again, he said, "Okay, enough of that," and smirked, which earned him a few more titters. "Getting back to our conversation, Yuri, what did they do after that?"

Yuri frowned as if he didn't understand the question.

"What did they do? Why, they left, of course. They went their way, and I went mine."

Now Stinislav frowned.

"That's it? They just left?"

"Yes, of course. I was clearly not a Nazi, so they left."

"Just like that?"

"Just like that," Yuri confirmed, but then paused to consider. "Well, I *did* punch one of them and gave the others a piece of my mind, too, of course."

Astonished gasps.

Stinislav said, "Wait a minute, let me get this straight. You actually punched one of them ..."

"With my fist," Yuri volunteered, balling up said fist for all to see.

"With your fist, as you say," Stinislav said thoroughly in awe, "and you're still alive to tell the tale." Shaking his head appreciatively, he said, "I would ask what you told them, but under the circumstances ..." he grinned at the audience and was answered with a great gust of laughter, as they tried to imagine the colourful language this gutsy Homstooder had used to see off the enemy.

Gauging the moment to a T, Stinislav, ever the professional, turned to the camera, and said, "All joking aside, this is what I mean when I speak of the courage of the Xorainian citizenry. A single man faced down an entire tank crew and sent them scuttling off with their tails between their legs. That, my friends, is courage, and *that*, by God, is Xoraina!" And then, amidst a wild outburst of applause, he said, "We'll be right back with more of Yuri's incredible story, but first here's a message from our sponsor."

When the producer signalled that they were off the air, Stinislav turned to Yuri, and murmured. "That went better than I thought."

"Do you really think so?" Yuri asked, scarcely daring to believe.

"Kid," Stinislav said, even though he couldn't have been more than a few years older than Yuri, "If you can keep this up for the rest of the show, I'll make you famous. Just continue doing what you're doing, only," he cautioned, "you might want to go easy on the language, yes?"

"Yes," Yuri assured him, "of course." Then, with visions of fame and fortune dancing before his eyes, he almost didn't hear the producer announce that there were five seconds before the show would continue.

At the signal, Stinislav looked into the camera, and said, "Welcome back to the *Stinislav Berkos Show*. Tonight, we are talking with Mr Yuri Zavlov from Homstood about his extraordinary journey to the Capital. If you've just tuned in, I can assure you that you missed out on quite a tale; but keep your chin up, there's more to come!" Then, turning to Yuri, he said, "So, Yuri, you just told us about your encounter with a Zlaimperian tank and how you sent it packing. However, you mentioned a second encounter with the enemy. Could you tell us a little about that?"

Infused with confidence from Stinislav's praise, Yuri settled back comfortably in his chair.

"Of course, I'd be happy to. You see, it was after I had travelled across occupied territory when I was approaching the front around the Capital. I was caught in an artillery barrage where I received this." He gestured at the pinkish scar on his temple. "It's just a scratch, really, but it was enough to daze me for a while, I can assure you."

Sympathetic murmurs.

Stinislav asked, "And then what happened?"

"Well, I was wandering around in the forest, not really in my right mind, you understand?"

Stinislav nodded that he did.

"When I came upon three Zlaimperian soldiers questioning a Xorainian prisoner, and they weren't being too gentle about it, either, if you know what I mean."

A few angry growls from the audience.

"Yes, I agree," Yuri assured them. "Treating a defenceless prisoner like that, it's shameful, that's what it was, shameful. Once I thought that Xorainians and Zlaimperians were brothers but I was very wrong. Perhaps we had been at one time but no longer."

"What happened to this Xorainian prisoner?" Stinislav asked. "Was he killed?"

"Well you might ask," Yuri replied, "but no." Cocking his thumb over his shoulder, he said, "That's him over there, standing in the wings, Captain Olesky, who I had mentioned earlier."

This was met with furious applause, and nothing would do but Olesky had to step out from the wings and wave at the audience before they would settle down again.

"That's quite extraordinary," Stinislav allowed, "and I'm happy that Captain Olesky is still here with us." At this, he led another round of applause in appreciation for Olesky's survival. When the audience grew quiet again, he asked, "Then what happened? Did you rescue him?"

"Not I," Yuri grinned affably. "It was the pig."

Stunned silence.

"Wait a minute," Stinislav said, clearly confused. "Did you just say a pig rescued Captain Olesky?"

"*My* pig, to be exact," Yuri told him. "And it wasn't just Captain Olesky's life he saved, but my own, as well."

Astonished murmuring from the crowd.

"He's a very good pig, as pigs go," Yuri assured Stinislav, "although, of course, he was drunk on mushrooms at the time."

In the silence that followed, Yuri thought he could hear someone in the audience drop a pin.

Hesitantly, Stinislav ventured, "Am I to understand that you brought a pig with you all the way from Homstood?"

"Why yes, of course."

"Over five hundred kilometres?"

Yuri shrugged. "Give or take."

Stinislav turned to the audience to gauge their reaction. Their astonishment caused the silence to change to quiet murmuring, which gradually began to grow louder.

Turning back to Yuri, Stinislav asked, "What in Heaven's name for?"

Yuri frowned. The subject had been the centre of his world for so long, he sometimes forgot that not everyone was aware.

"Why, to protest the new shipping tax, of course." Adding, "It's as much his problem as it is mine."

The murmuring died down again, although there was one astonished outburst of laughter.

"It's very unfair," Yuri assured them, "and should be rescinded immediately." Belatedly, he thought to add, "That's why I came to the Capital in the first place."

*

Closer and closer those terrifying explosions were creeping toward where the pig cowered in fear. Little electric shocks shorted the synapses in his brain, causing memories of that terrible day in the forest to come surging back with a vengeance. He wanted to scream. He wanted to leap up and run away from that awful sound as fast as his legs could carry him. But most of all he wanted the squire to reassure him and tell him that everything was going to be all right, but the squire wasn't there.

For the first time ever since starting out on this journey, the pig began to entertain doubts that he would ever see Homstood again.

And the ghosts continued to whisper.

Chapter Twenty-five

With the possible exception of a true Homstooder, the fact that Yuri had undertaken his incredible journey in order to protest a shipping tax, unjust or not, struck the average citizen of Xoraina as unlikely and that included the television audience. Sensing this, Stinislav, a veteran journalist, decided to push back against this incredible story story.

Levelling his most sceptical gaze at Yuri, he said, "Do you really expect us to believe that you walked all the way to the Capital through a war zone – no, as you say, through *two* war zones – just so that you could ship your pig to market? Come Yuri, we are not so simple as to believe such a tale." Turning to the audience, he demanded, "Are we?"

Doubtful murmurs.

Turning back to Yuri, more as an interrogator than a journalist now, Stinislav asked, "So come, tell us the truth, why did you take such a terrible chance?"

Yuri reared back in his chair as if he had just been struck, surprise stamped on every aspect of his being.

"I *am* telling you the truth!" he insisted with feeling. "A true Homstooder doesn't lie!"

Skilfully, Stinislav didn't press his challenge. Instead, he chose a different tack.

The very voice of reason, he said, "But you must be aware of how odd it seems to place yourself in such terrible danger over a matter some might consider to be trivial?"

Still rankled, Yuri riposted, "Trivial to some, maybe, but it's not *their* farm they're trying to save, is it? No, it's *my* farm, *my* east field, *my* sunflowers, if only I could afford the seed!" More subdued now, he added, "But I couldn't afford the seed."

Confused murmurs.

Irritably, Yuri continued. "You see, it's quite simple: I need five demlos of sunflower seed to sow the east field. My friend, Vasily Pomkin, is willing to sell it to me for forty-five lakons per demlo which comes to two hundred and twenty-five lakons." Turning to the audience as he had seen Stinislav do, he peered past the glaring lights, and asked, "Are you with me so far?"

He was rewarded with a few tentative nods, but most faces retained curious frowns.

"Although this was well below market price, it was still sixty lakons more than I could afford."

"So, you needed the money to pay for the seed?" Stinislav asked.

"Yes! My other friend, Hans Gromp, told me that the market in Lofstov was paying two lakons per kilo for pigs. Since my pig weighs fifty point four three kilos, that would give me enough to pay for the seed and possibly make some repairs to my barn." He shrugged, "Who knows, if there was any money left over, I might even be able to repair the roof of my cottage."

Although some faces in the audience wore amused smiles (which, thankfully, Yuri couldn't see) most bore a more sympathetic expression. But whether disdainful or sympathetic, all remained silent.

Understanding finally registering, Stinislav asked, "But you hadn't counted on the new shipping tax?"

"In the past, it used to be a matter of a few coins," Yuri said, still morose at the memory. "But the shipping agent told me that it would now cost fifteen lakons," amidst the astonished gasps, he finished lamely with, "which is more than I can afford." Gesturing helplessly, he said, "In Homstood, we work hard and pay our taxes. We know that life isn't fair, but so what? Life has never been fair for the likes of us. However, there comes a time, if we think something is *very* unfair, we feel that we must be heard."

Quietly, Stinislav asked, "So, you decided that you must come to the Capital?"

Just as quietly, Yuri replied. "It was the village administrator, he told me it was my only option."

More sympathetic murmurs.

However, still intent on getting to the bottom of things, Stinislav wasn't satisfied.

"That is all very touching," he said, "and, at any other time, I could certainly understand why you would want to come to the Capital to protest this new tax but," he said, raising a finger to make the point, "these are not ordinary times, my friend. Every day your life was in terrible danger – you yourself described horrific scenes of death and destruction – and still you insisted on coming. Why?"

Speaking reflectively, Yuri said, "Because I thought I would not be troubled along the way. I told myself that this was not my war. I could see no reason for such a thing. I thought it was ridiculous, and I still think that – ridiculous and barbaric. I told myself Zlaimperians and Xorainians were brothers, and neither would pose any danger to me." He shrugged. "I was wrong, I readily admit it, so very wrong. After all that I have seen, I can tell you that the Zlaimperians are nothing but cold-blooded murderers.

"Once, a few days ago, Captain Olesky took me to the front so that I might speak with our soldiers. *They* are not murderers. They are heroes, willing to fight, even to die, for Xoraina."

"Yes," Stinislav replied, "so noble."

"Noble, yes," Yuri agreed, and then blundered. "But still we must make peace."

Gasps of astonishment and unsettled murmuring.

Stinislav's brow knit on the instant. "Did I hear you correctly, Yuri? Why would we make peace with such people? You yourself said that they were murderers."

Having put his head in the noose, Yuri tightened it with, "Because our young people are dying in their hundreds, in their thousands. They are the flower of our country, our hope for the future, and we're wasting them for no good end. Sooner or later Zlaimperia will win. It's inevitable."

Speechless for once, Stinislav's face was frozen in amazement. The silence of the audience was absolute for precisely two seconds. Then, all at once, everyone was on their feet shouting their outrage.

The outcry was deafening, and all of it directed at Yuri.

He sat in his chair, blinking his surprise. This reaction was far stronger than he had anticipated. The din of so many angry voices, all shouting at once, was impossible to decipher as a whole, but he thought he heard more than one cry, "Take that *nevcheniy* bastard outside and shoot him!"

Rising to his feet, he held out his hands placatingly, shouting, "But surely it's obvious. It can't be otherwise. The perimeter around the Capital is shrinking every day in spite of the valiant efforts of our army. We must be honest with ourselves; the situation is not sustainable!"

It was doubtful if anyone could have heard what he said, but the outrage of the audience actually increased until Yuri thought he could feel vibrations of their wrath rise up through the very floor of the building.

The situation was precarious and in imminent danger of becoming violent. Indeed, one or two from the audience-turned-angry-mob attempted to reach him, hands extended like claws, but were held back by some of the crew. However, it was clear it wouldn't be long before they were overwhelmed.

Seeking inspiration, Yuri looked up at the ceiling and frowned at a light fixture swaying back and forth, causing it to flicker.

"Stupid man," someone screamed, "you've no right to talk that way. My son died for this country, and I won't have you sully his memory!"

A lesser man would have beat a hasty retreat, and although the notion was appealing, Yuri, like any true Homstooder, stood his ground, his stubborn sense of justice rising to the fore.

"It isn't my intention to sully the memory of anyone," he cried. "But I don't want your son's sacrifice to be repeated by others. The insanity must stop!"

"You're telling me that he died for nothing?"

Never known for his diplomatic qualities, Yuri replied, "Yes!"

"You bastard," the angry voice shouted, "I'm going to kill you with my bare hands!"

"Do I not have a right to my opinion?" Yuri shouted back.

"You have a right to be soundly thrashed!" came the enraged reply.

"And a right to be shot!" shouted another, which was met with tumultuous cries of approval.

More and more frequently, Yuri could feel the vibrations rising from the floor ... and a distinctly separate one coming from his breast.

Frantic, with the show threatening to spin out of control, he turned to Olesky for aid just as he always had ever since arriving in the Capital; but the captain, his face buried in his hands, wasn't looking. Clearly, there would be no help from that quarter.

Then, finally, having recovered from his astonishment, Stinislav raced to the front of the stage, arms outstretched, pleading for the crowd to settle. So great was the uproar that at first he was ignored, but so commanding was his presence that gradually, one by one, they began to acquiesce.

Oddly, however, the vibrations continued, both from the floor and from Yuri's breast.

Eventually, the crowd began to quiet until he could hear that the vibration was accompanied by a ringing sound. Everyone else in the studio could hear it, too. Curious, Yuri reached inside his shirt ... and withdrew his hand holding the defence minister's phone.

It was ringing.

Yuri stared at the instrument with the same amazement Stinislav had stared at *him* only moments earlier. Left with the shock of his encounter with the minister, followed by the terror of being in the studio in front of the entire nation, he had forgotten all about that one little detail.

Sensing that he was in serious trouble now, he held the phone out to Stinislav, offering it to him.

"Here," he said. "I don't want it."

Frowning angrily, for in all his years on television, not once had Stinislav's audience got so out of control and he, rightly, placed the blame squarely on Yuri's shoulders.

"Here, give it to me," he said, snatching the phone from Yuri's hand. Glancing at the screen, he demanded, "Didn't anyone backstage tell you that you're not supposed to …"

At this point he stopped, his eyes growing wide with shock. Instead of looking at Yuri, slowly, he turned to face the audience.

Holding up the phone for all to see, he said, "It's a text message," and his professionalism wouldn't allow him not to pause for effect, "from the Zlaimperian dictator himself!"

The audience inhaled as one. On every face was a look of utter astonishment.

Then all eyes swivelled to Yuri.

"It's not mine," he explained weakly.

"Let's get him!" someone cried, and might well have done, for the studio crew, astonished as everyone else, no longer showed any intention of trying to hold them back; but at that very moment, several soldiers stormed onto the stage, followed by a man dressed in the uniform of a Xorainian general.

"SILENCE!" he thundered, and the audience, quelled by his authority, obeyed.

Addressing Yuri in a voice loud enough for all to hear, the general said, "Yuri Yurivich, you are to be commended, for you have rendered your country a great service."

Yuri, and a good many of the audience, managed to gape but that was all.

"Allow me to introduce myself," this newcomer said. "My name is General Antonenko. It was I who you so cleverly informed of the nefarious intentions of a certain minister."

Having overheard, the audience buzzed with confused murmuring.

Antonenko continued. "It was during your meeting with the minister just this morning. I had sent him a text apparently at the same time he was divulging his information. Your quick thinking saved the day by recording the conversation." Noting Yuri's uncomprehending expression, the general produced his own phone, touched the screen, and said, "Here, listen for yourself."

Spellbound, Yuri listened. Although the first voice he heard (his own) was noticeably nervous, the minister's angry response erupted from the speaker loud and clear.

Yuri: *"A-and just how am I to expose the president, Excellency?"*

Minister of Defence: *"You defame the bastard! You tell the country that he's leading them down a road to destruction, that the situation is hopeless, and that he alone is responsible! You bury him with lies if you have to. I don't give a damn. After that you can leave the rest to me. Do I make myself clear? Good! And be sure that you do, otherwise it will go hard for you, Mr Zavlov, very hard, indeed. Never forget that. Now, get out, I have much to see to."*

General Antonenko shut off the recording, just as the entire building vibrated and Yuri felt another tremor run through his body. Glancing around, he saw that, while a handful of people appeared to have noticed it, too, most eyes were still on him and the general.

While the audience continued with their astonished murmuring, Antonenko said, "I don't know how you came into the possession of the minister's phone and," dipping Yuri a wink, added, "perhaps that's just as well, eh?"

Puzzled, Yuri frowned, and asked, "But how did you know it was me?"

Antonenko shrugged. "We made a few calls. The minister's secretary told us that he was in a private meeting with you at the time and said that you had left in an – how shall I say? – *unsettled* state? As for the rest, a visit to Lieutenant Shevchenko, the minister's equerry, was enough to confirm your voice on the recording."

Still confused, Yuri said, "But I didn't record our conversation ..." and then he stopped as he recalled his fumbling with the minister's phone just prior to tucking it into his shirt.

Guessing correctly at Yuri's hesitation, the general laughed, and said, "Ah, then you recorded the conversation by accident! I've often done the same thing myself." Then, shaking his head woefully, he said, "It's a pity; while this may be enough to drive the Minister of Defence from office, and possibly cause his political allies to distance themselves, there's not enough evidence here to send him to prison." More to himself than anyone, he added, "What we need is something damning."

It was then that Stinislav, who had been studying the contents of the minister's phone, spoke, his voice taut with excitement.

"I think that you may have it now, General,," he said, offering him the minister's phone.

There was a text displayed across the screen, and in the moment it took to read it, Antonenko's face grew visibly pale. Just as the building gave another shudder, he looked at Yuri, and said, "It's from the Zlaimperian dictator." Then, offering him the phone, he invited, "Here, see for yourself."

The building gave another shudder, this time eliciting an outcry from the audience. At the same time Yuri's subconscious identified the mysterious trembling as the result of artillery fire, and it was getting closer.

Gazing into the screen, below the dictator's name, he saw a text consisting of little more than a single line: *"Has your puppet performed his task?"*

The general's face twisted into an ugly grimace suffused with the triumph of vengeance.

"We've got him!" he cried.

However, before Yuri could reply, a soldier, with his face blackened, and blood seeping through a bandage inexpertly wound around his arm, burst onto the stage, presenting himself to the general.

"The Zlaimperians have broken through the perimeter!" he cried.

*

The explosions were coming closer and closer, each one shaking the building that housed the pig's enclosure, causing continuous clouds of dust to drift down from the rafters.

Terrified, the pig cowered in a corner, not daring to open his eyes. It was happening again, just as it had that terrible day in the forest. The blinding flashes closely followed by the explosions, so near they had been deafening, and how could he ever forget the searing pain as something cut into his flesh. Oh, the pain! Oh, the agony! Oh, the terror of it all, and he wasn't alone. All around him he could smell fear as workers ran hither and thither, seeking shelter.

Then memory became reality as a piercing whistle became a blinding flash as something penetrated the roof, the explosion that followed destroying everything in its path.

It was the neatly stacked bales of hay at the edge of his enclosure that saved him, having absorbed most of the blast, but still the pig was driven to his knees, rendering him senseless.

He came to a moment later, dazed and confused as he watched the resulting flames already beginning to devour the barn and its contents. However, it wasn't until they were licking at the planks of his enclosure that his panic asserted itself with a vengeance.

Squealing in terror, he ran blindly, scarcely noticing as the well-chewed boards gave way, and he was careening toward the open door.

With angry flames and the wails of ghosts at his heels.

Chapter Twenty-six

Yuri hadn't waited to be asked or, indeed, given much thought to his actions, when, in the face of the emergency, General Antonenko had ordered every available man to the front. He had simply attached himself to Captain Olesky as he raced outside in search of transport. Indeed, the captain showed no surprise when he was able to flag down a taxi and Yuri bundled in with him.

After he'd given the cabbie terse directions, to no apparent person in particular, he said, "The general told me that the bastards had broken through in the Bravo sector. That's where my boys are," but Yuri felt sure that he'd been speaking to him.

The taxi sped through the darkened streets of the Capital accompanied by a chorus of a racing engine and burning rubber. They arrived at the battalion headquarters in record time, but the driver wouldn't accept any payment. Instead, he said, "Stop those fuckers!" and set off back to the city, leaving in his wake the sound of screaming tires and choice invective aimed at the advancing Zlaimperians.

"Come on," Olesky said, "we've got to report to the colonel," and sprinted off into the night with Yuri hard at his heels.

However, after they had rounded a final corner, they were greeted with a devastating sight that caused Yuri's heart to sink like a stone. There before them, the headquarters building was little more than a burnt-out shell.

"Shit!" Olesky cried, and led the way forward. Kicking the remnants of the door open, the captain switched his phone to the flashlight mode and led the way inside.

All was darkness with the stench of smoke and something that smelled suspiciously like roasted meat. Soon they were choking from the still smouldering wreckage and stumbling over bodies, most charred beyond recognition. They found the adjutant on his back staring sightlessly up at the gaping hole in the roof and the colonel sitting at his desk, with what was left of his face resting on its surface.

Grimly, Olesky said, "There's nothing we can do here," and led the way back out to where the air was much cleaner.

Reaching a decision, Olesky said, "We'd best kit up. Let's see if the armoury is still standing," and set off again.

They found the building deserted, but more or less intact, although a near miss from an artillery shell had shattered the windows and blown the door off its hinges. Stepping inside, Olesky led them unerringly toward a room stocked with the accoutrements of war. Moving from shelf to shelf, he chose various items of equipment and handed them to his companion.

"Vest, helmet, and ammunition pouches. That'll have to do for now. Follow me," he said, leading them to an adjoining room. Seconds later, Yuri found that a Kalashnikov had been thrust into his hands. "Don't drop it," Olesky warned, "or even try to load it until I have time to show you how, understand?" Yuri replied with a single, tense nod and they raced outside again.

Caught momentarily in indecision, Olesky called out to a soldier approaching at a run; the man didn't seem to hear him and only stopped when Olesky grabbed him by the arm.

"Where's my company?" he demanded.

The soldier turned to him, eyes wide with terror.

"How the fuck should I know?" he shot back. "Everyone's dead, the colonel, my captain, sergeant, my comrades, they're all dead!" He tried to move on, but Olesky wouldn't release his grip on his arm.

"Where are you going, lad?"

The man, scarcely more than a boy, stared at the captain as if he'd just lost his mind.

Pointing in the direction from where he had just come, he cried, "Away from there!" and broke down in tears. "Tanks, rockets, artillery," he sobbed, "they just kept coming at us, wave upon wave of the bastards, until most of us were dead. Those of us who were left ran for our lives!"

"What's your name, soldier?" Olesky demanded, hoping that by referring to him as such would serve to stiffen his spine.

The trick seemed to work, if only momentarily, as the boy dried his eyes, and replied, "Bondar." Belatedly noticing the bars on Olesky's epaulettes, he thought to add, "sir."

"Right, Bondar, you've still got your rifle, do you? Excellent. Come with me."

"But, sir," the boy confessed, "I'm afraid."

To which Olesky replied, "So am I, Bondar. So am I." Then, not unkindly, he said, "Come along, now, let's get moving." But when he paused to check some minutes later, the boy was gone, his allotment of courage having been worn so thin that there wasn't enough left for him to be of any further use that evening.

Putting the matter from his mind, Olesky reasoned that, in lieu of finding his own company, the best course of action was to head to where the fighting was most fierce. Judging by the din of explosions and the rattle of small arms fire coming from the direction Bondar had just vacated, it was a good guess that that would be the place to start.

They had barely covered a few hundred metres when they were bracketed by a stick of mortar bombs, some falling uncomfortably close. At the same time, Olesky spotted a trench just a few metres away.

"Come on!" he cried, and leading the way forward, dove headlong into it, with Yuri tumbling in a split-second later.

"You're late, Captain," Kuzma said, adding, "You didn't bring much in the way of reinforcements, did you?"

Struggling to his feet, Olesky grasped his friend by the shoulders. "Kuzma, what luck! It's good to see you."

This was answered by an evil grin and, "Careful, Captain, the others might get jealous."

Paying the feeble jest scant recognition, Olesky wasted very little time., "Who's in charge here?"

"Well," Kuzma replied, "considering that Lieutenant Melnyk is dead and all the sergeants with him, I would guess that it's Kovalenko, if he's still alive."

"Where is he?"

Gesturing with a twitch of his head down the length of the trench, Kuzma said, "Last I saw, somewhere down there."

"Get him."

"You bet," and the incorrigible fellow disappeared down the line, returning minutes later with the gigantic Corporal Kovalenko in tow.

After a jubilant bellow of "Captain!" and Olesky being subjected to another bone-crunching embrace, it was time to get down to business.

Hunkering down on the floor of the trench, Olesky said, "So, tell me, Illya, what's the situation?"

The corporal didn't mince words. "It's bad, sir, they hit us with everything they had, artillery, missiles, you name it, and in far greater numbers than ever before. We lost the lieutenant and twenty percent of the company before the bastards even sent in the infantry. As you know, we were in support of the front line but, considering our casualties, you can imagine what theirs must have been. All we saw of them was the odd man running away. Considering that the enemy's advance hasn't been checked, we can only assume that the others must either have been taken prisoner or they're dead."

Remembering how broken Bondar had been, Olesky merely said, "Go on."

"They came at us with tanks and infantry, hordes of them. Our own artillery must be knocked out because there was nothing to oppose them except us. We had some tank support to begin with but they didn't last. I tell you, sir, nothing could survive in the open for very long in that barrage." Visibly shaken, the corporal passed a hand over his brow, and continued. "So, we fought on alone, as hard as we could, and managed to account for a good many of them, but for every one of theirs that fell, two more took his place. Meanwhile, our own casualties continued to mount. In the end, we had to fall back, but the pressure was so great that we lost more men over the open ground."

"What's our present strength?"

Kovalenko shook his head. "I don't know, sir. Seventy percent? Maybe less."

Absorbing this horrible news, Olesky asked, "What is your opinion, Illya? Can we hold?"

Again, the corporal shook his head uncertainly. "You know as well as I do, sir. These are good lads here, but they've been taking a beating for weeks now." He shook his head yet again. "Tonight, well, we were hit harder than we've ever been hit before. You know what they say about courage being finite, yes? Right now, we're running close to empty." He swore, and added, "Like I said, sir, these are good lads, and they're willing to fight, but they need hope. They have to believe they can win." Gesturing into the darkness of no man's land, he said, "And I just don't see that happening any time soon." Frustrated beyond endurance, he pounded his massive fist into the wall of the trench. "What we need, sir, is a fucking hero!"

For the first time since he'd known him, Yuri saw that Olesky was visibly shaken by the news but seemed determined to carry on in spite of everything.

"Look, reinforcements are coming," he promised. "Until then, we'll hold on as long as we can. Now tell me, what do we have for munitions, everything from machineguns to mortars, and MANPADS, how many of those do we have left? There must be something we can throw at the tanks when they come."

While Illya provided the answer (which was meagre enough) Yuri sidled up to Kuzma, who peered at Yuri in the dubious illumination of a star shell bursting overhead.

"Why, if it isn't that old-timer from two weeks ago. What the hell are you doing here?"

"That's a good question," Yuri conceded, dazed by the nightmare surrounding him. Then, offering Kuzma his rifle, apologetically, he said, "Olesky said that he would show me how to use this but, as you can see, he's busy. So, I was wondering ..."

Taking the hint, Kuzma snatched the rifle out of Yuri's hands with a look of disgust. Muttering something about what the army was coming to these days, he plucked a magazine from one of Yuri's pouches, and said, "Okay, pay attention." Holding up the magazine, he said, "This contains your bullets …"

"I know that," Yuri replied, managing to sound indignant.

"I don't know what you fucking know and what you don't know," Kuzma retorted unapologetically, "and there's no time to find out. So, I'm going to assume you don't know shit, okay? Right, so this is a magazine." Holding it to the loading chamber on the underside of the rifle, he said, "It goes in here, like this." He slapped the magazine into the chamber, saying, "Make sure you shove it in good and hard …" and stopped, with an evil grin at the unexpected double entendre. Elbowing Yuri in the ribs, he chortled like a satyr, and said, "Shove it in good and hard, get it? Laugh it up, Father, that was funny!" Then, chuckling, he wagged his head in appreciation of his supposed cleverness.

Yuri, who had never been gifted with much of a sense of humour, was both appalled by the joke as well as its timing.

Noting this, Kuzma shrugged his disappointment, and said, "Anyway, make sure it's well-seated, otherwise you're just begging for the fucking thing to jam. With me so far?"

Belatedly realising that Kuzma might not be able to see him nod, Yuri replied, "Yes."

"Good." Then, pulling back and releasing the bolt, Kuzma said, "Now you've got a round up the spout." Flicking a switch on the side, he added, "This is the safety. Remember to switch it off before you fire." Then, examining it more closely, he indicated another switch. "This sets it to automatic or semi-automatic. That means …"

"I know what it means," Yuri said.

Kuzma nodded. "Leave it on semi-auto. We're short of ammunition as it is." Holding up the rifle, he peered through the sights. "Make sure the stock is jammed tight against your shoulder, then just aim and squeeze the trigger in bursts of three. Got it?"

"Got it," Yuri replied.

Whereupon, Kuzma tossed the rifle back (which Yuri only just managed to catch) and said, "Welcome to the Armed Forces of Xoraina, Father. Oh, and one other thing ..."

"Yes?"

"It's *Captain* Olesky, got it? Or Captain, or 'sir.' Not just Olesky. The man deserves some respect."

Humbled, Yuri replied, "I hear you."

By now, the captain had finished speaking with Kovalenko and been brought up to date. He said, "Very well, Corporal. Disperse the machine guns equally down the line and place the mortar crew in the centre. Understood?"

After Illya left, Kuzma sidled up to Olesky, and asked, "What are your orders, Captain?"

"Simple enough," Olesky replied. "We wait."

"Wait? Is that all?"

Levelling his rifle over the parapet, Olesky peered through the sights, and said, "Either our reinforcements arrive on time, or ..." and left the rest unspoken.

Feeling a shiver run down his spine, Yuri tried to swallow, but his mouth had suddenly gone as dry as he could ever remember. Therefore, finding himself with nothing left to say, he stepped to the parapet alongside his captain and followed suit.

*

Street after street, the pig ran to escape from the cries of the ghosts and the shrieks of the demons. Racing blindly down one dark pathway after another, his hooves rattled a rapid tattoo on the broken pavement. But brilliant flashes and horrifying explosions continued to dog him everywhere he went. Beyond panic, he gave in to his fear, squealing at the top of his lungs, expecting at any moment to feel a cold, lifeless hand on his back to carry him down to the Old Place.

Squealing loud enough to wake the dead (who, in truth, were already awake) he found a final burst of energy and ran, and ran, and ran. Just when he thought he was going to collapse from exhaustion, he burst through a maze of streets, and came to an abrupt stop, while he stared with uncomprehending amazement.

For as far as he could see the entire world was on fire.

Chapter Twenty-seven

Apart from distant sporadic small-arms fire, at the moment, all was relatively quiet in the sector. Yuri fervently hoped that it remained so.

Through the eerie ghost light of star shells, he could just make out the ground in front of him and failed to gain any encouragement from it.

They were situated on the very outskirts of the Capital, pushed back by the relentless pressure of the Zlaimperian advance. To his front, Yuri could see the smouldering remains of building after building, broken beyond repair, and a street cratered by artillery. The ground had been especially shredded around a single Xorainian tank, orange flames still billowing from where its turret had once been.

"So, why did you come?" For Olesky, waiting was the most difficult part of all. Once he had given his orders he was desperate for conversation.

"To tell you the truth, I don't really know," Yuri replied. "I still don't believe in this war."

"And yet here you are," Olesky pointed out.

"Yes," Yuri agreed, "here I am." Musing, he said, "I doubt if anyone in this trench believes in it, either."

"On the contrary," Olesky said, "we are all highly motivated."

"Oh, I don't mean that," Yuri assured him. "I'm quite impressed with their determination. What I mean is they would rather there was no war at all."

Olesky was silent, so Yuri continued.

Indicating the far side of no man's land, he said, "I'll even go further and say that I very much doubt if the Zlaimperians want any of this, either."

Quipping, Olesky said, "Why don't you ask one of them?"

Pondering the question seriously, Yuri replied, "Maybe I will."

Pointing out the obvious, Olesky said, "If you're still alive to get the chance."

"Yes," Yuri agreed, "there's always that; but the point I'm trying to make is that no one really wants to be here. It's the powerful who are the cause of it all."

"In this case, just one man."

"Just one man," Yuri repeated, with a note of wonder. "How is that possible?"

Olesky shrugged, also indicating the Zlaimperian side. "They allow it."

Yuri frowned. "Well, they shouldn't, should they?"

Olesky offered a sad smile. "No, they shouldn't."

After a lengthening silence, Yuri asked, "Do you still feel that it's not inevitable that they will win?"

Olesky shifted uncomfortably, gripping his rifle with renewed meaning. "At least they'll know they were in a fight if they do."

"But why?" Yuri asked. "Why must so many throw away their lives for a cause that must be lost?"

Olesky tilted his head so that he could see his friend. "Like I said, here you are. Perhaps that is a question *you* should answer, not me."

"Yes," Yuri allowed, "you are right, but I'm not sure that I can. After all the killing has stopped, it still won't be any easier to get my pig to market."

"If we win," Olesky suggested, "at least you can still try."

Frowning, Yuri pondered over this a good deal, and said, "You're speaking of freedom, Captain. Such a grand idea, freedom, but listen to me: I'm only a poor farmer. What is freedom to the poor? What use have we for grand ideas? Whoever wins, I will be just as poor as I am today, or my ancestors were in the past."

Acknowledging the point, Olesky said, "I hear you, Yuri Yurivich. That is an issue that must be addressed." Then, reciting from memory, he said, "*No man on earth is truly free; all are slaves of money or necessity. Public opinion or fear of prosecution forces each one, against his conscience, to conform.*"

"Yes," Yuri said, "those are my thoughts exactly."

"Euripides would be relieved to hear it," Olesky said dryly, before continuing. "I can't find fault with his words even though I don't embrace them as you seem to. You and I can agree that we must learn to live with our imperfections, but that's where it ends. Whereas you regard them as carved in stone, I will never resign myself to accepting that we can never change. I believe that we must constantly strive to improve who and what we are, both as individuals and as a social order." Quoting again, he said, "We must continue to have '*an infinite expectation of the dawn.*' Which means that we must become accustomed to believing in a better future."

"Was that more Euripides?"

Olesky offered a dry chuckle. "No, just some badly paraphrased Thoreau."

Yuri said, "It is not my intention to mock you, Captain, but you've set your sites rather high."

Olesky snorted another dry chuckle. "Indeed, I have, but that's all the more reason never to stop trying." Then, more seriously, he said, "See here, Yuri, I freely admit that everyone wears chains to some extent, that is not the question, but consider this: some chains are heavier than others."

The furrows in Yuri's forehead deepened. "Why is that do you suppose?"

"It is the same as what I said earlier, about the consequences of one man's hubris: it is because the Zlaimperian people have allowed themselves to be bound by the heaviest chains of all."

Yuri was about to reply, but just then, they were distracted by a sound that both men knew well – the sinister squeal of tracked vehicles approaching.

At that point the conversation was over. Speaking softly, Captain Olesky said, "Illya?"

Corporal Kovalenko, who had been standing on the other side of Olesky throughout the debate, saying nothing, but bored to tears, answered, "Captain?"

"Tell everyone to hold their fire until I give the signal."

"Very good, sir."

"Oh, and corporal."

"Sir?"

"Bring up the new American missiles. I think we're going to need them."

*

The squealing of the tracks from the approaching tanks was quite loud now, as well as the muscular rumble of their engines. Yuri could count three of the monsters illuminated in the artificial glow of a star shell. Furtive shadows, drifting to and fro behind their advance, indicated that they were supported by infantry, as well.

Yuri swallowed hard, wishing that he had thought to bring a water bottle with him. Fear had a way of making a man thirsty.

Now the lead tank opened fire and the remains of a building to their front disappeared in a flash of brilliant flame, the force of the explosion causing the ground to tremble. In an effort to discover the exact whereabouts of the Xorainians, it was attempting to provoke a response.

Now all three tanks opened fire, with machine guns as well as their cannon, spraying waves of bullets over Yuri's head, outlined by brilliant streams of tracers.

Still Olesky didn't give the signal. Instead, he calmly stood in the trench with the launching tube of the anti-tank missile resting on his shoulder, waiting.

"If anyone's interested in my opinion," Yuri murmured nervously, "I think now would be a good time to open fire."

Peering through the sights, the captain smiled but did not reply.

Meanwhile, the Zlaimperians drew nearer.

The fire from the tanks was incessant now, the ground trembling by the mere rumbling presence of the monsters. Yuri could feel his legs trembling, too, but whether that was from the ground or from fear he wasn't entirely sure. He hoped that it was from the former but suspected that it might not be the case.

Dirt and gravel flew up from the ground in front of him, stitched by machinegun fire as the enemy continued in their efforts to seek them out. *'Never mind, you Zlaimperian bastards,'* Yuri thought vengefully, *'you'll find out soon enough,'* but couldn't help adding nervously, *'but when?'*

At that moment, there came a low growl from the launcher on Olesky's shoulder as it locked onto its target, followed by a loud 'WHOOSH' and a streak of light as the missile leapt from the tube and raced toward the unsuspecting tank like an avenging angel. Seconds later, other missiles followed suit up and down the Xorainian line. At the same time, their machine guns came to life, hammering streams of tracer into the gaps between the armoured vehicles. Then everyone opened fire and all was an indescribable din.

Yuri peered through his sights at one of the flitting shadows and squeezed the trigger as Kuzma had taught him, only remembering to release the safety when nothing happened. His concentration was such that he wasn't even aware when, one after the other, all three tanks exploded, or that the massive percussions had driven him to his knees; but he was up again and firing without actually realising that he had fallen. The adrenaline racing through his body was such that, all he could think of was the urgent need to stop the enemy.

With their tanks burning furiously now, depriving them of their cover, the only options the Zlaimperians had was to retreat or advance without them. To stay where they were would only mean they were a prime target for the one last mortar the Xorainians still retained. However, by now, they could see that the single trench causing so much havoc was just metres away. Flush with the success he had thus far enjoyed, the Zlaimperian commander gave his answer.

A great shout erupted out of the night and the ground between the trench and the blazing tanks was suddenly filled with Zlaimperian soldiers dashing forward.

The firing in the trench redoubled sending a hail of bullets into the invaders, cutting them down in swaths, but still they came on, desperately attempting to come to grips with the Xorainians.

Aiming carefully, Yuri rapidly squeezed the trigger – one, two, three – the butt of the Kalashnikov slamming into his shoulder with every round. He swivelled to the next screaming figure – one, two, three – and on to the next. There was no time to see if he had actually hit what he was aiming at – that screaming horde was approaching closer by the second – there was only time to fire and fire and fire again and hope that it was enough.

As it turned out, it very nearly wasn't.

A giant Zlaimperian – almost as big as Kovalenko – emerged from the haze of smoke and confusion, his face twisted with fury as he screamed his challenge. To Yuri, it seemed that he was charging directly toward him.

With growing panic, he squeezed the trigger, again and again, but still the brute came on. It was all that Yuri could do to stand his ground when every instinct he possessed told him to throw away his rifle and run. Forcing himself to concentrate, he tried to ignore the bursts of flame erupting from the muzzle of the Zlaimperian's rifle, while he desperately sought to kill this man who was just as desperately trying to kill him. A bullet whizzed past his ear, another tugged at his sleeve as he levelled his weapon, concentrating on a spot just above the man's protective vest, and squeezed the trigger.

And still the man came on.

Somewhere between affronted and terrified, Yuri glared at the screaming Zlaimperian over his sights, unable to believe that he had missed. At the same time, his bladder gave way, and he was vaguely aware of a warmth beginning to spread from his groin. Before he could attempt one last shot, the Zlaimperian dropped like a stone, barely ten metres from the trench, a bullet from Kuzma's rifle having torn out his throat.

That was as close as any Zlaimperian came during the assault. After that man fell, those of his comrades who still lived began to melt away, firing sporadically as they retreated. Eventually Olesky gave the order to cease fire, and the night grew eerily silent. The Zlaimperians had fled the field, leaving in their wake the dead, the dying, and three furiously burning tanks.

Yuri remained on high alert, his rifle levelled, ready for danger from every corner, even as his body shook like a leaf.

At his side, Kuzma said, "Your rifle, Father."

Reluctant to tear his eyes away from the battlefield, Yuri risked a quick glance and saw Kuzma standing, unconcerned, with his hand held out expectantly.

Turning back, eyes scanning the ground for any sudden Zlaimperian incursions, he said, "They could be back at any time."

Unperturbed, Kuzma merely said, "Please."

Uncertain now, Yuri asked, "Are you sure?" but instead of replying, Kuzma continued to hold out his hand, inviting Yuri to pass him his rifle.

Slowly, tentatively, reluctantly, Yuri complied.

Seizing the gun, Kuzma ejected the empty magazine, slapped in a fresh one, flipped the switch to safety, and handed it back.

"You ran out of ammunition several minutes ago," he said, and, glancing down, helpfully added, "Also, you've soiled yourself." After which he returned to his post.

Yuri blinked, and thought, '*So, that's why the bastard wouldn't die.*' Realising how close he'd come to being a victim of his own negligence caused his stomach to suddenly convulse and the remains of his last meal splattered around and over his boots. He'd just learned a valuable lesson and was extremely thankful that he was still alive to realise it.

"You all right, Father?" It was Illya this time.

Still shaken, Yuri related what had just taken place and, to his surprise, the hulking corporal bellowed with laughter.

"Par for the course," he chuckled. "The first time I saw action Kuzma had to save my life, too." Then, seized with a thought, first he checked the ground at Yuri's feet, and then his groin. "Yep," he said, nodding, "that, too."

Helpless, Yuri was floundering to reply when Captain Olesky came navigating his way up the crowded trench.

"Not too bad," he allowed, "two dead and twice as many wounded." Gazing out over the carnage that had been the Zlaimperian assault, he said, "I'd say we gave better than we got."

"Far better, sir," Illya agreed.

Turning to his corporal, Olesky said, "Check the ammunition, would you? Make sure that it's distributed evenly. One other thing …"

"Yes, Captain?"

"No one is to leave the trench, is that understood?" Explaining, he said, "I think we can expect to receive a barrage at any moment."

"Sir!" Illya was about to take his leave when he noticed the still-shocked expression on Yuri's face. "Don't worry, Father, you'll be fine … as long as you stay alive." Then, with a final wink, he was gone.

Puzzled, Olesky watched him go before turning back to Yuri.

"What was that all about?" he asked. After Yuri told him, he grinned, and said, "Don't let it bother you. Kuzma shit his pants during *his* first action, *and* wet himself, besides."

Appalled, Yuri said, "I might have been killed."

"Yes," Olesky agreed, "you might have been, but you weren't." More brusquely, he said, "Enough of that for now, we've got bigger fish to fry."

Yuri, who, at the moment, found it difficult to comprehend that there could be anything of more importance than his life, said, "Do you really think this isn't the end of it, that they're actually going to bombard us?"

"I think that's a definite possibility," Olesky replied, "They'll want to soften us up before they try again." Then, gazing at the luminous dial of his wristwatch, he said, "We have to hold on until …" Cocking his head as if to listen, he stopped in mid-sentence and cried, "Get down!" shoving Yuri to the floor of the trench.

Finding his face ground into a mixture of mud and his own vomit, Yuri philosophically supposed that this was no more than what a true Homstooder could expect, just as the ground shook with a deafening roar, and a shower of earth rained down on his back.

The barrage, that Captain Olesky predicted, had begun.

*

More explosions, more ghosts, more screaming. Brilliant flashes of light seared the pig's retinas as he continued his mindless charge in his effort to escape. He no longer took note if he was running away from or toward the menace; he was only aware that he had to keep running and squealing, to prove to himself that he was still alive. Oh, what wouldn't he give to be with the squire right now?

He had been running so long that he was past the point of exhaustion. His tongue lolled from the side of his mouth, the hairs on his back stood up like prickly spines, and his tail streamed out behind him like a useless appendage. Inevitably, his pace began to slow.

But then, there came an unholy scream followed by the most gigantic explosion of all, showering him with earth, and a searing burn as a splinter of shrapnel cut through his cheek.

Squealing with panic and pain, he ran on, and on, and on.

Chapter Twenty-eight

If Yuri had been terrified before, there was no word to adequately describe how he felt now.

Round after round, missiles slammed in and around the narrow trench, Xoraina's last bastion before the Zlaimperian hordes broke through into the Capital. As far as Yuri was concerned, they could have it and welcome.

They had taken casualties, he was sure of it, judging by the agonized screams he had heard over the ear-splitting explosions up and down the line. He had endured this for hours, until the coming of the dawn, and he'd long-since reached the conclusion that he couldn't take any more. And yet the shells continued to rain down, and somehow, he continued to endure.

The captain had told him that they must stay alert, that the Zlaimperians would attack under the cover of the barrage; but it was impossible. The barrage was so intense that the shells fell like rain, the ground constantly erupting in blossoms of fire and earth and a continuous hail of shrapnel. To a man, the Xorainians cowered in their trench, praying that none of those death-dealing missiles would find them.

With the coming of first light, Olesky roused himself enough to peer over the lip of the parapet, crying "Stay sharp, men!" but was immediately flung to the back of the trench by a whirling piece of shrapnel. Stunned, his helmet a shredded ruin, his legs folded under him as he slowly sank to the ground.

Appalled, Yuri stared at the captain, willing him to rise again, but Olesky continued to lay where he'd fallen, exhibiting no sign of life. Elsewhere, Xorainian soldiers huddled in the trench, instinctively shielding their heads against the most fierce barrage they'd ever experienced. Every one of them praying for it to end.

But it didn't end. Instead, it increased.

There came a roar like a thousand locomotives and the sky was crisscrossed with the fiery trails of rockets arcing over their heads, plunging down to seek them out. The ground was a constant tremble now, immediately dislodging anyone who found the courage to scramble to his feet.

Now missiles were landing in front of the trench, as well, chewing up the ground that the Zlaimperians had recently abandoned, filling the air with shrapnel and the limbs of those who had already fallen in the initial charge. One of the cursed projectiles slammed into the ground a few metres from the Xorainian position, deafening scores with the explosion and collapsing that section of the trench, abruptly silencing the terrified cries of the Xorainian soldiers as they were buried alive.

On the far side of a traverse, Corporal Kovalenko, furious at their helplessness, leapt to his feet, screaming defiance. For a brief moment Yuri saw the massive giant, outlined by the oily flames of a burning tank, arm outstretched, pointing accusingly at the enemy. Then there was a brilliant flash and a deafening explosion at his exact position. Yuri ducked instinctively behind the parapet; when he lifted his head again, Kovalenko had vanished.

Struck dumb with shock, Yuri was unaware of the tears streaming down his face, or of his own rage at the madness of it all. This was beyond all human endurance. To attempt to continue was utter insanity. Acting without thinking, he rose to his knees, then seizing the wall of the trench, he clawed his way up until he could peer over the top.

Scanning from right to left, he saw that the ground had been chewed into a moonscape of craters. The burnt-out hulks of the three Zlaimperian tanks had been reduced to piles of twisted metal, no longer recognisable as machines of war. Even the street across which their trench spanned, was obliterated, with no trace of the macadam whatasoever. Beyond, the sound of their approach obstructed by the din of the barrage, came more Zlaimperian tanks with soldiers arrayed behind them.

Transfixed by the sight, Yuri couldn't tear his eyes away when he screamed, "They're coming!"

But there was no fight left in the company. Those who had survived the bombardment remained curled fetally on the ground, hands covering their heads, screaming for their mothers, or God, or both, their bowels letting loose as they gave in to their fear.

The Zlaimperian tanks began to fire, their aim more sure now that the Xorainians had given away their position. Round after round slammed into the trench with devastating effect, the screams of the injured and dying only adding to the general din.

"This is impossible," Yuri muttered to himself, and in truth, who could blame him? After enduring the unendurable, they must now suffer the vengeance of the enemy who was about to descend upon them with overwhelming force.

"This is impossible," Yuri repeated, and giving in to his instinct to survive, he said, "I must make them stop!" Then, having confessed as much, he proceeded to the next logical step. "We must surrender!"

He was on the point of tearing a strip from his shirt, hoping that the soiled remains would be accepted as a white flag, when something caught the corner of his eye.

Inexplicably, streaking across the broken ground between the opposing forces, covered in muck, streaming blood from a dozen wounds, out of his mind with pain and terror, screaming like a banshee, was what appeared to be a demon from the fiery pits of Hell, but, in fact, was none other than Yuri's pig.

Even as the brute raced across his front, tongue streaming from his gaping mouth, the pig stumbled, disappearing into the cratered ground. At the same instant the scene was obliterated by the fiery ball of an exploding shell.

Horrified, Yuri screamed, "PIG!" and before he knew what he was about, he was over the lip of the trench and racing toward the spot where the beast had vanished.

Scarcely believing his eyes, Kuzma stared as Yuri screamed something that was drowned out by the sounds of battle, then watched, horrified, as he leapt over the lip of the trench like a man half his age, and raced off toward the approaching tanks. He had to admit that it was an amazing stroke of bravery, even as he noted, with an exasperated curse, that the thrice damned *nevcheniy* Homstooder had forgotten to take his rifle with him.

*

Olesky slowly woke as if from the deepest of sleeps, his head throbbing like the very devil, when over the roar of the cannonade, he heard Yuri shout, "They're coming!"

It took the greatest force of will to open his eyes in time to see the Homstooder shout, "PIG!" and leap out of the trench. At the time, he thought that it was the oddest of all battle cries, although that was only in the back of his mind. All that he was aware of for certain, as he watched Yuri race forward to face the enemy alone, was that, at last, Xoraina had found her hero.

Although summoning the strength for Olesky to open his eyes had been difficult, it seemed as child's play compared to the struggle to regain his feet. For a moment, the world swayed sickeningly around him, and he almost gave up the struggle. How easy it would have been to surrender to the urge to crumple back to the ground and let the war be someone else's problem. Instead, he shook himself, much like a bear, and the resulting pain in his head brought him back to the present.

Bracing himself against the pounding in his skull, he cried, "They're coming lads! Prepare to receive them!"

No one moved. Instead, they remained huddled on the ground, driven to a catatonic state by the terrifying furore of the barrage.

Furious in his own right, Olesky screamed, "What is this?" Pointing to where Yuri was racing forward, he cried to those who still survived, "Surely you're not going to let that old man show you up for cowards?" At last, this produced a reaction. One by one, eyes began to open, but they were reacting far too slowly. Past all patience, Olesky spat, and sneered. "Very well, you bunch of old women, I'll go on my own!" Then, cocking his rifle, he leapt out of the trench, trying to ignore the pounding in his head as he set off after Yuri, the heroic *nevcheniy* farmer from Homstood.

Meanwhile, Kuzma, who, ordinarily, would not have left the relative safety of the trench for a pension, also spat angrily when he saw his captain rush forward. Turning to his comrades, he cried, "You heard the captain. On your fucking feet and let's get tore into those bastards!" and with that, he was over the lip of the trench, giving chase as fast as his legs would carry him.

By now the men were roused, and shamed by their captain's anger, they responded with their pride. First, one by one, and then in their dozens, they surged out of the trench seeking their own vengeance.

*

Even though wounded, Olesky was young and fit, so had halved the distance to Yuri when he noticed the turret of the nearest tank begin to turn toward him but decided that it no longer mattered. Far better to die out here in the open than cowering in that trench waiting for the enemy to put him out of his misery. For that much he was grateful.

Suddenly, there was a piercing scream followed by a streak of light, and the tank exploded in a whirlwind of flame. Seconds later, the next tank erupted to join it, two Roman candles blazing furiously in the dawn.

Instinctively, Olesky turned his face to the morning sky. High up, he saw a speck that might have been a soaring eagle but which he knew to be a drone. That could only mean one thing, that the Xorainian artillery had finally re-joined the fight. Even as he watched, he saw it veer off to the north, searching for more targets to destroy.

Meanwhile, the third tank was turning toward him.

Olesky knew he should dive for cover, for the lethal rattle of the tank's machine gun couldn't be far behind; but his defiance had been raised to such a level that he merely spat his hatred and waited for the end.

It was at that moment that a missile screamed past, and slamming into the tank, set it ablaze with a gigantic 'WOOSH!'

Surprised, for knowing that the spotter drone had left the area, Olesky had no idea how the missile had found its mark, until he thought to glance over his shoulder.

Standing just beyond the trench, was a soldier from a different company, the empty tube of the anti-tank missile still resting on his shoulder. Looking beyond him, Olesky could see a full dozen Xorainian tanks, the ugly snouts of their cannon pointing toward the enemy. Behind them, struggling to keep up with the racing behemoths, came Xorainian infantry in their thousands.

At last, the reinforcements had arrived.

The Zlaimperians, deprived of their tanks, and now with their artillery slowed to a trickle, faced the mad charge of the Xorainians with growing uncertainty. At the same time, Olesky tripped over the uneven ground just as a mortar shell landed between him and Yuri, who was still racing forward for all he was worth. Just before he hit the ground, it occurred to him that the farmer from Homstood didn't appear to be carrying his rifle.

The resulting explosion was deafening, flinging shrapnel and debris everywhere. Had he not tripped, it would almost certainly have cut Olesky to ribbons. Coughing in the putrid air, when next he looked, Yuri had vanished.

Cursing, he sprang to his feet, and racing forward, found him lying in a shell hole, not moving, covered in blood, with one leg twisted at an impossible angle. Cradled in his arms, equally motionless and bloodied, was his pig.

At any other time, he would have stopped, reflecting at this blatant impossibility, beginning with the how and why had the pig ever found its way to this place? But, in the heat of battle, there was only time for a glance, not really knowing if either Yuri or his pig were alive or dead. With the Xorainian artillery once more involved and beginning to take effect, Olesky forced the Homstooder duo from his mind as he waved his men forward, routing, first the enemy from the field, and then all the way to the Zlaimperian lines themselves, where the enemy tried, but failed, to make a stand.

Thus it was that the Achilles heel of the Zlaimperian war machine was revealed. Never having been forced to retreat before, just like Napoleon's Old Guard at Waterloo, the consternation caused by its very inexplicableness soon turned to panic, compounding as one line collapsed onto the next, spreading like a pestilence, far and wide, unravelling what had once been considered a formidable juggernaut as easily as threads unravelling from a blanket.

On and on Olesky pushed forward, followed by his men, desperately pressing the enemy back until their retreat became a route. As the Xorainian pressure continued, the Zlaimperians, intent only on survival, dropped their rifles and surrendered on the spot, or ran for their lives, or died where they stood.

Such an end was poetic justice for those who had the temerity to invade this land.

Let them fertilize it with their blood, instead.

Chapter Twenty-nine

Yuri opened his eyes, not to the horrific sights and sounds of the battlefield, nor to the barn he had shared with the pig, nor to the Presidential Palace, nor to the cold embers of a campfire in the forest, nor even to his peaceful cottage in Homstood. Instead, it was to a large tent with rows of bedridden soldiers, all of whom appeared to be suffering from wounds. A field hospital then, somewhere far behind the lines. By his bed was an IV stand bearing a bag of clear liquid from which a plastic tube descended to a needle in his arm. On another stand, this one at the foot of the bed, a sling descended, supporting his left leg, encased in plaster.

"He wakes," Olesky said. Yuri swivelled his head to face him, wincing with pain. Although a bandage was wound around the captain's head and one eye blackened, he was still able to grin and dip him a wink. "Welcome back to the world of the living."

Instead of acknowledging Olesky's congratulations, Yuri demanded, "My pig. Where is my pig?"

"Calm yourself, Father," Olesky crooned. Gesturing, he said, "He's right here."

Ignoring the pain this time, Yuri turned his head a second time, and saw the pig lying asleep on a thick bed of old blankets, in a low wooden crate beside his cot. One haunch was wrapped in bandages, and two stitches were prominent in a jagged cut across his snout, with several lesser contusions covering the rest of his body.

"Poor fellow," Olesky said, "he's certainly been through the mill."

Yuri croaked, "I remember being caught in the blast just as I reached him."

"God, you sound terrible," Olesky said, offering a bottle of water. "Here, have some of this. Easy now, or it'll make you sick." Referring again to the pig, he observed, "Still, it looks a lot worse than it is. Regardless of all he's been through, he must be the luckiest pig in the world. The president personally called on the Headmaster from the National School of Veterinary Medicine to see to his wounds. The prognosis is excellent, by the way."

Yuri shifted uncomfortably, but it wasn't enough to keep a relieved smile from his face. "That's wonderful news. Please convey my gratitude to the president, as well as the good doctor."

"Certainly," Olesky agreed. "Although the doctor should be around in a day or two to check on his patient. As for the president, you can expect a visit in the next few minutes."

Yuri gaped. "The president? Here?"

"Oh, didn't I tell you?" Olesky smirked. "You're a national hero now, my friend. The attack you led caught the Zlaimperians completely by surprise, triggering a general retreat from the Capital. Your praises are being sung all over the country."

Scrambling to process so much information, Yuri frowned. "Attack? I led an attack?"

"Why yes, don't you remember?"

"I remember trying to save my pig," Yuri replied honestly, as any good Homstooder would, "but it was never my intention to lead an attack. In fact, it was quite the opposite."

Olesky considered Yuri's explanation and smiled. "Your intentions aren't important. What matters is that the attack was made at precisely the right time, when the enemy least expected it, and was exactly what was required to give the country hope. So," he said, with an air of finality, "you can just damned well accept the adoration and like it!"

Yuri was no less confused than before, but he shrugged knowing that Olesky wouldn't be swayed. In the end, because all this talk of his being a hero was making him feel uncomfortable, he decided to change the subject.

"And you, my friend, how are you feeling? I thought you were dead."

"As I no doubt would have been if not for my helmet," Olesky agreed. "As it is, I am as you see. A few bruises, a headache but no concussion. And you, Father, how are you feeling?"

"Truthfully? Like I lost a fight with a truck," Yuri admitted.

"I'll get the doctor," Olesky replied. "He will be relieved to know you're awake." But no sooner had the words left his mouth when he noticed a figure dressed in a surgeon's gown approaching, and said, "Ah, here he is now."

The doctor, tired and unshaven, arrived with a folder tucked under his arm.

"Excellent, you're awake, Mr Zavlov, and still in the land of the living, I see. How are you feeling?"

"Like shit," Yuri replied, before modifying that with, "a few aches and pains and a little dizzy, but I suppose I'll get by."

"Headache?"

"Not worth mentioning."

"Good," the doctor said distractedly, taking out various x-rays, one by one, and holding them up to the light. Apparently satisfied, he said, "You're a lucky man. Your body armour and helmet absorbed most of the blast – there are no broken ribs or signs of compression damage – but you had a concussion, not to mention several lacerations to the buttocks as well as a broken tibia and fibula – both clean breaks, by the way." Then, taking the stethoscope draped around his neck, he inserted the earpieces and, after warming the diaphragm with a few short rubs against his palm, placed it over Yuri's heart. Listening carefully, he gave a single nod, and repeated, "Good," before moving the diaphragm over one lung and then the other. Finally, draping the stethoscope around his neck again, he said, "Yes, very lucky. Your lungs appear to be clear enough, although your heart rate's a little slow but that and your dizziness are most likely due to your medication." Taking up the clipboard from its hook at the foot of the bed, he scribbled something that was all but indecipherable, and asked, "Are you hurting anywhere specifically?"

"You mean other than my arse and leg?" Yuri asked pointedly. "Not really, I'm fit as a fiddle."

Failing to pick up on Yuri's sad attempt at levity, the doctor replied, "That's to be expected. You should be right as rain in about six weeks. Meanwhile, if you can make your way around on crutches, we can probably let you out of here in two or three days." Glancing at the clipboard and then his watch, he added, "The nurse should be by shortly to give you something for the pain, okay?" Then, replacing the clipboard, he said, "Now, if there isn't anything else, I must get on with my rounds."

Just as the surgeon was leaving the ward, a nurse edged by him pushing a medicine trolley. Possibly in her mid-forties, but no older, she flashed a brilliant smile while calling out greetings to all the patients. This was met by wolf whistles and cat calls from men who only moments before appeared to be at death's door. The cheerful smile never left the nurse's face as she trundled past them and stopped at the foot of Yuri's bed. Taking up the clipboard just as the doctor had, her smile grew even sweeter when she said, "Good morning, Brother."

"Good morning, nurse," Yuri replied. Then, attempting to make a jest, he gestured at Olesky, and said, "At least you didn't call me Father like this young pup."

To which she raised her brows, and said, "Oh, I would never do that. You're far too young." Then, with Yuri unable to hide his pleasure, she asked, "And how are we feeling today?"

"Fine. Absolutely fine," Yuri heard himself reply, while doing his best to ignore Olesky, who was standing behind the nurse with raised eyebrows and a lecherous smirk. Well he might, too, for Yuri had never seen such a beautiful woman in all his life.

The nurse (whose name tag on her blouse proclaimed her to be Anastasiya) managed to laugh and scoff at the same time.

"You men," she said, wagging her head. "You just got out of surgery, so you're nothing of the sort. Now, just lie back and let Nurse Ana take good care of you," as if Yuri had any choice or, to be honest, any desire to do otherwise. At that moment, he couldn't think of any other place he would rather be, even when she jammed a thermometer in his mouth and ordered him not to talk. Retrieving it a minute later, she announced her satisfaction. Next, she produced an evil-looking hypodermic needle and a phial of medicine from the trolley, but Yuri hardly even noticed. All he saw was the perfection of her face. Frowning at his leg in traction, she said, "Obviously I can't give you your pain injection in your bum, so your thigh will have to do."

Eager to assist, Yuri flung the blankets aside, only then noticing that all he was wearing was a hospital gown and that it had somehow managed to crawl up past his waist.

Nurse Ana's eyes widened considerably.

"Very impressive," she said. Then taking a cotton swab soaked in alcohol, she cleansed an area on Yuri's thigh and plunged the needle in before he could recover from his embarrassment. "I suppose now I can tell you that I could just as easily have given you the injection in your arm."

Bewildered, Yuri gaped at her while Olesky burst out laughing.

"But you said …"

Allowing a smirk to play across her lips, she explained, "A girl can be curious, can't she?" While Olesky collapsed, helpless with laughter, she said, "Ordinarily, a shot in the arm would be more difficult but," she let her eyes fall to Yuri's bicep, honed by a lifetime of physical toil, "I could see straight away there wouldn't be a problem with you." Then, having seen her fill, she tucked the blankets back over his torso.

By now, Yuri's face had grown a deep red, for he had never met such a bold woman before and was at a loss as to how to respond. Which was just as well, one might suppose, because from that moment on, during all the time it took to take his pulse (which, opposed to what the doctor had said earlier, was now racing slightly) to his blood pressure, Nurse Ana did most of the talking, all the while performing her duties with practiced ease.

Should you be wondering, the topic she chose, in the most glowing terms, was Yuri's heroic charge that had broken the Zlaimperian stranglehold on the Capital, not allowing Yuri to get a word in edgewise. She also managed to elicit from him that he was a widower within seconds of her mentioning that she was divorced. Finally, her inspection complete, she pronounced her overall satisfaction, and said, "I understand you're from Homstood?" When Yuri cautiously allowed that he was, she said pointedly, "It sounds wonderful. Nice and peaceful. I'm ready for some of that." She said it in such a matter-of-fact way that it couldn't even rightly be described as suggestive. Then, glancing across Yuri's bed, she saw the pig slumbering in his pen.

Eyes glowing, she said, "So this is the fellow you mentioned on the *Stinislav Berkos Show*! What a lovely boy!"

While Ana scurried around the bed the better to see the pig, Yuri admitted, "He's the reason why I'm here." In answer to Ana's questioning gaze, he took a deep breath and explained, inwardly trembling that she would think the less of him.

However, when he had finished, Ana merely laughed. "That's an even better story!"

"Do you really think so?" Yuri asked shyly.

Smiling down at the pig, Ana asked, "Well, he is a Xorainian pig, isn't he? I'd say he's certainly worth saving, wouldn't you?" While Yuri grinned like the village idiot, she leaned over the pen with her hands on her knees. Gazing down at the pig, she asked, "Does he have a name?"

Yuri came perilously close to bursting out laughing at the mere thought – a name for a pig, who had ever heard of such a thing – but he caught himself just in time.

"No," he admitted, but the more he thought about it the less ridiculous the idea seemed.

With a last warm smile at the snoring beast, Ana said, "Well, that's something we'll have to work on, won't we?" Then, having tarried for as long as was decently possible, she reached into her pocket, producing a pen and pad. She wrote down a number in a neat, feminine hand, and tearing off the sheet of paper, handed it to him. "I understand you're new to the Capital. Give me a call when you're feeling better. I'd love to show you around." With that, she winked at Yuri, blew the pig a kiss, and set off down the ward, trolley to the fore, leaving Yuri to wonder if it was his imagination or was there an exaggerated sway to her hips as she walked away? He certainly hadn't noticed it before.

Although having since recovered from his bout of laughter, Olesky was still far from sanguine when he chortled, "To the brave go the spoils!"

Still bewildered, Yuri shook his head, and said, "That was all meant for you, you know."

Continuing to smile, Olesky said, "What does it matter who led the charge? It wasn't me; I was only following *you*. Anyway, you are welcome to the recognition. All I care about is that the Capital has been saved."

Thinking of Kovalenko and other comrades they had lost, Yuri pointed out, "At considerable cost."

More sober now, Olesky quietly replied, "Yes." Then, in the ensuing silence, he broke the mood that had suddenly grown so sombre. Glancing at his wristwatch, he said, "That's it for me, I'm afraid, I've been ordered to battalion headquarters to meet the new commanding officer."

"Off you go, Marko. Our charge should be safe enough in my hands."

For the first time, both Yuri and Olesky realised that the president had managed to approach unnoticed.

After the greetings had been made, Olesky said, "Right then, I'm off." To Yuri, he added, "I'll try to stop by later if time permits."

"Which it won't, I'm afraid," the president murmured as soon as Olesky was out of hearing.

"Sir?" Yuri asked.

The impish grin on that ogre-like face was a sight to behold, but the president seemed to be thoroughly enjoying himself when he said, "I must confess that I've been guilty of a bit of subterfuge." In response to Yuri's questioning look, he explained, "A little surprise has been prepared for our friend, Marko. You see, he was ordered to battalion headquarters to meet the new commanding officer. Imagine his surprise when he discovers that said commanding officer is none other than himself! So, you see, if I'm any judge, he'll be far too busy for the foreseeable future."

"Ah," Yuri replied, enlightened, "a promotion! That's very good, Excellency. He deserves something from all this."

"Indeed, he does," the president agreed.

"Especially if it is I who am to gain all the recognition when it's so undeserved," Yuri confessed guiltily.

When the details had been explained to him, the president laughed. "You know? I actually thought as much when I was told how they found you with your pig, but Marko is right, it makes no difference. Right now, the country needs a hero more than ever, and what better choice than the man who expressed such doubts on the *Stinislav Berkos Show*?"

Unable to meet the president's eyes, Yuri looked away. Speaking slowly, he confessed, "There's something that needs to be said about that."

"Yes?" the president asked,

"I may not have been *entirely* correct," which was about as close as any true Homstooder would come to admitting that he was wrong. "In light of recent events, I'm not convinced that a Zlaimperian victory is as inevitable as I once thought."

Nodding soberly, the president replied, "That you are willing to admit as much is all the more reason for making you the man of the hour. If the people see that *you* can change, what sort of message would that send to all of those who feel the same way?" Levelling his gaze, he said, "You have done your country a greater service than you imagine, Yuri Yurivich. By your actions you have given the people hope and managed to unite them like never before." Offering his hand, he said, "And for that you have the thanks of a grateful nation."

Yuri accepted the hand, whereupon the president said, "But hope without something concrete behind it isn't enough. Later this evening the people will have even more reason for optimism." Explaining, he said, "I will be announcing to the country that, after talks with the Americans and their allies, they will be supplying us with weapons of the latest technology – weapons that will shoot farther, faster, higher and more accurately than anything in the Zlaimperian arsenal."

Yuri said, "That's wonderful news, sir!"

"It is," the president acknowledged. "After all, the West has even less desire to see the return of the old empire than we do. Xoraina has been put in the position to confront the ogre. Very well, we will fight, both for ourselves and the free world. We are willing to do so, but we must be given access to Western weapons and technology. That, combined with the indomitable spirit of the Xorainian people, must see us victorious in the end."

The two men shared tentative smiles while they contemplated the arrival of that day. Then, remembering what the president had said earlier, Yuri admitted, "I wasn't aware that you had watched the *Stinislav Berkos Show*."

"I wouldn't have missed it," the president assured him. "The Minister of Defence is in prison now, by the way, and has made a full confession. It turns out that he was not only plotting treason but was in league with the Zlaimperian dictator before the invasion even began." Very soberly, he added, "Apparently he had been promised my position when Xoraina had once more become a Zlaimperian vasal state."

"What will become of him?" Yuri asked, for he had no wish to see the minister again.

The president mused. "I would like to tell you that he will stand trial for his crimes and, if found guilty – which would certainly be the result – he would be punished to the fullest extent of the law." Suddenly irritable, he shrugged. "But we live in a political world, my friend, where conclusions are seldom so simple. It *is* possible that events will unfold as I have just stated – and nothing would make me happier – but the minister is a powerful man with powerful friends. It is more likely that he will languish in prison until a suitable exchange can be made with the Zlaimperian tyrant. I believe that is the best that can be hoped for."

Yuri thought about this for a moment and then accepted the president's prediction. He wasn't a man who required vengeance, only the assurance that the minister would no longer be capable of inflicting harm on his country.

"I shudder to think that I was very much like him," Yuri admitted, "and that he tried to make me spy on you."

"'*Was*' being the operative word," the president pointed out. "That is the past, Xoraina is only interested in moving forward into the future." Almost as an afterthought, he said, "By the way, I am happy to see that you have come to recognise the benefits of a democratic society."

"It's not perfect," Yuri pointed out.

"No, of course not, but that is something we can work toward, don't you agree?"

"Possibly," but Yuri didn't sound convinced.

"Tell me, Yuri," the president said, "have you ever voted?"

"Not I," Yuri scoffed. "I don't get involved in politics."

Gently, the president chided, "Everything is political, my friend. How can we make Xoraina a better place if people like you, who are so stout in your beliefs, don't become involved? Every day, we need better people with better ideas if we are to evolve. We need the old ways to be challenged at every turn."

"Even you?" Yuri asked, intending it in jest, but the president didn't laugh or even smile.

"*Especially* me," he said emphatically, "for I am from the same time as our former Minister of Defence. The old ways are all that I have known, and the path forward isn't always so obvious." Attempting to clarify, he said, "Twenty years ago, when the Zlaimperian dictator first came to office, he was widely regarded as a good man; but as time passed, absolute power poisoned his mind until he became the corrupt ogre that we see today. Power is a wonderful thing, Yuri, but like Tolkien's ring, it must be taken in moderation. In due course, it poisons the mind, and if left too long, it poisons the soul, just as it has in the dictator's case. I have no wish for that to become my fate, as well."

Yuri stared at the president, not knowing what to say. For the first time he had been introduced to the world of ideas and was intrigued. This good man was so passionate about Xoraina that he would be willing to give up power if it was in the best interests of the people. It was a concept so completely out of the scope of his experience that he needed time to digest the idea.

Sheepishly, he admitted, "Whenever I met with my friends in the market after church, the only thing we ever discussed about politics was to complain about the government."

The president offered a dry chuckle. "Possibly for good reason," he said and then brightened. "Which reminds me, I have given much thought to the issue and though it took much cajoling and cost me more than a few political favours, I have succeeded in rescinding the shipping tax on livestock." Then, smiling like someone who had just achieved the impossible, he said, "I trust that this pleases you?"

Yuri turned from the president to the pig lying asleep in his makeshift pen. After all the struggle, all the blood and tears spent in the endeavour – the greatest, by far, that he had ever undertaken – he had finally achieved his goal. Now he could ship the pig to the Central Market in Lofstov and sow sunflowers in the east field, and if the crop was as bountiful as he had reason to hope it would be, he would be able to fix the barn and repair the roof on the cottage, and possibly even afford another pig but this time one with papers. It was all within his grasp. The future looked brighter than he could ever remember, except …

Turning back to the president, he murmured, "Erm, yes … about that, Excellency, perhaps you should sit down; I have something to tell you …"

Epilogue

Yuri finished his inspection of the farm. Pyotr and Borys trotted at his heels, their tongues lolling in the warm summer morning. Over by the woodpile, Svetlana sat, gazing with intense concentration at something – a mouse perhaps – in its depths. Along the lane, wildflowers were in bloom with bees flitting from one to another, just as they had since time began.

The people had returned to Homstood, or most of them anyway. All everyone could talk about were of Yuri's heroic exploits during the battle for the Capital. Homstood was proud of her son and had treated him like a conquering hero. Of course, the pig had been with him, too, both of them having fully recovered from their wounds.

On a day set aside for the occasion, the entire village assembled in the market where the village administrator had proudly presented Yuri with a new radiator hose for the Kamaz. A photograph of that momentous occasion appeared in the *Homstood Weekly* the very next day, with the administrator beaming professionally at the camera and Yuri staring at the lens like a rabbit caught in the headlights of an automobile. That aside, however, it had all been quite satisfying. Mother Oksana had even said that she was proud of him, and she was sure that dearest Daryna – may she forever rest in peace – would be smiling down on him from Heaven.

Yes, it felt good to be back. It was what he had dreamed of ever since leaving four months earlier. The farm looked good, as well. With her limited resources, Mother Oksana had worked wonders, it could not be denied.

Ana would be pleased, too, he thought.

With her acting as his guide, his impressions of the Capital had been forever altered. Not that they had seen all that much of it – the urgency of war didn't leave time for courtship – but the memories they had been able to create together left him with emotions he hadn't felt since his wife had passed.

Deep in contentment, he adjusted his pack and slung the Kalashnikov over his shoulder. Yes, the future looked bright, even if it must be delayed for a while.

Reflecting, he thought of that terrible night when he'd been so terrified, and pondered the question all over again: why, when he had been so convinced of the inevitability of a Zlaimperian victory, had he accompanied Olesky to the front? At the time, he supposed that he'd simply been caught up in the excitement and that was probably true. Other times, he recalled the soldiers who were risking everything to keep the Zlaimperians at bay. When they had offered him that bottle of vodka, he had hesitated because he hadn't shared their views. They had accepted him under what he felt were false pretences. Now, in his mind, he had earned the right to share the bottle should it ever be offered again.

Ruefully, he recalled that his determination had been short-lived when he had made that failed attempt to surrender, but later, when he had confessed as much to Olesky, the captain had simply smiled and told him that there was no such thing as an atheist in a trench.

Yuri had wondered about that a great deal since and decided that Olesky meant that, if under such conditions, there were no atheists, maybe there was no reason, either. In the face of impending death, there was only a primordial urge to survive.

However, although all these thoughts were compelling and not without grounds, in his heart, Yuri came to understand that the real answer was that, when faced with his own moment, he knew the time had come to make a stand – to send a message to the Zlaimperian dictator that *'the way things were'* was no longer acceptable and needed to change.

So, now he was in uniform, just as his friends, Hans Gromp and Vasily Pomkin, were, as well as most of the other men in Homstood. But Yuri never dwelt on that decision. For him, the reasons were clear: all the ghosts – of the girl who had hung herself, of the people who had died in the caravans, in the villages, the tortured soul of Hanna Gorchenko, in fact, everyone who had paid a heavy (and all too often ultimate) price because of the diseased vanity of one man – all combined to form the soul of the land. While the Zlaimperians were no longer at the gates of the Capital, they still posed a grave threat to the south and east of the country. The tortured soul of Xoraina could never rest as long as those threats remained.

The president said that the people needed a hero, but the truth of the matter was that no longer applied. The people were their own heroes and needed no other. Yuri had declared that it was governments who fought wars and in the old autocratic days that may have been true. But, in Xoraina, the government *was* the people, but more than that, their determination made it a people's war on a level the Zlaimperians could never hope to match.

He had always thought that the yoke of occupation had been inevitable, but he had been wrong. For the dictator, the war had been lost the moment Xorainians had decided that they were unwilling to return to the days when they had a Zlaimperian boot on their neck. Everything else was just playing out a role, a role that Yuri wanted to be part of, toward the ultimate goal of victory.

The kitchen door next to the herb garden swung open and Mother Oksana stood at the threshold, the tantalizing smell of borscht and verenyky emanating around her. There were tears glistening on her weathered old face but still she managed to smile.

For at least the sixth time that morning, she asked, "Are you all ready?"

Patiently, Yuri smiled, and replied, "Yes, Mother. My ride will be here any minute now."

Yuri knew that she hated his decision to go off to war, but he also knew that she would never admit it, not even on the grave of her long-dead husband. Homstood women were every bit as strong as their men. Still, she looked troubled.

"Perhaps I should prepare another lunch for you," she said uncertainly.

"You have already prepared enough for the entire battalion." Yuri reminded her with a wink.

"Oh, you!" she scoffed, but still she appeared, if not pleased, at least a little less troubled. Then, looking over his shoulder, to the forest verging onto their property, her wrinkled old face softened, and she pointed with a finger painfully swollen from arthritis.

"Someone else has come to see you off."

Turning, Yuri saw the pig standing at the edge of the forest, his snout lifted, twitching interrogatively as he tested the air.

Of course, he had never shipped him off to the market in Lofstov. How could he after all they had been through together? Not to mention the pig was as much a hero of Xoraina as Yuri was himself. If not for the pig, Yuri would never have left the trench, and probably would have died there along with everyone else in the company. Sometimes fate was suspended on a razor's edge and the destiny of a nation might depend on nothing more than the whim of a pig. It sounded ridiculous, of course, but that didn't make it any less true. Therefore, all things considered, it only seemed fair to give the pig the same freedom they were all fighting for.

As the sound of a truck engine coming down the lane heralded his ride, Yuri raised his hand and waved, but of course, the pig never waved back. He was a pig, after all, a short-sighted creature not given to such social niceties even if he had noticed the gesture.

The truck came to a stop in front of Yuri and he went around to the back to hand his rucksack and rifle to willing hands already inside. Just prior to climbing in to join them, he turned to look one last time, but the pig was gone.

Swallowing the lump in his throat, Yuri accepted the helping hand offered by a comrade, and rode off to war.

*

The pig didn't rightly know what brought him to the edge of the forest that day, but he knew before he arrived, he could smell it in the air. The squire was leaving again, this time without him.

Of course, the pig was sad about that, the squire was the best of all friends. Never late with the swill, always making sure there was a pleasant wallow close by, why, he even tended him when he was feeling poorly. Not to mention the great adventure they'd had the last time they went a-journeying. Now that had really been a tale for the ages!

However, as sad as that made him, there was a small part of the pig that was also relieved. After all, that adventure hadn't exactly been a pastoral meadow filled with sunshine and roses, had it? No, indeed not.

He hadn't cared for all the angry humans trying to hide their fear, nor did he like the rat-a-tat of something he didn't understand, but whatever it was it smelled of even more fear and sorrow, and he certainly didn't like those brilliant blossoming flames or the thundering 'BOOM!' of the explosions that always seemed to accompany them. But most of all, he had grown to be terrified by the wails of all the ghosts. He knew it was because they couldn't rest and he wondered if they ever would? Every night he awoke on the verge of screaming, thinking that terrible time was happening all over again. Those dreams left him tired and shaken every morning. The message was clear: there was an affliction upon the land, and although he was never really sure what it was, he knew that it had to be overcome and the land given time to heal.

He had been free to roam in the forest for a mere matter of days now, and although he had at first been reluctant (perhaps even suspicious) when the squire left the gate of his sty open, his natural curiosity had eventually carried the day. He'd followed his snout out into the world, unfettered by leash or the guiding hand of the squire. First little steps, but then his stride grew longer and more confident when he discovered the forest and began to explore, as was the way of his kind. In time, he had forgotten all about the sty or any inclination of returning to it. Sometimes he'd root for grubs and other toothsome things and sometimes he'd find a pleasant place for a good wallow by a stream. Other times, he spent entire afternoons doing nothing but lying in the warm sunshine listening to the wind murmuring through the leaves. He hadn't been visited by the nightmares since he'd set hoof outside, and while he was aware that this was so, he would have been amazed at the thought, that instead of becoming healed itself, it was the land that was healing him. *He knew that the explosions and the balls of fire and the wailing ghosts were still out there. Sometimes he could smell them on the wind when it came from the wrong direction, but they were all far away from the forest. Not here ... not here.*

Glancing at his side, he offered a piggy grin and felt his heart swell the way it always did when the kindest, most beautiful sow in all the world smiled back at him. Uttering a long, contented grunt, he sent the squire his own farewell, and with his companion by his side, returned to the forest.

Although he couldn't see or hear him, he had sensed the squire say farewell but that he would be back again, just as soon as he had fixed the world. Maybe then it would be possible for his own healing to begin.

Unconcerned, the pig knew he would recognise the day of his returning; the trees would whisper his name; he would smell him on the wind.

Until then, he would wait.

THE END

Afterward

You may wonder why I chose to write a story about two fictitious countries instead of about the real struggle occurring in eastern Europe today. I'll attempt to explain.

First, if I were to write a story based on the current war (there, I said it – special military operation my arse!) there would be too many ancillary details impossible to verify clouding the issue. The second reason might be the most obvious: that it saved me untold hours of necessary research that, I feel, would not only restrict the scope of the story but would have only limited value. The third answer is that, by making Xoraina a fictitious country it would make Yuri easier to explain. You see, the story demanded a character of such extremes that I'm almost certain that attaching him to a real country would be viewed by that citizenry as a mortal insult, and I wouldn't blame them. After all, farms in eastern Europe are just as modern as farms anywhere else, not to mention the owners are hardly likely to go around wearing homespun clothing or ship their pig off to market as if they were sending it on a holiday. I wanted to simplify Yuri's own operation for ease of comprehension and that meant simplifying Yuri to the most basic level. Thus we find a field left fallow instead of adding hydrogen to the soil, excess grain used for seed with no mention of having it cleaned, omitting the application of fertilizer as well as any other additives that it takes to grow a crop in today's world, and last but not least, an insistence on a pay-as-you-go operation rather than simply stopping in at the nearest bank and demanding an operating loan. Had Yuri been a modern farmer in that sense it would have clouded the issue with unnecessary details that might detract from the main issues later on. So, I had to make him just about as basic as possible, without actually turning him into a *moujik*. However, you'll note that I *did* allow him the Kamaz, even though it was, admittedly, on its last legs.

So, very well, the two countries had to be fictitious. What should I call them? This turned out to be more difficult than I imagined. Not being happy with my first attempts, I turned to my friend, Olga Rudnitsky, who is fluent in Ukrainian. By cobbling together the words for 'evil" (*zla*) and 'empire' (*imperia*), I was able to come up with Zlaimperia for one. Then, by using the same technique, I crammed together the words for 'good' (*xorosha*) and 'country' (*kraina*) to come up with Xoraina for the other. I should add that this was not intended as a slight to the people of the Evil Empire, merely to the dangerously deluded and self-serving autocracy that rules over them.

One final note, my physical description of Xoraina's president is in no way intended to reflect the current president of Ukraine. The poor man has enough on his plate already without my adding to his troubles.

CW Lovatt

Biography

CW Lovatt is the award-winning author of the best-selling Charlie Smithers Collection and the critically acclaimed Josiah Stubb trilogy. He lives on the Canadian prairies and is the self-appointed Writer in Residence of Carroll, Manitoba (pop +/- 20).

Further Works by the Author

The Adventures of Charlie Smithers (2013)

Wild Wolf's Twisted Tails (2013)

Josiah Stubb: The Siege of Louisbourg (2014)

Charlie Smithers: Adventures in India (2015)

Charlie Smithers: Adventures Downunder (2015)

And Then It Rained (2016)

Josiah Stubb: Interim (2017)

Josiah Stubb: The Plains of Abraham (2018)

Never Taken Road (2018)

The Little Mouse (2018)

Dolly Pleasance (2021)

Charlie Smithers: Adventures in Arran (2021)

Charlie Smithers: Adventures in the Great White North (2023)

www.ingramcontent.com/pod-product-compliance
Lightning Source LLC
Chambersburg PA
CBHW070139100426
42743CB00013B/2766